British Society and Social Welfare

Also by Vic George and Paul Wilding:

Ideology and Social Welfare
The Impact of Social Policy
Welfare and Ideology

British Society and Social Welfare

Towards a Sustainable Society

Vic George

and

Paul Wilding

MACMILLAN

First published 1999 by
MACMILLAN PRESS LTD
Houndmills, Basingstoke, Hampshire RG21 6XS
and London
Companies and representatives
throughout the world

ISBN 0–333–71975–1 hardcover
ISBN 0–333–71976–X paperback

A catalogue record for this book is available
from the British Library.

This book is printed on paper suitable for recycling and
made from fully managed and sustained forest sources.

10 9   8   7   6   5   4   3   2   1
08 07 06 05 04 03 02 01 00 99

Editing and origination by
Aardvark Editorial, Mendham, Suffolk
Index prepared by Frank Merrett
Typeset by T&A Typesetting, Rochdale

Printed and bound in Great Britain by Creative Print and
Design (Wales), Ebbw Vale

Contents

List of Tables and Figures

Tables

Figures

Acknowledgements

A Leverhulme Emeritus Fellowship enabled Vic George to carry on his work at the University of Kent and to complete his share of the writing of this book. Paul Wilding was awarded a Leverhulme Research Fellowship for the academic year 1996–97 to work on this book. We are very grateful to the Trust for its support.

The authors and publishers wish to thank the following for permission to use copyright material:

Office for National Statistics for material in Tables 2.1, 2.2, 2.3, 2.4, 2.5, 5.8, 5.9, 5.10, 5.11, 5.12 and Figure 6.1;

Stationery Office for material in Tables 4.1, 4.3, 5.6, and 5.7;

Low Pay Unit for material in Table 2.8;

Child Poverty Action Group for material in Table 5.4;

British Medical Association for material in Table 4.2;

Institue of Fiscal Studies for material in Table 5.3;

OECD for material in Table 2.9.

Every effort has been made to trace all copyright holders and if any have been inadvertently overlooked the publisher will be pleased to make the necessary arrangements at the first opportunity.

Introduction

This book is the product of concern about two contemporary issues – the stability and sustainability of contemporary British society and the need for new approaches to social policy if the problem of sustainability is to be tackled effectively. It was the Brundtland Commission which introduced the concept of the sustainable society to social and political discourse. The Commission's primary focus of concern was with environmental sustainability, although it took a broad view of what that meant. The use of the term 'sustainability' as adopted in this book is rather different – and broader still. It is concerned with more general sustainability – with society's ability to hand on the norms, values and commitments that will ensure its survival; with its capacity to provide the economic prerequisites of sustainability, for example work for all and a reduction of gross inequalities; with its capacity to sustain and nourish families so that they can effectively socialize the next generation and care for those who are dependent; with its capacity to sustain and maintain informal and formal mechanisms for maintaining order and law; and with its capacity to make the moral and collective decisions needed to protect the environment for the future at the expense of present gratification. Society's sustainability depends on the health and well being of key social institutions, hence the focus on particular areas of society's life.

The focus on stability and sustainability as central elements in a society's welfare does not imply that they are the only elements in the good society. Stability can be achieved at too high a cost in terms of individual liberties or the maintenance of long standing inequalities. The real challenge is marrying stability with justice and development. Economic and social changes are constant features of any modern society and, by their very nature, tend to generate instability because change nearly always destabilizes – either temporarily or permanently. Change has to be managed. The focus of the analysis here is on the political and social instability that has characterized Britain in recent years, even though that same instability has been accompanied by many changes that most people would see as advances.

For example, there have been major improvements in the position and opportunities of women. Society has become less hierarchical, and there has been less deference towards authority. A growth in concern about the disadvantages and discrimination suffered by ethnic minorities, gay people and people with disabilities has occurred, and action has begun to right some of those historical wrongs. The consumer has been discovered, and there has been a start made in the reining in of the overweening power of professionals and bureaucrats. A new sensitivity has developed towards environmental issues. The central issue is, how can society enjoy the advantages of change yet contain and manage the instabilities that inevitably accompany change? How can a rapidly changing society be made sustainable?

Rapid economic, social and cultural change seems to threaten key aspects of society – the family, work, law and order, social cohesion and the environment. The strain on key social institutions is exacerbated by the failure of social and public policy to respond effectively to the new stresses and challenges.

The years 1945–73 were years of economic growth, full employment and social stability. It looked as if capitalism could, indeed, be managed and transformed into welfare capitalism. In retrospect, these years were, in fact, the product of a series of historical accidents rather than a final resolution of capitalism's inherent contradictions. The economy expanded; real incomes rose, full employment was maintained; the welfare settlement laid down between 1945 and 1948 seemed to be an effective answer to contemporary social problems and social needs. The financing of welfare out of economic growth was relatively painless.

The economic problems that emerged in the early 1970s showed that historical problems had not been solved and that global forces had a direct impact on domestic policies. Threats to the sustainability of the contemporary economic and social order became clearer, exacerbated by an ideological backlash against the policies and practices of the previous thirty years.

The book explores the problems in five areas – work, family, the environment, social division, and law and order. A range of factors – economic, social and cultural – have led to changes, strains and tensions in all these areas. In all of them, it is possible to look back to a recent stability that seems to have disappeared. It is no longer possible to talk sensibly about 'the family', only about families. The pattern of paid work has changed dramatically – less full time work, more part time work, more work for women, less for men. No one seems to expect a return to traditional full employment. Rates of recorded crime and victim surveys show dramatic rises in crime, lawlessness and disorder. The poor get poorer, and the rich get richer. Society puts even greater pressure on what is increasingly recognized to be a fragile environment – and we seem unable collectively to take the decisions to preserve it that individually we know we need to take.

Problems in these areas are the product of economic and social change, and of the failures of government to see the significance of what is happening and to respond effectively. The successes of public and social policies in the years of economic growth lulled governments into a false sense of security and satisfaction. It seemed as though the parameters of social policy had been successfully laid down once and for all.

The result is that, at the end of the twentieth century, British society and British social policy face an uncertain future. Thinking has not moved on to develop policies to protect and preserve those key social institutions threatened by economic and social change. Society has not taken seriously the fact that work, for most people, is the main source of welfare. Policy has been slow to take account of the new stresses and strains that face families today and to see support for families as central to the sustainable society. Governments have failed to respond creatively to growing concern about law and order. There has been little constructive response to the emergence of a two thirds society divided much more sharply than in the recent past. And the world seems unwilling and unable to respond effectively to the emergent knowledge of the threat of environmental disaster.

Academics and policy makers alike have continued to think of social policy in traditional terms – health, education, housing, social security, social care – with a focus primarily on individuals rather than on societal needs and institutions more generally. Order, stability and the future have been taken too much for granted, and there has been a failure to see the need for policies with a societal rather than an individual focus. Society has continued to define social welfare in narrow, largely individual, terms and has assumed that it could be achieved by the establishment of a limited range of social services.

The problem of stability and sustainability is the product essentially of four factors – developments in contemporary capitalism, changes in social values towards greater individualism, a failure to recognize the exceptional character of the years between 1945 and the early 1970s, and a failure to develop social policies in line with economic and social changes. The welfare settlement of 1944–48 was essentially a response to the instabilities of the years before the Second World War. Even with the modifications of recent years, it does not constitute an answer to the problems of the 1990s.

Certainly, many of the pressures after 1979 were new, but the central, essential failure of those years was the rejection of the centrality of social policy to societal sustainability. The government looked to economic growth and trickle-down as the way to preserve social stability. The strategy failed. There were increases in productivity and there was economic growth, but it failed to trickle down and provide crucial social cement. Meanwhile, the need to develop new social policies to counter the destabilizing impact of the Conservative economic project was rejected. The result was a crisis of sustainability, a societal crisis.

The Structure of the Book

The core of the book is five chapters exploring substantive areas in which we see acute problems of stability and sustainability – work, the family, the environment, social division, and law and order. We see these areas as vitally important to the overall well being of society. In each area, six sets of questions are explored:

1. What has been happening? What have the recent trends been?
2. Why have things been changing as they have?
3. What has the government response to these changes been?
4. What are the broad implications for society?
5. What proposals have been made by conventional policy sources?
6. What proposals have been made by radicals?

There is inevitably some overlap between the chapters because of the linked nature of the issues. This shows that the issue with which we are dealing is a systemic one – one to do with the very nature of society rather than one which is confined to particular policy areas.

That understanding underpins the first and last chapters. Chapter 1 explores the nature of the stability and social cohesion that characterized the years from 1945 until the early 1970s and why this stability was replaced by a seemingly much less stable society in the years that followed. It also outlines the major preconditions for a sustainable society. Chapter 7 draws the argument together and provides a more personal interpretation of the issues.

Obviously, we are trying to cover a very wide area in one volume. This inevitably means that the presentation of the issues will be in summary form. We hope, however, that our analysis of the problems facing British society today and our proposals for solving these problems will stimulate others to look at these issues from a systemic, societal position rather than from an individualistic or a social service perspective.

1

The Stability and Instability of British Society

What really strikes early 1990s eyes about those brave, semi collectivist years of mid century Britain is the combination of hope and public purpose. (Hennessy, 1993, p. 453)

Introduction

The half century since the Second World War can be divided rather crudely into two periods. The first, which lasted until the early 1970s, was one of general confidence, growth and stability. The second was characterized by declining confidence, a bumpy economic record, a sense of declining stability and greater assertiveness by hitherto neglected and silent groups – women, ethnic minorities, gay people and people with disabilities. In the 1980s and 90s, these destabilizing trends became clearer and stronger, for example in rapid and significant changes in families, in increasing crime, in sharpening social division and in the declining availability of work.

There are obviously both general and more particular reasons for the disturbing trends. In later chapters, we will explore each in turn. The general, however, can easily get lost in the particular. It is the general problems that underlie the particular, and the general issue is the maintenance of a sustainable society in a market economy driven by individualism and concern for the short term without regard for the well being of society as a whole. In some societies, at certain times in history, market-driven development will not seriously threaten social order. At other times it will and it does.

Contemporary British society provides major challenges to social policy. What is needed is what might be termed better 'social management'. Market societies are no longer necessarily self-sustaining. Market systems may deliver economic growth but at destructive social costs that threaten longer-term sustainability. Markets can only function acceptably if supported and modified

1

by a range of polices designed to preserve the order that they threaten. If that central truth is ignored, society's sustainability is threatened.

The evidence for this argument can be found in trends and developments in the 1980s and 90s. In all five areas examined in the book, there are deeply worrying trends. Not all can be attributed directly to market-driven development. Economic trends and the putting of the economy always first have contributed to rapid changes in all these areas. The stability of the social fabric has been assumed and thus neglected. The result is a rash of socially threatening situations, a shortage of work, increasing social division, worrying changes in 'the family' and a sharp increase in crime.

The Nature of Stability

This chapter tries to tease out what made for the relative stability of British society in the thirty or so years after 1945 and why it then became less stable. Obviously, such an analysis can be no more than suggestive, but it provides a necessary background to later chapters.

Seven factors seem to have contributed significantly to the stability and thus to the sustainability of early postwar British society – full employment, economic growth and affluence, satisfaction with the postwar settlement, confidence in the future, dominant social values, a sense of social solidarity and an acceptance of their deprivations by disadvantaged social groups.

Full employment was perhaps the greatest achievement of the postwar years. 'Unemployment', says Fraser, 'had indeed been the central issue of the inter war years. Its malignant canker had poisoned millions of homes; it had blighted whole industrial regions; it had disinherited a generation' (Fraser, 1984, p. 198). In the postwar years, Giant Idleness seemed to have been vanquished. It was not until 1971–72 that unemployment in Britain averaged 3 per cent over the year.

Full employment provided a regular income, security, a purpose, hope. It bound people into society. It provided at first a trickle of jobs for married women and then a flood, which led to a revolution in women's lives and to the affluence of the two-income household. It contributed to a culture of contentment, a sense of collective well being. It extended opportunities.

Economic growth, which was almost a new concept in political and economic discourse in the postwar years, was also crucial to social stability. From 1948 until 1973, Britain's rate of economic growth averaged 2.8 per cent per year. Between the early 1950s and the mid 1970s, the earnings of male manual workers doubled in real terms. Consumer goods that had been the privilege of a minority became much more widespread. The number of cars on the road increased from 2.5 million in 1951 to more than 6 million in 1964. In 1951, there were only 1 million TV sets in Britain; by 1964, there were 13 million. Owner occupation doubled between 1945 and the mid 1960s, reaching 50 per cent in 1964.

A third important element in the stability of postwar Britain was the nature of the postwar settlement. As Beer put it, Britain 'began to create a social and economic order that promised to cope with many of the disorders and deprivations of industrial society' (Beer, 1982, p. xii). Of course, there were disappointments, but Hennessey points out that 'The bundle of social and economic problems the welfare state was designed to break open and solve proved tough to crack. But real progress there was; progress on a scale and a duration never surpassed in the nation's history' (Hennessy, 1993, p. 2).

Health care was provided for all citizens, free (or almost so) at the point of use. There was free secondary education for all. There was universal social insurance undergirded by National Assistance. It amazed and satisfied contemporaries. It instituted a new form of relationship between citizen and society, between citizen and government.

It is easy to be critical of the postwar settlement. In a sense, it was backward looking, but those were the problems people knew and had suffered. There is, too, a substantial amount of truth in the argument put forward most forcibly by Corelli Barnett (Barnett, 1986) that Britain voted itself a nice peace when it should ideally have been putting its energies into rebuilding the economy. Keynes had voiced the same fears about reconstruction plans as early as 1944 (Barnett, 1995, p. 128). Be that as it may, the postwar settlement did inaugurate thirty years of prosperity and stability. The Conservative Party recognized in 1950 that the settlement was so generally popular that acceptance of it was politically inescapable. Anything less would have been political suicide.

A fourth element in the stability of the years after 1944–45 was the widespread confidence in government. Government had emerged from the war with immense prestige. There was confidence that the knowledge and techniques existed to manage the economy in order to avoid the mass unemployment of the interwar years. There was its successful commitment to providing health care and education for all. There was the seeming abolition of poverty.

Initially, there were no doubts about the capacity of the new health service to improve the nation's health, of free secondary education for all to achieve genuine equality of opportunity, or of the new National Insurance and National Assistance legislation to abolish poverty. There was no sense of insoluble problems facing society. There was great confidence that a new order had been brought into being and that it could defeat the giants that Beveridge had seen barring the road to reconstruction.

The fifth important element contributing to stability was dominant social values. 'There endured after 1945', says Morgan, 'a powerful civic culture, a commitment to hierarchical and organic values, to crown and parliament, to law and order, to authority however it manifested itself' (Morgan, 1985,

p. 327). It was a profoundly traditional society in its acceptance of hierarchy, its male-dominated nature, its deference to authority and its acceptance of the past as the best guide to the future. There was an emerging sense of social rights, but it remained weak. Expectations in terms of increases in income and the provision of services were low. There was still a war-induced sense of collective purpose and collective solidarity. Confidence in the future operated as a restraint on demands in the present.

There was also a strong sense of solidarity. In part, of course, it was war induced, a sense of suffering endured and victory achieved, of shared memories and aspirations. War helped to create a social capital on which postwar governments drew for a generation. Quantifying such a sense of solidarity is obviously difficult, but there is the vigorous middle-class support for Beveridge's proposals even though most respondents did not hope to gain directly themselves. There is the fall in the level of crime between 1945 and 1950. There is the successful wage restraint policy pursued by the government between 1945 and 1950. From 1940, says Addison, 'egalitarianism and community feeling became, to a great extent, the pervasive ideals of social life: whether or not people lived up to them, they knew what they ought to do' (Addison, 1977, p. 18). He argues that the national unity of the postwar years generated a new political consensus that shaped the agenda of government for the three postwar decades and reflected and reinforced war-induced solidarity.

Finally, there was an acceptance of their deprived position by disadvantaged social groups. There were few demands for greater equality for women before the mid 1970s. Concern about the unequal position of ethnic minorities emerged strongly only a little later. People with disabilities remained silent. Sexuality was a private rather than a public issue. Groups that suffered discrimination or oppression had little sense of their right to be heard or to more equal treatment. From the perspective of the late 1990s, it was a strangely acquiescent society. Protest there certainly was – for example the student movement in the late 1960s – but it was political issue based rather than focusing on social rights, and it did not connect with other potential social movements.

Seeking the basis of social stability means potentially dangerous generalizations and a risky mix of history and social analysis. There are exceptions to all the points made here. There were pockets of unemployment even in the years of full employment. There was growth and affluence but not all benefited. There were many who had hoped for a more radical settlement than was actually put in place in 1945. Although there was widespread confidence in the future, there were others with doubts. Certainly, there were values that made for order and sustainability, but affluence was beginning to nurture a less deferential, more individualist society seeking more immediate gratification. The old society contained within itself the seeds of the forthcoming new, less stable society.

There is also the point needing to be emphasized that stability is not in everybody's interests. It benefits 'insiders' because it maintains the *status quo*. By preserving the *status quo*, it perpetuates inequalities of power, status, reward and opportunity. There is a clear hierarchy of gainers and losers from stability. Men gained, women lost. Whites gained, while blacks lost. Stability might have been for 'the general good', but the general good as defined by dominant interests means the good of the majority in dominant groups, and that may be (and usually is!) sustained at the expense of minorities of various kinds. Stability and order may be central to welfare and thus to sustainability – but they have a cost, and that cost may at times be heavy in terms of social justice and the denial of fundamental rights. The post-Second World War world scored high on stability but lower on longer-term social justice and sustainability.

Nevertheless, looking back on the early postwar decades from the 1990s, the sense of order, stability and collective purpose is what stands out. It was a society without the open anxieties and the troubles that emerged from the 1970s.

The Decline of Stability

Pinpointing the moment when stability becomes an issue is impossible. What is very plain, however, is that the society which had emerged in Britain by the mid 1970s was widely felt to be less stable than the society of the immediate postwar years. A series of interrelated economic, political and social factors accounted for this gradual shift.

Economic Factors

Economic factors were crucial in the emergence of a less stable society. The sharp increases in oil prices after 1973 were a blow to the international economic order, but by then the difficulties of the British economy had already become apparent. The essential problem was one of decline relative to competitors and relative to expectations. Brittan, for example, calculates that real output per head in Britain between 1960 and the mid 1970s grew by around 2 per cent a year. In West Germany, however, it grew by nearly 4 per cent, in France by around 5 per cent and in Japan by nearly 10 per cent (Brittan, 1977, p. 127). Britain's share of world manufacturing exports was 15.7 per cent in 1961; by 1970 it was down to 9.5 per cent (Leys, 1989, p. 85). There was mounting evidence, too, of poor productivity. The 1970 Central Policy Review Staff study of car production showed that, when holding key factors constant, output in British factories was only half that of plants in continental Europe (Leys, 1989, p. 89).

By the mid 1970s, Britain's economic difficulties were having a major social impact. They were making it increasingly difficult for government to meet the expectation of ever-increasing personal incomes and higher standards in social services. The search for steady economic growth became the dominant theme in politics, but the search was unsuccessful. The failure to achieve publicly acceptable levels of growth had a profound effect on society. Middlemas wrote of 'the cosmic despair of the mid 1970s' (Middlemas, 1986, p. 336) when real incomes failed to rise in three successive years. The result, in Kavanagh's words, was 'greater social tensions, group rivalries and growing dissatisfaction with the incumbent authorities' (Kavanagh, 1980, p. 156).

Britain's declining competitiveness and reduced share of international trade led to the re-emergence of unemployment as a significant social and economic problem. Unemployment reached almost one and a half million in 1977, after averaging around 400 000 for the first twenty years after 1945, and throughout the 1970s, there was continuing concern over youth unemployment as firms reacted to their problems by not recruiting new workers. Then the problem became more general as unemployment reached 3 million in the early 1980s. The whole of the workforce is affected as unemployment generates underemployment and a pervasive job insecurity and drives down wages.

Modern societies, says Dahrendorf, are 'work societies' (quoted in Leisink and Coenen, 1993, p. 7). They are shaped by patterns of work. Work is one of the great stabilizing elements in society. Hence, the absence of work and insecurity of employment profoundly affect social order. Substantial numbers of people are excluded from mainstream society. They lack what they need to acquire social status and social identity and become stakeholders. They cannot establish and support families.

Political Factors

Political changes also played a part in the gradual decline of the stable society of the early postwar decades. There are a number of now classic expositions of what was feared to be happening in, and to, politics in the 1970s. There is Brittan's work on the emergent economic contradictions of democracy, in which a combination of excessive expectations and the uninhibited pursuit of group self-interest, in his view, placed an excessive burden on the sharing out functions of government and threatened the continued survival of liberal democracy (Brittan, 1975).

Then there is King's work on overload in government. Expectations of government as the creator of the future have vastly increased its range of assumed responsibilities at the same time as governments' capacity to deliver on their new responsibilities has declined. A range of connected factors has made Britain harder to govern. Governments, therefore, fail more frequently, with consequential damage to their chances of future success (King, 1975).

Rose explored the much discussed issue of ungovernability and of whether Britain was, in fact, becoming ungovernable as the effectiveness of government programmes and government's ability to secure consent became questionable. Programmes became more expensive and the resources to finance them became more difficult to secure (Rose, 1979).

The problem, in essence, was that of managing distributive conflicts in a society that had strong expectations but was not creating the wealth to meet them, and where any sense of self-restraint to further the common good seemed to have ebbed away. Economic growth had made it possible, in the 1950s and 60s, painlessly to fund better public services and growth in personal incomes. In the 1970s, this ceased to be possible. Government, as an institution, suffered. So did society. So did the economy. It was partly this disillusionment that brought Mrs Thatcher to the leadership of the Conservative Party in 1975 and to power four years later.

Beer's thesis was that the political failures of the mid 1970s were the inevitable product of collectivist policies: chickens were simply coming home to roost (Beer, 1982, p. 4). Government authority sank 'in a swamp of pluralist stagnation' (Beer, 1982, p. 17). The nature of the earlier reform had been mechanical rather than moral, to borrow Plant's analysis of the Thatcher project post-1979 (Plant, 1996, p. 174). Affluence, and then a dashing of hopes for more, showed that individual and group interests were still more powerful than collective concerns. Politics was less able to manage the conflicts. What Beer's analysis underemphasizes, however, is the divided nature of society. He fails to connect the political failures of the 1970s with the still sharp divisions that characterized British society thirty years after the postwar settlement. He seems to assume a much more cohesive society than was the reality. Political problems must therefore, in his view, have political origins. Others would prefer economic and social explanations.

Changes in Values

Changing social values have also contributed to the emergence of a less stable society. Beck, for example, sees reflexive modernization as dissolving the traditional parameters of industrial society, with class culture and consciousness, gender and family roles being dissolved 'in a social surge of individualisation' (Beck, 1992, p. 87). Affluence certainly generated a new emphasis on individual rights and freedoms. The individual was asserted at the expense of the collective. Demand for rights came to overwhelm the belief in duties.

There is considerable discussion in the literature that explores the sustainability of capitalism in relation to two issues relevant to our discussion. The first is capitalism's need for a supporting social morality. Hirsch argues this very strongly, that the principle of self-interest, the motor of capitalism, only operates effectively in tandem with some supporting social principles because of the need for other principles that check and modify self-interested behaviour (Hirsch, 1977, p. 12). Fukuyama argues a similar case: that if the institutions of capitalism and democracy are to function properly, they must coexist with certain pre-modern cultural habits that ensure their proper functioning, for example duty towards community (Fukuyama, 1995, p. 11).

The second issue is the way in which capitalism is alleged to destroy the morality on which it depends. Schumpeter, for example, writes that 'in breaking down the pre capitalist framework of society, capitalism thus broke not only barriers that impeded its progress but also flying buttresses that prevented its collapse' (Schumpeter, 1970, p. 139). Brittan speaks of capitalism living off 'the moral heritage of the feudal system', which it eventually destroys (Brittan, 1975, p. 149).

Postwar Britain had a clear and established morality, the residue of a past age based on a pre-secular world. Affluence, individualism, the privatization of life, the emergence of adolescence as a separate stage of the life course between childhood and adulthood, and later on the prolongation of limbo life through youth unemployment, all contributed to a growth of normlessness and moral relativism. Respect for property, private or public, seemed to decline alongside respect for persons. The social ethic that had seemed so strong in the war and in the early postwar years seemed to be weakened by economic and social changes.

Writing about political culture in 1980, Kavanagh suggests that 'One way to summarise the change may be to speak of the decline of deference' (Kavanagh, 1980, p. 156). Beer entitles Part 3 of his book *Britain Against Itself* 'The Collapse of Deference'. Both authors are seeking a shorthand term for the decline in respect for authority, established hierarchy and the existing socio-political system. Goldthorpe stresses a slightly different aspect of the same fundamental problem in his analysis of what he calls 'the decay of the status order' (Goldthorpe, 1978, p. 197), the socially accepted evaluation of social worth and the resulting inequalities of reward, power and standing. He sees an accepted status order as legitimating both economic and social inequalities and the exercise of political authority. The decay of the status order deprives economic inequalities of their legitimacy. He speaks, for example, of 'an increasingly delegitimated structure of class inequality' (Goldthorpe, 1978, p. 208). In modern capitalist societies, the status order is progressively weakened and, with it, one of the essential underpinnings of stable capitalism.

An accepted status order inhibits both political dissent and substantial wage demands because it fosters an acceptance of the *status quo*. Middlemas sees the 1960s as the decade of working-class emancipation (Middlemas, 1990, p. 10), emancipation from the inhibitions of deference and the acceptance of inequalities of reward and power. The result of such an emancipation is the growth of 'a recalcitrant, demanding public in the early 1960s' (Middlemas,

1990, p. 11). Exactly when deference weakened to reveal a mature working class is a matter for debate. What is not in debate is the weakening of those values and inhibitions that had helped to ensure a stable, deferential but profoundly unequal society.

The decline of deference is one element in a broader decline of civic culture and of those key social values that help to bind a society together – acceptance of authority, concern for the community and the common good, restraint in pursuing individual and group ends, respect for past practices and patterns, and an acceptance of the need for compromise and give and take. A range of commentators argue for such a decline from the late 1960s and more generally in the 1970s. Beer believes it is no exaggeration to speak of the 'collapse' of the civic culture in the 1970s (Beer, 1982, p. 119). Mackintosh wrote of 'a decline in the sense of common purpose among the various sections of society', of groups and individuals coming to regard society not as a vehicle for the advancement of common goals but as 'an orange to be squeezed by those with the strength or the nerve to extract more juice for themselves' (Mackintosh, 1976, p. 94).

The decline of deference and of the traditional civic culture, and the growth of individualism, had its positive aspect. For example, it made for a freer and more equal society. It made possible a new working-class assertiveness. It contributed to the challenging of traditional stereotypes of male superiority and of the rightness of the male monopoly, or near monopoly, of certain occupations and positions of power. It contributed to challenges to patterns of institutionalized discrimination. Minority groups of various kinds were given – or seized – space to assert themselves as the power of traditional patterns of ideology and authority weakened. This, of course, had both negative and positive sides. For Brittan, the more vigorous pursuit of group self-interest was one of the two endemic threats to liberal representative democracy, the other being the growth of excessive expectations, which was, in part, the product of the collapse of deference and the restraint to which it contributed (Brittan, 1975, p. 129). On the other hand, groups that had accepted oppression and disadvantage began to question their position and struggle with greater militancy to better their position, often outside customary conventional channels.

Hirsch sees the 1970s as a significant turning point in the development of capitalist societies because of a change in the balance between the individual and the social good (Hirsch, 1977, p. 178). The underlying legitimating belief of free market capitalism, that the pursuit of individual interest promoted the common good, was exposed as an inadequate basis for economic and social development because of the existence of social limits to growth. In Hirsch's famous phrase, if everyone stands on tiptoe no one sees better (Hirsch, 1977, p. 5). It raised the basic question of which kind of society could or should follow capitalism.

The Welfare State

In the immediate postwar years, the British welfare state was seen both as an expression of social solidarity and as promoting it. Its achievements were recognized by virtually everyone. Heclo's judgment in 1980, however, was that, in spite of its achievements in improving physical well being, 'none of this has produced social solidarity as the welfare state founders had hoped' (Heclo, 1980, p. 40). The hoped for solidarity 'has become enveloped', he argued, 'in a politics of recrimination and confrontation' (Heclo, 1980, p. 54).

The result was that the welfare state itself became a focus of conflict as groups sought to promote and secure their interests at the expense of other groups. Skidelsky writes of the chief flaw of collectivism as being the fact that 'outside exceptional periods, the degree of consent for the reshaping of the economy and society is always more limited than the ambitions of the collectivists' (Skidelsky, 1995, p. 26).

What the development of the welfare state does is to transfer some of the distributive conflicts endemic in society from the marketplace into politics (Esping-Andersen and Korpi, 1984, p. 202). In times of steady economic growth and strong and effective government, that transfer is unproblematic. When growth slows or stops, and when the authority of government is challenged and threatened, those distributional conflicts take on a new significance. The claims, demands and needs of a range of groups – new and established – that see possible advantages to be gained from the pursuit of their interests through the political marketplace gives a spur to these conflicts. The change offers them a new sphere in which to pursue their cause.

Another element in the British welfare state's inability to reduce social conflict and to promote stability was the limited definition of the role of social policy with which it worked. British social policy has always had a primary focus on individual welfare rather then societal welfare in a broader sense. Social policy has not been used in any very committed way to facilitate economic and industrial change, although there are counter examples, such as the introduction of earnings-related unemployment benefit in the late 1960s to encourage what was euphemistically described as 'shake out'. Nor has it been used vigorously to improve the skills of the labour force, or to retrain workers, or to encourage regional policies. It has shied away from concern with earnings or from creating a participatory society to give people a stronger sense of social belonging and commitment.

In the 1970s the tensions in the welfare state between rights and responsibilities first became clearly apparent. The emphasis in the early postwar years was all on individual rights and government obligations. What became increasingly obvious from the late 1960s was that the existence, let alone the extension, of social rights depended on some people assuming the responsibility for other citizens' social rights because rights had costs. There was a reluctance to do this. As groups asserted the 'rights' of their constituents to more and better goods and services after decades – or even centuries – of oppression, welfare politics became more issue based and thus more fragmented.

Welfare state-type policies can be a bonding force in society, promoting stability through policies that foster social inclusion, stress common needs and remove sources of grievance and gross inequalities. On the other hand, such policies can stimulate conflicts over rights and priorities and can raise expectations and then fail to meet them when the economy fails to deliver anticipated rates of growth.

By the mid 1970s, Britain had reached a point at which the demand for rights and higher expectations was putting great pressure on government, and government was trying hard to hold down increases in expenditure at a time of low rates of economic growth. The welfare state, as established in 1945, had plainly not secured a permanently sustainable society. For a range of reasons, whose precise significance and relative importance are keenly disputed, the postwar settlement had failed to generate the levels of economic growth or the range or kind of social services that people had come to expect and demand.

A New Philosophy

The final factor to be considered here among factors contributing to a decline in social stability is the new economic and social philosophy and policies that developed in the Conservative Party from the mid 1970s and became the formal ideology of government in 1979, albeit somewhat muted in the early years.

This philosophy was, in many ways, a reaction to what was defined as the failure of the so-called consensus politics of the previous thirty years. It sought to re-establish social order and the authority of government. What it did, in reality, was to contribute to further instability. Four elements in the government's approach weakened social stability and raised questions about the sustainability of the society that was emerging.

First, there was the policy of giving single-minded priority to the economy. Economic growth was the government's overriding concern. Putting the economy first was seen as the way to escape from the sluggish growth rate of the previous decade. The social implications of giving an overriding priority to growth, for example the links between high rates of unemployment and crime, or the links between deprivation and urban disorder were ignored or denied.

The government's thinking had all the virtues and shortcomings of simplicity. Giving priority to growth would increase the likelihood of achieving it. The fruits would, in the longer term, benefit everyone and be a powerful bonding force in society. The unpleasant reality was that a concentration on growth without regard to the social costs exacerbated social division, contributed to social exclusion and sharpened other social problems. The government also put the responsibility for slow growth on supposedly high rates of public expenditure, a gross oversimplification.

Second, there was the government's model of how such growth was to be achieved. There were several crucial elements in the growth strategy – tight control or, better still, cuts in public expenditure, a vigorous attack on inflation, holding down or driving down wages and, finally, the promotion of inequality.

Overall, public expenditure was not significantly reduced. There were, however, major cuts in certain areas, most obviously in housing. What the government did was to hold down increases in spending so that spending failed to rise in line with the increases in need resulting from an ageing population, new possibilities in health care and needs arising from the return of mass unemployment. At a time of rapid and significant economic change, public expenditure has to rise to ease and soften the impact of change. In Britain in the 1980s and 90s, it failed to do that, and the social implications were considerable.

The government saw inflation as the result of existing levels of public expenditure and as a key element in Britain's failure to secure higher rates of economic growth. It saw higher rates of unemployment as a price well worth paying to achieve the conquest of inflation. Unemployment became a central element in the government's economic strategy, to hold down wage increases, to ensure a buyer's market for labour and to weaken the power of the trade unions.

Inequality was seen as both necessary and inevitable in a dynamic economy, necessary in that the effort required to secure economic dynamism should and must be rewarded and in that, to stimulate such effort, failure must at the same time be punished. Inequality was seen as inevitable to secure the necessary dynamism and development. The successful must be rewarded, and failures must be allowed to fail and suffer accordingly. The outcome was a much more unequal and divided society.

There was also the attack on the state and the denigration of government, of its ability to spend wisely, to manage the economy, to achieve social goals. Government action was problematized as inefficient, ineffective and parasitic on the wealth-creating private sector. The great solvent of social ills was the market rather than the state.

Finally, there was the vigorous promotion of individualism and individual responsibility. Individuals must be encouraged – even compelled – to take responsibility for themselves and their families. It was good for them as moral beings, good for society and good for the economy if individuals' claims upon it could be diverted or reduced. State welfare provision was defined as destructive of individual responsibility and as disabling.

Mrs Thatcher's notorious statement that there is no such thing as society, only individuals and families, captures the government view all too accurately. Such a view, of course, militates against any generalized concern for the well being of society as a whole, any sense of, or concern for, the common good, and any sense of a collectivity that is somehow more that the sum of a number of individuals. Hutton's verdict, writing in 1995, was that 'the sense of belonging to a successful national project had all but disappeared' (Hutton, 1995, p. 2).

The new philosophy of the 1980s was a response to a particular interpretation of the problems that had emerged in the 1960s and 70s, and of particular beliefs as to how a particular model of the good society could be re-established. Our argument is that the government's approach of giving priority to the economy, pursuing a particular growth policy, promoting individualism and denigrating government sharpened rather than eased the crisis of stability and sustainability that was brewing in the 1960s and 70s. The result of eighteen years of economic liberalism was to make instability more obvious and sustainability more problematic. Destabilizing trends accelerated. Free market liberalism stood revealed as being unable to provide the cement required to hold society together. 'It may be', said Skidelsky optimistically, 'that marketisation itself creates the voluntary associations needed to socialise it' (Skidelsky, 1995, p. 193). In Britain, it did not.

Neither the Keynesian welfare state nor the Thatcherite espousal of free market solutions seemed able to deliver a sustainable society. The Keynesian welfare state failed to generate either the economic growth needed for the painless financing of social services or the support for self-restraint on which its social policy success depended. The Thatcher project also failed to generate the economic dynamism which alone might have held together the social order that economic and social strategies put under such strain.

In Summary

The major justifications for what has been attempted so far in this chapter are threefold. First, there is the need to provide the backcloth for the more detailed discussion of specific policy problems that follows. Second, there is the need to illustrate how both the Beveridge and the Thatcher approaches to state welfare provision failed, although for different reasons, to achieve economic growth and social stability. Third, the analysis makes the case for a Third Way of ordering the country's economic, political and social affairs – the sustainable society approach – which we set out in more detail in the chapters which follow and in the Conclusion.

Preconditions for a Sustainable Society

The concept of sustainability was defined in the Introduction. In brief, sustainability is society's ability to sustain a commitment to common social purposes, to maintain social order, to extend the opportunity of work to all, to achieve tolerable living standards for all, to ensure adequate care for the dependent and to have proper regard for the natural order and its future – all within a spirit of enterprise and fellowship.

Here, the conditions and preconditions of sustainability in advanced industrial democratic societies are explored in greater detail. Obviously, much depends on history and on expectations, and there are actual and potential trade-offs and conflicts between conditions. Ten conditions are outlined below under three headings.

Economic Preconditions

1. Work for all, a commitment to full employment is a, if not the, key precondition of sustainability. Work gives people a role, a stake in society, the chance of independence, the best way of escaping poverty, a way of realizing their aspirations. Work is also important in helping to avoid the emergence of an alienated underclass.

   Commitment to full employment may not mean that full employment is always achieved. Dynamic economies generate short-term unemployment. The important condition is that a society should be committed to full employment and should not manage the economy in such a way as to perpetuate high rates of unemployment in the pursuit of other supposedly desirable economic and social goals, such as the reduction of inflation. Traditional full-time full employment is clearly no longer possible, and a new approach to full employment is necessary.

2. An active commitment to abolishing poverty and reducing economic inequalities is essential. Excessive economic inequalities eat at the heart of social stability by the way in which they generate and sustain social division, produce alienation, weaken a sense of the common good and feed resentment and a sense of injustice. They also, of course, impose heavy costs on society in terms of educational failure and extra demands on the health care and criminal justice system.

   Inequalities are inevitable, but, for the sake of sustainability, they need to be reduced to levels that do not threaten social stability and social order. Inequalities of gender, race, geography and, above all, socio-economic inequalities need to be tackled.

3. A balance between economic and social development is of central importance. An overriding commitment to economic growth can be destructive of social stability if it ignores the social costs that it can impose. A preoccupation with social development without regard to the health of the economy can be equally threatening to sustainability. Economic development is vital to preserve the competitiveness on which future employment depends and to generate the resources required for the achievement of social purposes.

    The appropriate balance will obviously vary from society to society and from time to time. The crucial element, in our view, is a commitment to holding the goals of economic and social development as being of equal importance. Social and economic policies should be seen as of equal worth to society, and they should be planned in ways that are mutually reinforcing. That is the only way to ensure balance and sustainability.

Social Preconditions

4. There must be a strong commitment to meeting basic needs, to abolishing poverty and to ensuring an acceptable living standard for all members of society. Poverty is socially divisive. It feeds alienation and a sense of injustice and hopelessness. It contributes to educational failure and thus becomes self-perpetuating. It imposes heavy costs on the rest of society. By its very nature, it tends to hit some groups particularly hard, among them families with children, so imperilling society's future. A commitment to a national minimum is an expression of society's concern with its collective well being and its collective future. Poverty and deprivation are fertile breeding grounds for unsocial and antisocial behaviour.

5. There has to be a commitment to environmental protection. Without a concern for the future costs of present ways of living, there may well be no future. A species that destroys its habitat destroys itself. Protection of the environment requires a commitment to the future and, at times, the subordination of present advantage to future well being. It rests on a strong commitment to the common future good. It can impose costs in the present. Certainly, any society concerned for its future stability and long-term sustainability must make a commitment to the protection and preservation of the environment as protection of the environment improves the welfare of present and future generations. For national environmental goals to be achieved, government needs also to take account of the needs of people in the developing world: the environment issue is international.

6. Socialization of the next generation must be accepted as a shared responsibility. Society's future depends on inculcating appropriate norms and values in each succeeding generation. In a more individualistic and more pluralist society, that responsibility can no longer be left solely to families. It is too important and difficult, and has therefore to be shared between families, society and the state. The socialization of the next generation is crucial in a range of ways, most obviously, perhaps, for law and order. Government action will be required to protect the very young from depriving life circumstances as well as from undesirable influences.

7. Caring for elderly people and those with handicaps has to be seen as a key element in society's life and a central concern for government. Caring is one of the great central human activities. A massive proportion of a society's resources in terms of money, time and energy is devoted to caring. The length and degree of dependency in old age has been greatly extended. Society has strong incentives to see that caring is carried out effectively. A neglect of caring responsibilities leads to a coarsening of the national life that can undermine stability. Leaving the burdens of caring to lie where they fall is a recipe for inadequate caring, weakening any sense of the ultimate value of people and any sense of society as a collective enterprise.

Political Preconditions

8. There has to be a balance between rights and duties. A commitment to rights which ignores the fact that one person's rights constitute another person's duties is destructive. It feeds a concern for individual and group needs, wants and aspirations without regard for the common good. Equally, an emphasis on people's duties and obligations that fails to take account of economic and social change, and people's capacity to perform such duties, can be punitive and alienating. It can damage relationships between individuals and weaken any sense of belonging to a society.

   In the first thirty years after 1945, there was too much stress on rights and too little on duties and obligations. In the 1980s, there was an attempt to reassert duties and obligations, for example the duty of the unemployed actively to seek work and to take any available job so that they were not a 'burden' on the rest of society. Little was done, however, to make a reality of people's right to work.

   Individual rights depend on society for their achievement. For its flourishing, and indeed survival, society depends on people showing a sense of their duties and obligations. There has to be a balance. Stressing one and ignoring the other is a recipe for social conflict. There are no abstract answers to achieving the proper balance; any answer has to be pragmatic and situational. However, the sustainability of society depends on being alert to the need to get the balance right.

9. Contemporary society in Britain will only survive as a living, collective enterprise if people feel involved in decisions about its life and their future. Sustainability depends on consent, and people must feel that their voice counts. A sense of powerlessness breeds frustration and alienation, and a weakening of any sense of commitment to common goals and purposes. Democratic participation means much more than voting every few years in central and local government elections. It has to be extended to a range of other social institutions and situations. The stable, sustainable society depends on popular commitment to its aims, purposes and the methods of achieving them. That means a thorough democratization of national life.

10. Government has to accept a key role in economic and social affairs. Markets are institutions of compelling power and potential for good and for evil. Only the state can hope to harness their potential for good and limit their potential for undermining social stability. This means, in our view, a major role for the state in economic affairs, in securing adequate levels of investment, in stimulating employment, in providing the necessary infrastructure and in carrying out the necessary redistribution of resources. As regards meeting social needs, government is only one of a variety of institutions, including families, voluntary bodies and the private sector, involved in such responsibilities. Only the government, however, ultimately has the power and resources to ensure that needs deemed important by society are met. We see government acceptance of a central responsibility in economic and social affairs as essential to stability and sustainability.

Any list of the conditions of sustainability is inevitably and inherently ideological because it involves judgements about the nature of the desirable society. Any debate about the future direction of society and social policy has to face this difficulty. If we are to address the issue of sustainability, it is important to set out the preconditions of that desirable state. These preconditions inform our approaches to the five areas – work, family, the environment, economic and social division, and law and order – that we now go on to discuss.

Further Reading

Barnett, C. (1995) *The Lost Victory*, London, Macmillan. Barnett argues that Britain took a sadly wrong turning in 1945 and that all our problems have followed from that gross error.

Beck, U. (1992) *Risk Society*, London, Sage. This book is a forceful statement of what goes wrong if societies do not pursue balanced development.

Hennessy, P. (1993) *Never Again*, London, Vintage. An excitingly readable account of the history of the years 1945–50.

Hutton, W. (1996) (revised edition) *The State We're In*, London, Cape. A compelling account of just why we are in the sad state we are in.

Hutton, W. (1997) *The State To Come*, London, Vintage. The follow-up to the earlier book. Perhaps rather less convincing than Hutton's analysis of the past, but that is true of most prescriptions for the future.

2
Work

Employment is the umbilical cord connecting the individual to society... tolerating unemployment is the fastest way to put communities at risk. (Derber, 1994, p. 34)

Reducing unemployment by the required amount will certainly involve some sacrifices. In particular, society will have to face up to the fact that investment – private and public, in industrial capacity and in people – must take priority over consumption for a period of years. Economic renewal and the need to offer every citizen a full stake in society demands this. Social justice also demands that the burden of the adjustment from a largely acquisitive society to one that seeks to further the common good must fall primarily upon those most able to bear it. (Philpott, 1997, p. 27)

Introduction

Industrial societies are structured around the institution of work for both economic and social reasons. The work ethic is their central social value, and paid employment is the major source of income for both individuals and societies. Without paid employment for all, these societies lose their affluence and cohesion, and become conflict ridden and impoverished.

Work is important to society in more than economic terms: it is significant for social and emotional reasons too. It provides the opportunity for individuals to develop their abilities and talents, to fulfil their ambitions in life, to develop the social networks that are so important for individual and family stability. It structures people's lives, it allocates workers to their social statuses, it acts as a stabilizing force in society and it reduces the risks of anti-social behaviour of all types.

High levels of unemployment can demoralize individuals and families, sharpen inequalities and divisions in society, undermine social cohesion and generate feelings of frustration, pessimism and hopelessness, all of which threaten society's sustainability. The payment of unemployment benefits is no real solution to these problems. Three out of four respondents in the British Social Attitudes Surveys during the mid 1980s to mid 1990s preferred to work rather than have an income from the state (Hedges, 1994).

It is important, however, not to romanticize or idealize work as it has another rather different face. Many jobs are uninteresting, hazardous, physically demanding and low paid, and lead not to self-fulfilment but to soul destruction. As Macarov has warned, there is a great deal of evidence showing not only that there is 'widespread unhappiness at work', but also that this has been increasing rapidly in recent years (Macarov, 1996, p. 196). Government policies need to pay as much attention to the quality as to the quantity of work, not only for social and economic reasons, but for reasons of law and order as well, as low-quality employment is strongly associated with crime among young adults (Downes, 1995, p. 141).

It is paid employment that has traditionally been considered as work by governments. In recent years, however, there has been a half-hearted acceptance that other forms of work, such as caring for children or dependent adults, merit government recognition and remuneration. Change at work is a natural process and is always taking place. Industrial societies are today, however, going through yet another major industrial revolution, which will increase productivity but may not increase the number of jobs. We shall return to this issue later in the chapter.

First, however, we need to examine the major trends in the area of work during the postwar years, indicate the winners and losers, and perhaps gain some idea of possible future developments.

What Has Been Happening?

The major achievements of governments in Western Europe during the postwar period down to the mid 1970s were high rates of economic growth and low levels of unemployment. Living standards improved for all as a result of both rising earnings and expanding welfare provision. People enjoyed security of employment, and many looked forward to good career prospects. Security at work was matched by family stability and community cohesion. Inequality and poverty declined as a result of the improvement of wages, the expansion of the welfare state and the progressive nature of direct taxation systems.

It was, however, a period when employment rates for women were low, discrimination at work widespread and technical innovation rather slow. World wide, there was little trade competition from the countries of Asia and South America. The industrial supremacy of Western Europe and North America was absolute. In retrospect, it may also have been a period when current consumption was overemphasized at the expense of investment for the future.

Numerous changes have taken place over recent decades, and the world of work in the 1990s is different in many ways from that of the 1950s and 60s. We outline the major changes below.

The Size and Composition of the Workforce

To begin with, the size of the workforce grew only modestly over the postwar years, reflecting primarily the entry of women, particularly married women, into the labour force in large numbers.

The status of employees

The majority of the workforce has always been in the category of employees even though there has been some decline in its relative size – from 89.3 per cent of the UK workforce in 1959 to 86.2 per cent in 1997. The decline is compensated by the increase in the number of self-employed persons from 8.3 per cent of the workforce in 1959, as Table 2.1 shows, to 12.4 per cent in 1997.

Table 2.1   Composition of the workforce in employment, UK (percentage), 1959–97

	1959	1971	1997
Employees	89.3	89.7	86.2
Self-employed	8.3	8.8	12.4
HM Forces	2.4	1.5	0.8
Work related government programmes	–	–	0.6
Total (per cent)	100.0	100.0	100.0
Total in thousands	**23997**	**24636**	**26774**

Source: Government Statistical Service, 1994, Figure 2, p. 4 and Table 1.1, p. 7. For 1997, *Labour Market Trends*, April 1998, Table 0.2, p. S4.

The occupational structure

The occupational structure of the country has changed quite substantially in recent years. Employment in manufacturing declined steadily for both men and women – from 35 per cent of men in 1978 to 26 per cent in 1997, with an even steeper decline for women, from 22 to 10 per cent, as Table 2.2 shows. On the other hand, service employment and financial services came to dominate for both men and women. Parallel to these occupational changes has been the decline in the number of unskilled jobs and the rise in employment requiring training and professional qualifications. Educational achievement has now become a central requirement for opening up employment opportunities.

Table 2.2   Employees by industrial sector and gender, UK (percentage),
1978 and 1997

	Males		Females	
	1978	*1997*	*1978*	*1997*
Distribution, hotels, catering and repairs	15	20	24	26
Manufacturing	35	26	22	10
Financial and business services	9	16	11	19
Transport and communications	9	9	3	3
Construction	8	7	1	1
Agriculture	2	2	1	1
Energy and water supply	5	1	1	–
Other services	16	19	38	40
Total	100	100	100	100
ALL employees in millions	**13.4**	**11.7**	**9.4**	**11.3**

Source: Office for National Statistics, 1998, Table 4.8, p. 78.

Gender and employment

In gender terms, the change over the years has been remarkable: a decline in the number of male employees and a rise in that of female employees so that by 1997 they achieved virtual parity in numbers, as Table 2.2 shows. Unlike men, however, the probability of women's employment depends on their marital status and the presence of children in the family. Women without children are more likely to be in employment than are married women with children, who are, in turn, more likely to be in paid employment than lone mothers. Also, as we shall see below, most of the rise in women's employment is in part-time employment.

This rise in female employment applies to all advanced industrial societies, although it varies in degree depending on the ideology of the country concerning women's employment, demographic factors and the role of the state. The employment of married women receives more support from society at large, and from husbands in particular, in some countries than others. In Europe, Denmark tops the list, the UK lies somewhere in the middle, while Luxembourg and Ireland show the least support (Deshormes La Valle, 1987). Demographic factors also exert an influence on women's employment. The reduction in the birth rate means that women have more opportunity for employment, while the rise in the number of the very elderly means the exact opposite as women are the main carers. Whether one talks of community care or care in the community, it is mostly women who are the carers, paid or unpaid. The role of the state is the third important factor manifested in such policies as the provision of child care facilities, child benefits and maternity and paternity benefits.

Lewis correctly argues that all European welfare states began with the twin assumptions that men are the breadwinners and women the carers. With the passage of time, however, they have drifted away from this model in varying degrees. She identifies three current categories of welfare state in terms of gender: weak, moderate and strong 'male breadwinner states' (Lewis, 1992). The Scandinavian countries are seen as weak male breadwinner states because their welfare provisions treat women as being equal to men and provide sufficient services and benefits to enable them to be free from many of their caring responsibilities in order to partake fully in the labour market. Britain and Germany are examples of the strong male breadwinner states because of women's inferior position in the social security system and the state expectation that they will carry out most of the family caring duties on their own and largely unaided by the state.

Despite the rise in female employment, women are underrepresented in highly paid managerial jobs and are overconcentrated in the lower socio-economic groups. As Table 2.3 shows, however, there has been some relative improvement in the position of women in the two higher socio-economic groups. Although the proportion of men in these two groups increased from 20 per cent in 1975 to 28 per cent in 1995, the corresponding rates for women rose from a mere 5 per cent to 12 per cent.

Table 2.3   Socio-economic groups by sex, Great Britain (percentage), 1975 and 1995

Socio economic Group*	1975			1995		
	Men	Women	Total	Men	Women	Total
Professional	5	1	3	7	2	4
Employers and managers	15	4	9	21	10	15
Intermediate and junior non-manual	17	46	32	17	49	34
Skilled manual and own account non-professional	41	9	24	35	8	21
Semi-skilled manual and personal service	17	31	24	15	22	19
Unskilled manual	5	9	7	4	8	6
Total	**100**	**100**	**100**	**100**	**100**	**100**

* The socio-economic group shown is based on the individual's own job (or last job if not in employment).

Source: Government Statistical Service, 1998a, Table 4.4, p. 49.

These changes in the occupational and gender structure of the labour force have had significant implications for the political and social life of the country. The decline in manufacturing employment has meant a weakening of the significance of traditional class politics and of the traditional class forces in support of the welfare state that emerged at the end of the Second World War. A more complex system of social relations has emerged that emphasizes the political importance of consumption patterns and of social movements as much as allegiance to conflicting social classes. Political parties have to take account of this new situation and reflect it in the policies that they advocate. In the social domain, the growth in the employment of women has contributed to the development of less inegalitarian gender relationships both within the family and society directly as well as indirectly through the stimulus it has given to the growth of the feminist movement.

Working Time Flexibility

The traditional pattern of standard work schedules has been in retreat in all industrial countries during the 1980s and 90s. Working-time flexibility is the emerging pattern, involving part-time work, unsocial hours, more overtime and a relaxation of labour market regulation and social protection legislation. The driving force behind all these changes is the desire or necessity for employers to reduce wage costs and increase productivity, competitiveness and profitability in a globalized world market.

Part-time employment

Part-time employment has become a central feature of the British economy. While full-time employment declined, the number of part-time jobs almost doubled from 15 per cent of all jobs in 1971 to 28 per cent in 1994. Women dominate part-time employment, while men do likewise in full-time employment. Thus, in 1993, 81 per cent of part-time employees were women, while 63 per cent of full-time employees were men (Government Statistical Service, 1994, p. 9). Interestingly, the majority of part-time women workers come from households that already contain employed men, suggesting that part-time employment is not financially attractive to women in other types of household.

Most part-time women workers belong to the 25–39 year age group, when they have dependent children, while most part-time men are beyond the age of fifty when they lose their appeal to employers for full-time employment. In other words, child care reasons dictate part-time work for women, while labour market reasons are the explanation for men. Eighty per cent of women attributed their part-time work status to the fact that they did not want a full-time job because of their family responsibilities (Naylor, 1994, p. 480). It is not, therefore, unexpected that the recent expansion of part-time employment has been taken up by 'over-qualified women rather than by unskilled and less educated women or men' (McLaughlin, 1994, p. 185).

In occupational terms, for both men and women in part-time work, 'the highest proportions are in sales and service jobs, while managerial and indus-trial occupations remain predominantly full-time' (Naylor, 1994, p. 476). Several studies have shown that part-time workers *vis-à-vis* full-time workers in most countries 'face a double bind: lower hourly earnings are severely compounded by less than **pro rata** employee benefit packages' even after taking into account 'human capital differences and a range of job characteris-tics' (Gornick and Jacobs, 1996, p. 4). Seen from a gender perspective, this indicates a large number of over qualified women attempting to perform the difficult dual role of mother and wage-earner, and being exploited in the process.

Unsocial hours of work

Side by side with this rise in part-time work, there has been an increase, albeit on a much smaller scale, in the number of people working unsocial hours – nights, weekends, away from home, shift work and even hours of work decided at will by employers. Gender is an important variable in all these patterns of work. As a recent study concluded: 'Men are more likely to be involved in shift work and unsocial working-time patterns than women, but men appear to have more autonomy in the choice of working-times' (Fagan, 1996, p. 86).

Employment and Unemployment Rates

Although most attention tends to be given to unemployment, it is important to look at the broader concept of the employment or labour participation rate. In other words, it is important to discuss not only those who are regis-tered as unemployed, but also the larger group of the non-employed of working age.

Employment rate

The non-employed section of the working age population, excluding students, comprises those officially classified as unemployed and the economically inactive – those who have officially withdrawn from job search. The non-employed section of the population is clearly bigger than the unemployed section. The employment rate, or labour participation rate, of a country, takes both of these groups of non-employed persons into consideration.

For the UK, the employment rate has remained constant during the past twenty years – 70.7 per cent in 1975 and 70.0 per cent in 1995. This overall figure conceals significant gender variations: for men the figures were 88.6 and 77.0 respectively, for women the corresponding figures 54.3 and 62.8 (European Commission, 1996, p. 162). Another way of expressing these changes is that the inactivity rate for men, that is, the proportion of men of working age who are not students and who neither work nor are registered as unemployed, increased over the years, while for women it declined, although still remaining substantially higher than that of men. It suggests that there are significant reserves of labour that could be employed if the number of jobs created were to rise. It also suggests that governments have to create substantial numbers of new jobs for the unemployment rate to drop significantly. It is quite possible for many new jobs to be created without the unemployment rate falling as many of the new jobs are taken up by those not on the unemployment register.

Unemployment

Unemployment in the UK increased substantially during the 1980s, and, although it declined during the 1990s, it is still well above the low levels experienced during the 1950s, 60s and 70s. This is despite various government redefinitions of unemployment, which have had the effect of reducing the number of those classified as unemployed.

Long-term unemployment, that is, the proportion of the unemployed out of work for a year or more, has risen much faster than the overall unemployment rates: while only 12.1 per cent of the unemployed were long-term unemployed in 1955, the corresponding proportion in 1995 was 43.5 per cent. Desegregating long-term unemployment by gender only aggravates the severity of the problem for men, with a rate of 49.6 per cent in 1995, and softens it slightly for women, whose rate drops to 32.3 per cent.

The level of unemployment varies considerably by socio-economic grouping. As Table 2.4 shows, it is higher, for both men and women, among the semi-skilled and the unskilled than among other groups. Age has also been a significant factor, the young and the over-55s suffering most.

Most ethnic minority groups suffer more from unemployment than do the rest of the population even when educational qualifications are taken into account. It is an indication of the significance of the discrimination that ethnic groups suffer in employment in Britain. Table 2.5, based on the returns of the 1991 census, shows not only that unemployment rates for all ethnic groups are double those of the white population, but also the variations among the various ethnic groups by gender. The Chinese have the lowest unemployment record for both men and women – rates that are almost the same as those of the white population.

Table 2.4   Unemployment rate by socio-economic group, Great Britain (percentage),* 1995

	Men	*Women*	*Total*
Professional	1	3	2
Employers and managers	4	3	4
Intermediate and junior non-manual	6	6	6
Skilled manual and own account non-professional	10	10	10
Semi-skilled manual and personal service	16	7	13
Unskilled manual	24	6	14
Total	**9**	**6**	**8**

* Definition of socio-economic group as for Table 2.3.
Source: Government Statistical Service, 1998a, Table 4.5, p. 50.

Social Focus on the Unemployed (Government Statistical Service, 1998b, p. 14) provides more up-to-date data for 1996–97 although not in the same detail. It shows an unemployment rate for Pakistanis and Bangladeshis of 23 per cent, for Indians of 9 per cent, for black groups generally of 20 per cent and for other ethnic minorities of 13 per cent. The unemployment rate for whites was just 7 per cent.

Unemployment in EU countries

Unemployment rates are high not only in the UK, but also all over Europe. As a recent EC report put it, 'unemployment remains the major economic problem – both now and for the rest of the decade' (European Commission, 1994, p. 7). There are, however, minor variations between EC member countries in terms of both unemployment and labour force participation rates, as Table 2.6 shows. Leaving aside the Mediterranean countries, which have higher unemployment rates than the rest of the EU because of their lower level of economic development, the Scandinavian countries have the best record, partly because of their active labour market policies and women's higher employment rates. Although the overall employment rate is an important factor in a country's economic fortunes, it has to be seen alongside the country's labour productivity rate. Thus, although the UK has a better record than France and equals that of Germany in terms of unemployment and labour force participation rates, its labour productivity is lower – 'around 20 to 30 per cent behind France and Germany' (Barnett, 1998, p. 6).

Table 2.5   Unemployment rates among ethnic groups, Great Britain (percentage), 1991

Ethnic group	Men	Women
WHITE	10.9	6.5
ALL ETHNIC GROUPS	20.3	15.6
I. Black	25.3	16.8
Black Caribbean	24.0	13.8
Black African	28.9	24.8
Black, other	25.5	18.4
II. South Asian	19.2	16.5
Indian	13.5	12.6
Pakistani	28.5	29.5
Bangladeshi	30.8	34.5
III. Chinese and Other	15.6	12.1
Chinese	10.5	8.2
Other Asian	14.2	12.3
Other – other	19.7	14.9
ENTIRE GB POPULATION	**11.3**	**7.0**

Source: Owen, 1997, Table 3.13, p. 54

Table 2.6   Average unemployment and labour force participation (LFP) rates in EC member countries, 1980–96

	Unemployment	LFP
Belgium	9.3	62.1
Denmark	7.9*	81.1
France	10.0	66.8
Germany	7.7	68.7
Italy	9.4	59.0
Netherlands	7.3	58.4
Sweden	4.7	80.3
UK	8.2	75.0

* Denmark's figure for unemployment refers to the period 1988–96 and overestimates the average extent of unemployment for the period covered by the table.

Source: OECD, December 1997a, Annex Tables 19 and 22, pp. A22 and A25.

Deregulation legislation

In addition to the above changes in the labour market, there have been several legislative changes in the UK that have increased job insecurity. Reforms in employment legislation have made it easier and cheaper for employers to dismiss workers; the virtual abolition of minimum wage councils has exposed low-paid workers even further at a time when their labour is least needed; and legislation has also weakened trade union power in a period of high unemployment. All these changes have made it possible for employers to introduce insecure employment patterns that were almost impossible before. The practice of temporary contracts, which enables employers to take on and lay off workers at will in response to market demands, inevitably increases insecurity. Married women with children are the group most likely to suffer from this practice (Alexander and Radford, 1994). If the 1960s and 70s were the decades of trade union power, the 1990s belong to the employers.

Work insecurity is justified by the New Right as a necessary employment environment that helps to create a lean workforce striving for maximum efficiency. It can, of course, be argued that insecurity at work may have the opposite effect as it may act as an obstacle to both flexibility and innovation. Why should workers welcome technical or managerial change if it means redundancies or deterioration in working conditions? The difficult question is how to combine labour flexibility with work security. The recent agreement between United Distillers and the trade unions offering employees a three-year contract and wage rises just above inflation in return for flexibility and retraining is a welcome attempt to reconcile the two. Hain hails this agreement as 'the only route to higher productivity and investment – and sustainably higher earnings' (Hain, 1996, p. 16).

While imposing heavy costs on many sections of the population, labour deregulation has helped to increase profitability and has led to more foreign capital investment in the UK than in any other European country during the 1990s. Similarly, productivity rates have improved so as to arrest the decline that set in during the late 1970s, although they have not reached the high rates of previous decades or caught up with those of several European countries (OECD, 1994a, p. A63). Improved productivity rates, however, do not necessarily lead to higher rates of economic growth in the short term. Annual rates of gross domestic product (GDP) growth averaged 1.9 per cent throughout the 1970s and for the period 1980–93, well below the figure of 2.8 per cent during the 1960s (George and Taylor-Gooby, 1996, pp. 4, 8 and 9). Although all commentators will support the significance of improved productivity rates, they will disagree on how best to achieve them and on how the accruing economic benefits should be shared out.

What Has Been Happening?

The size and composition of the workforce
- Decline of employment in manufacturing
- Growth of employment in service industries
- Growth in women's employment
- Gender inequalities at work remain

Work flexibility
- Growth in part-time employment
- Growth in unsocial hours of work
- Growth in employment insecurity

Employment and unemployment
- Growth in unemployment in the UK and Europe
- Growth of deregulation legislation

Why Have Things Been Changing as they Have?

The rise in unemployment and underemployment, the move to deregulation, the growth in part-time work and the increase in unsocial patterns of work are complex processes that require complex explanations. Monocausal explanations can only capture part of the reality. Below, we outline and assess the contribution of three major explanations in this area.

The New Right Explanation

Governments in the UK have relied very heavily, sometimes exclusively, on the New Right explanation that places the responsibility for Britain's relative economic decline on the high levels of public expenditure. As the first White Paper by the first Thatcher government put it:

> Public expenditure is at the heart of Britain's present economic difficulties. (HM Treasury, 1979, p. 1)

The twin arguments in this thesis are that high levels of public spending mean high levels of employment in the public sector and high levels of taxation in order to finance the government's activities. The implications of the first argument are that public employment means not only too many people being drawn away from 'productive' industries into 'unproductive' public services, but also that this reduces the reserve army of labour that is necessary for industry to use when it is in a position to expand. The weaknesses of this part of the argument are that there has not been a general shortage of labour; that most of those employed in the public sector are women, while most of those employed in the manufacturing sector are men; and that the distinction between productive private employment and unproductive public service is crude and does not always stand up to scrutiny. In brief, the 'crowding out' of labour thesis has been 'generally discredited' (Gough, 1996, p. 216).

It is the second argument, the 'financial crowding out', that has carried more weight over the years. Direct taxes are said to have an adverse effect on people's willingness to work hard and to save, as well as on corporate decisions to invest in a country. There is a massive body of literature showing that the effect of direct taxes on individuals varies according to their economic and family circumstances. Some will be deterred, others will not, and still others may be forced to work harder in order to receive the net earnings that are necessary for their needs. Many, of course, have no opportunities to work harder in their jobs. While there is some disagreement over the overall effect, it is agreed that, whether negative or positive, it is an exceedingly weak influence on the economy.

There is, however, some evidence that seems to suggest that firms may relocate part of their operations away from countries with high labour costs to countries where such costs are low, and this involves issues of taxation and insurance contributions. We will examine this in more detail in the section below on globalization.

Comparative evidence on economic growth, public expenditure and taxation neither supports nor refutes this claim (OECD, 1994a, Annex, OECD, 1995, p. 73). Depending on which countries one compares over what period, and how one defines public or social expenditure, one can reach different conclusions. The only conclusion one can draw from such studies is that high as well as low rates of economic growth are compatible with both high and low levels of public expenditure (Pfaller *et al.*, 1991; George and Taylor-Gooby, 1996). Table 2.7 provides evidence that can be used both to defend and to refute the New Right thesis.

Historically, too, there is no evidence linking particular taxation rates with particular rates of economic growth. According to the OECD, the low levels of productivity of the 1970s were not so much the result of public expenditure or taxation volumes as primarily the result of investment deficiencies:

Table 2.7   Public and social expenditure, taxation and economic growth, 1984–94

	Public expenditure as percentage of GDP	*Social expenditure as percentage of GDP*	*Taxation as percentage of GDP*	*GDP growth percentage per year*
Denmark	60	29	52	2.2
France	52	27	44	2.0
Germany	47	26	41	2.8
Greece	45	17	36	1.7
Italy	52	23	38	2.2
Norway	47	25	45	2.7
Spain	42	16	34	2.7
Sweden	63	33	54	1.3
UK	42	21	36	2.3
USA	34	14	29	2.9
Japan	32	12	29	3.1

Sources: OECD, 1994a, Annex Tables 1 and 27; OECD, 1996, Table 1.1, p. 19; Richards and Madden, 1996, Table 1, p. 23.

If one single explanation had to be provided for Britain's record concerning labour productivity and foreign competitiveness, it would probably be found in the investment area. (OECD, 1977, p. 33)

The New Right explanation has recently concentrated on the effects of benefits for the unemployed as a major cause of unemployment. It has used the example of the USA, where benefits are far from generous by European and even British standards and where unemployment rates have been consistently lower. This is true, but the picture is very different if one uses the labour participation rate rather than the unemployment rate as the index of employment. Since welfare benefits for the unemployed are paid for shorter periods in the USA than in Europe, the US unemployed are less likely than their European counterparts to say that they are actively seeking employment and are thus excluded from the unemployment rate statistics. The risk of exclusion from the labour market may be similar, but the official unemployment rate is lower. McLaughlin provides evidence showing that, when both unemployment and inactivity are taken together, the US figures converge with those of European countries:

On average 12% of prime-age US males and 14.9% of UK males were out of work in the 1980s, compared with 9.1% in France and 12.2% in Germany. It is the

pattern, rather than the extent of unemployment and non-employment rates which is very different across OECD countries. (McLaughlin, 1994, p. 181)

The Neo-Keynesian Approach

The Neo-Keynesian approach sees unemployment as the result of a decline in overall demand in the economy, of the abandonment of the corporatist approach to industrial relations, and of the elevation of inflation containment as the primary economic concern of government. Reducing demand through cuts in public expenditure lowers purchasing power within society; adversarial industrial relations lead to more strikes that can affect productivity rates; and excessive emphasis on inflation control can lead to public and fiscal policies that increase unemployment both directly and indirectly.

It follows from this approach that governments wishing to prevent or reduce unemployment must pursue policies that stimulate demand through a variety of fiscal measures – financial aid to employers to create jobs, direct government job creation measures, active labour market policies, regional policies and similar approaches. Governments should also encourage trade unions and employers to negotiate wages, redundancies, training and other industrial issues in a spirit of compromise, with the national interest firmly in mind. High unemployment as a means of containing inflation is rejected. As Layard put it in relation to unemployment in the UK in the early 1980s:

> Until this deflation of demand is moderated, the hopes for unemployment are poor. For the quickest way to raise employment is to spend more now, and accept that inflation will continue at the present level. (Layard, 1986, p. 33)

Evidence in support of this view comes from the recent rise in unemployment in Germany, France and other European countries as a result of their efforts to reduce inflation in order to satisfy the criteria for joining the European Monetary Union (EMU). It is also instructive that the criteria for EMU membership do not include a reduction in unemployment level. Indeed, all three criteria for EMU membership can involve a decline in overall demand, which this approach sees as the major cause of unemployment.

The weaknesses of this approach stem from the very same features that constitute its strength as it 'is associated with the concepts of consensus building, social partnerships and dialogue as being the alternative to the impersonal workings of the market economy' (Mullard, 1995/96, p. 266).

Increasing demand in the economy through public spending over long periods can imply rises in taxation that may become electorally damaging for governments. There is no inevitability of this happening; but its possibility cannot be ignored. The success of corporatist approaches depends also on the degree to which the social partners play the game according to the rules. This, however, is not always the case. It is for this reason that some have argued that corporatist structures based on voluntary participation should be strengthened with some form of government backing that pressurizes both employers and trade unions to observe the rules of corporatism.

Neo-Keynesians reject the claim that deregulation creates jobs and reduces unemployment, as suggested by the American experience. Their argument, as mentioned above, is that if one looks at statistics not only of unemployment, but also of non-employment, the supposed ill-effects of generous unemployment benefits on employment levels are undermined. In countries with inadequate benefits, the unemployed are less likely to register and to appear in the official statistics – they simply disappear, but only to be included among the non-employed section of the population. Moreover, deregulation leads to the 'pauperization of work', that is, 'declines in job quality and security, as measured by earnings, continuity of employment, and provision by employers of nonwage benefits, notably health care insurance and retirement pensions' (Rosen, 1996, p. 37).

Globalization and Unemployment

Recent changes in technology, information technology, transportation systems and international legislation concerning trade and investment have greatly enhanced the power of large firms, particularly transnational companies (TNCs). These can move finance, trade and investment across countries very quickly with or without the consent of national governments. It is a political as well as an economic process as TNCs can greatly influence, some would say dictate, government economic and social policies (Cable, 1995; Strange, 1995). TNCs will locate their activities in countries where they can maximize their profits. Although there are several factors affecting this decision, labour cost is one of them.

It is difficult to know the extent to which the relocation of firms on grounds of labour costs has occurred. The experiences of countries with high labour costs in Europe, however, are indicative of the potential seriousness of the problem. Olsen argues that, in the case of Sweden, where labour costs are comparatively high, the process was well under way by the end of the 1980s. Large Swedish firms were employing more people and investing more capital abroad than in Sweden:

> Stronger, much more unified, and considerably less dependent upon Swedish labor and the domestic scene, Swedish capital has been able to pursue different strategies more suited to the emerging global order. (Olsen, 1996, p. 13)

Similarly, in Germany, Marsh argues that the high labour costs accruing from corporatist industrial relations have driven German capital to invest more abroad than at home in recent years. Most of this investment has been in the UK and the USA rather than in developing countries. He also points out that these shifts of capital investment:

> have far-reaching implications for Germany's social system and consensus-oriented system of management, based on traditional tripartite understanding between government, trade unions and employers. (Marsh, 1996, p. 395)

In addition to the problem of capital flight, there is the issue of the effect of imports of low-priced goods from developing countries. Estimates of the number of jobs lost in advanced industrial societies through this process vary, although it is agreed that it has happened even after taking into account the increase in the number of jobs through trade with developing countries. It is also generally agreed that it is the unskilled workers who have suffered most through this. The cautious conclusion of the International Labour Office is as follows:

> It is not, however, unreasonable to conclude that trade with the South has been at least partly responsible for the loss of unskilled jobs and the widening of wage differentials in the North. (International Labour Office, 1995, p. 53)

Almost irrespective of the party political nature of the government, globalization has resulted in welfare retrenchment in advanced industrial societies, which has implications for employment policies. As Lee puts it:

> Globalization is being accompanied by a worldwide trend towards smaller government, manifested in reductions in public expenditure, lower taxes, reduced political support for redistributive measures and widespread deregulation of markets, including the labour market. (Lee, 1997, p. 497)

In conclusion, globalization is a process that is compatible with the New Right approach as its advocates claim that unless labour costs are reduced, unemployment will increase. It raises difficult issues for Neo-Keynesianism because it questions its basic assumptions about government spending and corporatist structures of industrial relations. At the very least, it requires that certain adaptations be made to the Neo-Keynesian approach, such as making the payment of benefits to the unemployed, lone parents and other groups of working age more difficult and less generous. It increases the economic and political power of business and makes the achievement of traditional, secure full employment patterns more difficult. It is, however, an abdication of political responsibility to conclude that governments are impotent and totally subservient to worldwide economic trends. Their power may have been restricted, but it has not been abolished.

Why Have Things Been Changing as they Have?

New Right explanations

- High rates of public spending
- High rates of public sector employment
- High levels of taxation
- Financial crowding out
- Generous benefits for the unemployed

Neo-Keynesian explanations

- Decline in demand
- Abandonment of corporatist approaches
- Putting inflation containment as the primary goal

Globalization explanations

- Relocation of industry
- Capital flight
- Competition from developing countries

What are the Broad Implications for Society?

High rates of unemployment, particularly long-term unemployment, as well as high rates of labour deregulation have adverse effects on various aspects of life in a society that affect different groups in society differently.

Widening of earnings inequalities

There is compelling evidence that unemployment and deregulation contribute to the widening of earnings inequalities because of the downward pressures that they exert on wages in some occupations and the fact that the level of benefits is lower than earnings from work for the majority of the unemployed. Table 2.8 outlines the evidence for this. It shows that, while the earnings of the bottom decile of male manual workers as a percentage of the median earnings improved slightly during the postwar era, they declined consistently after 1976 with the application of New Right economic and social policies. The opposite trend applied to the earnings of the top decile group. The table also shows that, historically, earnings inequalities have remained fairly constant for a whole century despite intermittent fluctuations. It suggests that there are strong pressures in society that maintain wage differentials at a pretty constant – although not quite identical – level over the years.

Table 2.8 The spread of full-time male manual earnings, 1886–1996

Year	*Lowest decile as percentage of median*	*Highest decile as percentage of median*
1886	68.6	143.1
1906	66.5	156.8
1938	67.7	139.9
1960	70.6	145.2
1970	67.3	147.5
1976	70.2	144.9
1986	65.4	154.8
1996	62.8	160.5

Source: Low Pay Unit, 1996, Table 2, p. 9

There are different views on what is an acceptable wage level below which earnings are unacceptably low. If one uses the Council of Europe's threshold, then, in 1979, 57.6 per cent of full-time women employees and 14.6 per cent of full-time men had earnings that were below that level, corresponding to a total of 28.3 per cent of the labour force. In 1996, the corresponding proportions were 49.6 per cent for women – an improvement – 30.8 per cent for men – a deterioration – and an overall figure of 37.6 per cent (Low Pay Unit, 1996, p. 8). The only bright side to these trends is the narrowing of gender inequalities. In 1979, women in full-time employment had gross earnings, including overtime pay, that amounted to 63.6 per cent of those for men; in 1996, the corresponding proportion rose to 72.3 per cent (Low Pay Unit, 1996, p. 9). Although gender earnings inequalities remain, recent trends show some hope for the future.

Rise in poverty

Work – and its absence – is inextricably linked to poverty in a variety of direct and indirect ways. People at work with low pay have always been one of the major groups in poverty. This was much more the case in pre-1970 days than today with the introduction of the family credit scheme and the entrance of married women into part-time employment in large numbers. Unemployed persons and their families are more likely to be in poverty than are other groups on benefits because of the lower level of their benefits and the greater policing to which they are subjected. Unemployment, low pay and poverty are inter-connected as it is the low paid who are more likely to be unemployed and more likely to be in poverty. Similarly, low pay and long-term unemployment affect the future level of the state pension and even more so of any occupational pension. The claim that the low-paid worker of today is the retired pensioner in poverty of tomorrow has always been a fairly accurate description of poverty trends along the life cycle.

It has been argued that there is considerable upward mobility, with the result that low-pay jobs are simply the stepping stones to better-paid jobs. While this may be true for many workers, it needs to be also borne in mind that low pay can last for a long time. As Table 2.9 shows, this period is the longest in the USA and UK, and it is also longer for women than for men. There is also 'evidence of a "carousel effect" in all countries for which data are available: many workers seem to move back and forth from low pay to no pay' (OECD, 1997, p. 39).

Table 2.9 Number of years in low-pay jobs for persons continually employed in full-time employment, 1986–91

	Denmark	*France**	*Germany*	*Italy*	*UK*	*USA*
Men	1.4	2.6	2.2	2.7	3.3	3.8
Women	1.9	3.1	3.4	2.9	4.0	4.2
Total	**1.8**	**2.8**	**2.8**	**2.8**	**3.8**	**4.1**

*For France, the years are 1984–89.
Source: OECD, 1997, p. 39.

Mixed results of part-time work

The growth of part-time employment has its positive and negative aspects as far as family and individual incomes are concerned. In those cases where part-time work fits the wishes and requirements of the individual, it cannot but be welcome. In cases, however, where part-time work is imposed by employers contrary to the employee's wishes, it is an unwelcome practice serving primarily the interests of employers. The same, however, cannot be said of work insecurity, which is always contrary to individual and family welfare. It means that family income is precarious, it lowers wage levels, and it increases the stress on individuals and their families.

Work and health

Work is essential to the health of individual workers. It is not simply that it provides the necessary income for themselves and their families, but it also provides them with emotional and psychological stability. As always, however, there is the other side of the coin that points to the damaging effects of some aspects of work to health. There is now abundant evidence that modern pressurized forms of work can have adverse effects on people's physical and mental health. Chronic work stress can be damaging to health even when it is accompanied by increased individual affluence. Absenteeism from work in Britain is running at 8.26 days per employee each year, it is costly to the country as well as to the individual, and its two probable causes are 'stress and low morale' (Bassett, 1997, p. 48).

Unemployment and personal problems

The effects of unemployment on health have long been documented, from the recession of the 1930s onwards (Jahoda, 1979). All the studies have consistently shown that physical and mental health suffers as a result of unemployment. Recent evidence also shows unemployment to be related not only to ill health, but also to suicide and parasuicide (Brenner 1980; Platt and Kreitman, 1984). Fagin and Little's study demonstrated that unemployment affects the health of not only the individual unemployed person, but the immediate family as well (Fagin and Little, 1984). Long-term unemployment has also been linked to marriage break-up (Lampard, 1993) as well as educational underachievement. Evidence also shows that, subjectively, the unemployed consider their well being more unfavourably than do employed persons even after such factors as education, age, health and marital status are taken into account (Clark and Oswald, 1994).

The financial costs of unemployment

The financial costs of unemployment to society are very high: the loss of production; the loss of revenues to the government since the incomes of the unemployed are too low to be taxable; and the cost of benefits paid to the unemployed irrespective of whether these are insurance or assistance benefits.

In brief, unemployment continues to be a major social problem for individuals and society despite the provision of welfare benefits. Summarizing the evidence on the different types of costs incurred by unemployment, Philpott aptly concludes that 'while all unemployment is wasteful, long-term unemployment appears to be a total waste since it fails even to offer a pay-off in terms of controlling inflation' (Philpott, 1994, p. 144).

Employment and social security

The new employment practices and the high levels of unemployment raise serious questions concerning the appropriateness of the principles underpinning the social security system. The Beveridgean social security system was based on the insurance principle that envisaged full-time full employment for all except married women. We now have an employment situation in which part-time work is as widespread as full-time employment, where married women are employed in large numbers, where divorce and separation rates are high and where a large proportion of the working population does not satisfy the insurance contribution record to be entitled to benefits. There is clearly an urgent need to reassess the principles of the social security system in a way that enables all those at work and those who care for others to qualify for benefits.

Employment and sustainability

Full employment, as defined in this chapter, is an essential ingredient of a sustainable society. It raises living standards, supplies governments with the revenues to provide social services to all, enables individuals to be socially integrated in their communities, reduces the possibilities of crime and other antisocial behaviour and acts as the binding force that holds society together as a well-functioning entity. High levels of unemployment persisting over long periods of time have exactly the opposite effects.

What are the Broad Implications for Society?

- A widening of earnings inequalities
- A rise in poverty
- Unemployment is related to physical and mental ill-health, contributes to family breakdown and is costly to individuals, families and the government
- Flexible employment increases profitability but creates problems for many employees

---

What Has the Government Response Been to these Changes?

The response of Conservative governments during the 1980s and 90s to the problems created by unemployment, underemployment and deregulation is encapsulated in their core belief that 'unemployment is a price worth paying'. It is a central strand of New Right thinking that governments wishing to control inflation, improve productivity and raise rates of economic growth must create a deregulated supply of labour and an economic environment that makes it possible for employers to manage as they think fit. The implication of this was a series of measures during the 1980s that first reduced the generosity of existing provisions for the unemployed, second weakened labour and wage protection, third increased inequality and fourth reduced trade union power.

Benefits for the unemployed were made less generous in a variety of ways (Dean, 1994):

- From 1980, all benefits, including those for the unemployed, were to be increased annually not according to any rise in earnings but according to the rise in prices.
- A long series of changes throughout the 1980s and 90s made the definition of unemployment more stringent and hence reduced the number of those registered as unemployed.
- The qualifying criteria for unemployment benefit were made more stringent, with the result that fewer people qualified and those who did received lower benefits.
- Greater stress has been placed on the detection of benefit fraud and the prosecution of those involved in it.
- A greater proportion of the unemployed have had to rely on income-tested assistance benefit rather than on insurance unemployment benefit, a trend that has added to the stigmatization process of the unemployed.
- In the 1990s, workfare projects were introduced that made the payment of benefit conditional on accepting employment in low-paid, low-skill work.
- The regulations governing the payment of redundancy lump sums have been altered in order to reduce both the number of workers who qualify and the amount of the lump sum.

A series of legislative measures has reduced the protection of low-paid workers. The various wages councils that provided a minimum wage in certain industries and trades have gradually been abolished on the grounds that their work reduced labour flexibility and hence efficiency and profitability. Successive Conservative governments have defied the European Court on several employment issues and have doggedly refused to accept the Social Chapter of the EU.

The change in the indexation method of benefits, the increased use of assistance instead of insurance benefits, the taxation of unemployment benefit, the spread of low-wage employment and, perhaps above all, the sharp lowering of taxation rates on higher incomes inevitably increased income inequality. It was a policy that governments pursued in their belief that increased inequality sharpens work incentives and improves productivity rates. At the same time, the age-old view that the higher paid need not reductions but increases in their already high salaries in order to boost their incentives to work harder became the accepted wisdom.

Finally, major pieces of legislation were introduced with the direct intention of lowering the power of trade unions. This legislation and the high rates of unemployment inevitably tipped the balance of power firmly in favour of employers. Wage rises have been brought under control, while rates of profitability increased – a trend very much in line with government thinking that maximum labour flexibility and high profitability are essential to investment and economic growth.

Although it is too early to assess the policies of the new Labour government, the indications are that it will continue with most of the macro-economic policies pursued by previous Conservative governments. It differs, however, in its intention to introduce several micro-policies, such as a minimum wage, make better child care provisions, place more emphasis on the training of the young unemployed and the long-term unemployed and improve workers' rights at work.

What Has the Government Response Been to these Changes?

- The criteria for eligibility for unemployment benefits were tightened
- Benefits for the unemployed were made less generous
- Unemployed people became more dependent on means-tested benefits
- Protection for low-paid workers was reduced
- The power of the trade unions was reduced

What Proposals for Action Have Been Made by Conventional Sources?

In this section, we look at the proposals of the main political parties in the UK, the EU, the OECD and those academics who believe that it is possible to abolish unemployment and return to the traditional type of full employment.

The macro-policies of the two main UK political parties in relation to employment and unemployment are very similar as they are both firmly committed to fiscal discipline in public expenditure, the control of inflation and the pursuit of higher rates of productivity. They insist that public expenditure should be tightly controlled, that public debt should be reduced, that personal taxation should be lowered, that inflation should be kept low and that the UK should be made attractive to foreign investors. It is a fiscal scenario that is not conducive to rapid reductions of unemployment in the short term. Both parties have rejected the traditional Keynesian approach that argued for substantial increases in government expenditure in order to stimulate demand and thus reduce unemployment. It is therefore true that, in macro-policy concerning unemployment, 'it is becoming increasingly difficult to disentangle right from left in any simple way' (Shackleton, 1996, p. 6).

The two parties, however, disagree on some, but not all, of the micro-policies related to investment and labour market issues. The Labour Party is committed to a national minimum wage, while the Conservative Party is opposed to it (Conservative Research Department, 1995, p. 296). Much has been said about the incentive and the disincentive employment effects of a national minimum wage, while the evidence shows that its effects depend on the level at which it is set, the method of its introduction, the criteria used for its annual upgrading and the degree to which it is policed and enforced.

The second area of difference between the two parties concerns the European Social Chapter, which regulates the labour market in such areas as hours of work and annual holidays and which provides such benefits as maternity and paternity leave. The Conservative Party has steadfastly opposed it on the grounds that it 'would reverse the programme of deregulation which successive Conservative Governments have carried out' (Conservative Research Department, 1995, p. 296) and thus raise labour costs. While in opposition, the Labour Party supported the Social Chapter on the grounds of fairness to workers, in the belief that a satisfied workforce is a more productive one and because it already applied to the other member countries of the EU. In government, the Labour Party has wavered from this position to adopt a policy that supports some but not all the strands of the EU Social Chapter.

Both parties have abandoned the traditional, fairly passive approach to benefits for the unemployed. Both now feel that the payment of benefits should be made more conditional on the recipient's willingness to look for and accept jobs and training; that greater resources should be put into the detection of fraud by the unemployed; that the benefit system should be tailored so as not to act as a disincentive to employment; and that greater emphasis should be given to counselling and assisting the long-term unemployed to obtain jobs. On the employer's side, both parties give support to the payment of some sort of subsidy to encourage employers to take on the unemployed, particularly the long-term unemployed. There is also bi-partisan agreement that the benefit and tax system should be so harmonized as to minimize existing poverty traps. This is not to suggest a total unanimity of views but, instead, general agreement on the main conditions attached to the payment of benefits to the unemployed.

Even in the area of training, in which the Labour party has made ambitious pronouncements, the differences between the parties are not as great as they first appear. The Conservatives want the private sector to take the lead, the state providing a supportive hand, while the Labour Party talks in more ambitious tones about state involvement such as work or training for all young people aged 18–25 and the establishment of a University for Industry along the lines of the Open University. Any extra costs, however, will be financed not through normal sources but through a windfall tax on the profits of the privatized public utilities. Since its election to office in 1997, the Labour Government has shown a great deal of enthusiasm in pursuing these policies.

In brief, although the two parties start from different ideological perspectives, they converge a great deal. The Conservative Party favours deregulation of the labour market but accepts that training and education measures are also essential. The Labour Party lays great stress on the role of education in improving the quality of labour but accepts some of the deregulation policies. Their differences are even less significant when viewed within the macro-policy of fiscal discipline in state finance to which they both subscribe. It is perhaps for this reason that multinational companies are not unduly worried by which party is in power. No one doubts the power that multinational companies have to influence the economy of a country, and both political parties are anxious to enlist their support. Their political muscle is based on the brutal fact that, in 1993, 'global firms accounted for two thirds of world exports of goods and services. Half of this comprised exports from one part of a company to another' (Bush, 1997, p. 29).

To say that the macro-policies of the two parties are almost identical and their micro-policies very similar is only half the story. The other equally important half is that this convergence has come about as a result of the Labour Party's shift to the right, with the result that government policies to reduce unemployment in the near future will be based largely on some variant of the New Right approach. There may well be less unemployment, but, as in the USA, the number of the non-employed will rise and the social costs will also be high: more low-paid jobs, even higher poverty rates, greater inequality and deeper social conflicts along American lines.

One needs to look outside party politics in order to find advocates of the more egalitarian institutional approach to the creation of full employment. Boltho and Glyn, strong advocates of this approach, argue for increased public expenditure in order to create jobs directly in various sectors of the economy, including the public services, rather than providing subsidies to employers to induce them to take on the unemployed:

> A major advantage of additional public spending on goods and services is that it usually creates jobs directly and relatively predictably, whereas subsidies or deregulation have very uncertain effects. (Boltho and Glyn, 1995, p. 465)

They acknowledge that such a programme will mean higher levels of public spending, but they defend their case in two ways. First, the total net cost will be substantially lower than the gross cost through savings on benefits and the payment of taxes. Second, they feel that 'there is no coherent economic reason for aiming at a particular "optimal" size of the public sector' (Boltho and Glyn, 1995, p. 466).

They also concede that such a programme is politically feasible if (1) the public is willing to pay the higher taxes that are necessary to finance the public employment programmes designed to cut unemployment, and (2) the trade unions and those at work in general are prepared to accept that higher taxes should not be compensated for by higher wages. Without this, 'the whole process will be frustrated by a combination of reduced competitiveness, profits and investment, as well as higher inflation' (Boltho and Glyn, 1995, p. 467). Critics will be quick to point out that both of these conditions are problematic.

Many in this group, however, agree with Lee that 'there is no single measure that can restore full employment swiftly' (Lee, 1997, p. 49). Lee's list of policies consists of first raising the rate of economic growth in a non-inflationary way brought about not by deregulation but by a social pact between employers, trade unions and the government. Second, a series of labour market measures that fall into the category of active labour market policies: training, payment of subsidies to employers to take on unemployed workers, employment expansion in the social services, reform of the benefit system for the unemployed, in terms of both the way in which it is funded and the way in which it pays out benefits, and so on.

All advocates of this 'active government' approach accept that the reduction of unemployment is as much a political as an economic issue. It involves costs that will be borne by some groups in society so that the unemployed can be provided with work. Some even feel that it is more of a political than an economic problem. As Ormerod crisply puts it:

> Unemployment is in essence a political and not an economic question. A variety of potential solutions exists to the problem, but each of them entails costs. Different groups may bear the costs in different ways, but costs are unavoidable. (Ormerod, 1996, p. 21)

What Proposals for Action Have Been Made by Conventional Policy Sources?

- Firm fiscal discipline
- A tight control of inflation
- Increased productivity
- Benefits to be clearly conditional on a search for work
- More emphasis on training

What Proposals for Action Have Been Made by Radicals?

What unites the various proposals in this section is the belief that the age of full-time full employment is over and cannot be re-created. Most find this

regrettable but a fact of life, while a few welcome it as it presents the opportunity for a new beginning in the area of work and human welfare. They all
share the sentiment expressed in the quotation below:

> If we understand by full employment continuous full-time employment for all – 8
> hours a day, five days a week, 48 weeks a year for 45 years of our lifetime – then
> full employment is impossible. (Schmid, 1995, p. 429)

Three major reasons are given for the inability of governments to bring back
this type of full employment: the effects of modern technology; the globalization of production; and the entry of women into the labour market.

There is general acknowledgement that, in the past, technology created
more jobs than it destroyed, albeit in different sectors of the economy and
usually after a time lapse. However, it is argued, extrapolating from previous
technological revolutions is of little value because current and future technology is of a different kind. The silicon chip, with its low cost and high capa-
bility and versatility, is replacing not only human labour but the human mind
as well. Rifkin puts this most forcefully as follows:

> Earlier industrial technologies replaced the physical power of human labor, substi-
> tuting machines for body and brawn. The new computer-based technologies,
> however, promise a replacement of the human mind, substituting machines for
> human beings across the entire gamut of economic activity. (Rifkin, 1996, p. 18)

As a result, modern technology affects all types of jobs and all socio-economic
groups – not only the unskilled and semi-skilled as in the past, but also the
white collar and professionals. It leads to both higher levels of productivity
and higher levels of joblessness.

It is very difficult to assess the validity of this claim, although one cannot
but be overwhelmed with the advances in information technology and its
effects on employment in almost all aspects of life. This process will clearly
continue and gain momentum in the future, and its effects on employment
patterns will be substantial. Its effects on employment levels, however, are
much in dispute. Even those who believe in its employment potential qualify
it by insisting that this will only come about if education and training are
constantly improved. As Francis has argued, although 'there is no reason why
the new technology should inevitably mean a massive reduction in employment' (Francis, 1986, p. 23), countries that do not provide enough training
to their workers will suffer from unemployment. However, if all advanced
industrial countries pursue equally comprehensive education and training
policies, the competitive advantage of training to a country is surely blunted.

The globalization of finance, technology and trade means that, whenever
possible, production is likely to move to countries with low labour costs. It is
argued that however much European countries try to reduce their labour

costs and increase their productivity, they will not be able to compete with many low-wage countries in Asia and South America where educational standards are high and where labour productivity can also be high. Although there is some truth in this argument, it needs also to be borne in mind that labour costs are rising fast in some of these countries and that other factors are also important in deciding the geographical location of industries. Again, disagreements emerge, for while Mishan concludes that globalization means that 'there are hard times ahead for the working populations in the world's more prosperous countries' (Mishan, 1996, p. 156), Corry, in a reply article, rejects the threat to employment from Third World countries because rises in income in these countries will mean 'increased demand for our higher-tech exports' (Corry, 1996, p. 160).

On balance, it is difficult not to accept the conclusion of the International Labour Office cited earlier in this chapter that, so far, imports from developing countries have had a minor adverse effect on employment in the advanced industrial countries. In all probability, this is likely to continue in the future.

As shown in a previous section of this chapter, employment levels among men declined while women's rates rose during the past few decades. The argument is that this will continue as there are substantial reserves of married women who will enter the labour force if jobs are available. Thus, Bassett summarises the findings of a recent report on the future of employment in the UK by pointing out that half of the expected new jobs in the decade to 2006 will be in self-employment; of the other half, most will be part-time, mainly for women, and only a small number of full-time jobs will be mainly for men. The combined effect is that women will take up two thirds of the total number of new jobs by the end of the decade, with the result that the overall effect of this on unemployment levels will be minimal (Bassett, 1996, p. 26).

In brief, radical critics insist that a return to traditional full employment is not likely to be possible. If societies wish to abolish unemployment, they will have to adopt a series of new measures that broadly aim to (1) redistribute work and (2) blunt the distinction between employment and unemployment.

Redistribution of Work

A series of measures designed to redistribute work in order to reduce unemployment have been put forward by various writers: planned reductions in working hours, reductions in the levels of overtime, job sharing and reducing the working lifetime.

During this century, the number of hours worked per week has declined gradually but substantially in all industrial societies as a result of advances in technology, trade union power and government policies. It may well be that this will continue in the future. What is proposed, however, is something rather different: governments, preferably with the consent of trade unions and employers, should legislate a substantial and quick reduction in the hours of work in order to create more jobs. The most commonly suggested reduction is to limit the working week to 30 hours.

Such a policy, however, may carry a price tag: for employers, it can mean a loss of production, while for workers, it can mean wage reduction. It may well be that reduced hours of work will increase productivity per worker so that employers do not lose out. If this happens, however, there will be no good reason for employers to take on more workers unless there is strong demand for their products. In cases where product demand is stable, Gill states the dilemma as follows:

> The conundrum is that if productivity is increased to offset the cut in hours, no jobs are created; if it is not, employers' costs rise – unless they are offset by cuts in real pay. (Gill, 1985, p. 173)

Some supporters of this approach feel less pessimistic about the obstacles. Jossa has argued that there is 'a theoretically simple and clear way to get out of the dilemma: to agree that the work hour reductions must be strictly tied to the labour productivity increase, leaving wages unchanged' (Jossa, 1996, p. 3). In other words, workers should produce as much as they did before even though they are working fewer hours.

The other objection, that reducing the hours of work might simply result in more overtime, is comparatively easier to deal with providing the government, the employers and the trade unions are prepared to face up to the issue. This is clearly not an easy task, but neither is it an impossible one.

Reducing the hours of work will have child care and social benefits. It will make it easier for parents to work and to care for their children, and it will provide more time for personal educational, leisure or sports pursuits.

So far, the only cases of actual planned reductions in work hours have been designed to prevent redundancies. The much reported decision of Volkswagen in Germany in 1994 to introduce a four-day, 28.8-hour week in order to avoid reducing its workforce by 30 000 was made possible after the trade unions had agreed to a reduction of wages by 10 per cent. There have been several similar cases in other countries, all based on the principle of wage reduction to offset employers' costs. In all such cases, agreement was reached out of pragmatic considerations and not because of 'any inclination toward socio-cultural experimentation' (Bastian, 1994, p. 303). Such agreements also occurred in firms where wages were high.

The recent proposals by the socialist government in France to reduce the hours of work to 35 per week in order to take on more of the unemployed shows both the problems and the possibilities. It was electorally a vote-winning promise, it is supported strongly by the trade unions, it is opposed equally strongly by the business leaders, and the cabinet appears to be split on the issue.

Job sharing is different from conventional part-time employment. It 'involves dividing a full-time position into two or more positions while retaining all the rights and privileges attached to the full-time position. It is this which differentiates job sharing from part-time work, in that many part-time jobs do not carry **pro rata** terms and conditions, and they are very often poorly paid and low status' (Roch *et al.*, 1996, p. 143). The arguments in favour of and against job sharing in terms of productivity are largely ideological and are not based on any hard evidence. It is, however, generally agreed that for some workers, particularly mothers with young children and some older workers, job sharing provides a better fit to their circumstances than does full-time employment. Many governments in industrial societies have introduced legislation making job sharing possible, particularly among their own employees, from a variety of motives. So far, job sharing remains a minority practice because it inevitably means a reduction in earnings for employees. As far as employers are concerned, part-time appointments are a more profitable proposition than job sharing.

Reducing the length of people's working life time through such practices as sabbaticals, extended leave and early retirement is the third major proposal for reducing unemployment by redistributing work. Beginning with early retirement, evidence shows that it has spread quite widely, so that in 1991, the proportion of men aged 55–59 in employment ranged from 49.3 per cent in Belgium to 73.9 per cent in the UK and 74.5 per cent in Denmark; for the 60–64-year age group the corresponding proportions were 17.8 per cent, 48.9 per cent and 46.4 per cent respectively (Walker *et al.*, 1993, p. 95). This decline in economic activity, however, was due primarily to attempts by employers to reduce labour costs. It therefore means that early retirement does not lead to the creation of more jobs or even to the reduction of unemployment. Only in a small proportion of cases where there is agreement between employers and trade unions are early retirees replaced by young unemployed persons. A recent example of this again comes from Germany, where the trade union IG Metall reached an agreement with the employers for workers aged over 60 years to work half-time and to receive 82 per cent of their basic pay in order to free jobs for young unemployed workers.

In many cases, early retirement is imposed on older workers without sufficient monetary and pension compensation, with the result that it leads to higher poverty levels. Where early retirement schemes provide sufficient financial compensation, they involve high costs for governments, and their popularity waxes and wanes depending on the state of government finances. As far as sabbaticals and extended leave are concerned, they have rarely been used despite their high profile in the literature. Only in some professional sectors, such as university employment, have sabbaticals been used because, as far as employers are concerned, such schemes involve costs but do not guarantee any direct tangible returns.

Blunting the Distinction Between Employment and Unemployment

The various proposals for work redistribution are not mutually exclusive. Most commentators see them as complementary depending on the circumstances of different employers, occupations and so on. Indeed, some see them as part of a greater design that attempts to blunt the current sharp distinction between employment and unemployment by creating more acceptable work statuses.

A report by a recent French group proposes the creation of activity contracts to supplement employment contracts for individual workers. In the same way as employees are given employment contracts setting out their right and responsibilities under the law, they should also be given activity contracts that set out over a period of years their employment patterns: full-time work, part-time work, training, family leave and so on. The proposal was seen as an attempt to reconcile the demands of firms for more flexibility and the individual worker's desire for more security (Boissonnat, 1996).

More ambitiously, Gorz has proposed the idea of a Time Bank for all citizens throughout their working lives. Every individual should be expected to work a minimum number of hours during his/her working life – between twenty and thirty thousand hours over a lifetime. Individuals would decide when they would work these hours without loss of income. For this, they should be paid a basic wage, and they should be allowed to work longer and earn more if they so wish (Gorz, 1989).

Feminist writers and others have argued for all such forms of work as caring for children or adult dependents to be considered legitimate work and be treated on an equal footing with paid employment. As mentioned earlier, this has met with only a modicum of recognition by countries in Europe. It has not been fully accepted in policy terms.

Still others see part-time employment 'part-day, part-week, part-month and/or part-year' as the basis for the future organization of work. Such part-time work would be guaranteed by the state, the public sector acting 'as employer of last resort' (Delsen, 1997, p. 129). Only by restricting paid employment to part-time work will there be enough employment for all.

Family-friendly Employment Policies

With the rise in the proportion of women going out to work, there has been an increasing realization of the need to make employment more friendly to the needs of the family, particularly women. Government policies vary considerably on this issue not only with regard to the provision of pre-school facilities, but also in relation to maternity and paternity pay and leave, as Table 2.10 shows. The USA stands out as a minimal provider of such policies. Radicals and others have argued for an increased provision of such policies not only on family and child care grounds, but also on pure employment considerations – such policies improve work incentives and work productivity.

Table 2.10   Family-friendly employment policies

Country	Maternity leave	% of previous pay on maternity leave	Parental leave*	Mother/father
Britain	14–18 weeks	90 initially	–	–
France	16–26 weeks	100	3 years	Entirely
Germany	14 weeks	100	3 years	Entirely
Italy	22 weeks	80	6 months	Entirely
Japan	14 weeks	60	1 year	Entirely
Netherlands	16 weeks	100	1 year	6 months
Spain	14 weeks	100	3 years	Entirely
Sweden	14 weeks	75	1 year	Most
USA	12 weeks+	0	–	–

* Parental leave means that the previous job is preserved but the pay is mostly minimal.
Mother/father refers to whether the parental leave is transferable.
Source: *Economist*, 1998, p. 13.

What Proposals for Action Have Been Made by Radicals?

- To seek a new kind of full employment
- To redistribute work
- To blunt the distinction between employment and unemployment
- To establish family-friendly employment policies

Conclusions

Proposals for reform need to be based on an understanding of recent and future trends in work and employment. We will therefore outline these trends before we go on to assess the contrasting proposals for a full employment society.

- Most of the new jobs to be created in the future will not be in the manufacturing but in the service sector. In the past, the expansion of jobs in the service sector was as much and sometimes more apparent in state social services than in private services. In Sweden, most of the new jobs created during the 1970s and 80s lay in the state social services, whereas in the USA, most of the new jobs were in private services, the so-called 'McJobs', low-paid and insecure. The experience of other countries falls somewhere between these two extremes. Expansion of state service employment, however, appears unlikely if the present political antipathy towards the role of the state continues. Expansion in the number of 'McJobs', however, looks certain to continue, although it is very unlikely that this increase will be high enough to offset the decline in both state service jobs and the manufacturing sector.

- The supply of labour will continue to be plentiful. Women will continue to enter the labour market in increasing numbers, thus offsetting the number of those retiring early. In addition, several European countries have raised their retirement ages in recent years. If the culture of early retirement reverses itself, and if retirement ages are increased by five years and equalized between the sexes, the pool of labour will increase even further.

- Labour will be more educated than in the past, but the belief that education necessarily creates jobs is a half truth for, beyond a certain level, education may simply act 'as a discriminating device in order to allocate too many workers to scarce jobs' (Boyer, 1995, p. S56). Moreover, the current emphasis on education, although welcome for educational reasons, has to face up to the fact that many of the new jobs created do not require all that much skill or higher educational achievements. It begs the question not about the emphasis on education but about the quality of jobs being created.

- The drive towards increased productivity may intensify in order to ward off increasing competition from other firms or other countries, with the result that a catch-22 employment situation sets in: 'productivity is key to the survival of high wage jobs, but productivity improvements means fewer employees are required' (Gunderson and Riddell, 1995, p. 125). The dream of generations of free thinkers that higher technology will liberate men and women from endless toil recedes once again as increased productivity is used primarily to increase profits for the few rather than reduce workloads for the many. As Rifkin puts it:

  > Ironically, the closer we seem to come to the technological fruition of the utopian dream, the more dystopian the future itself appears. That's because the forces of the marketplace continue to generate production and profit, with little thought of generating additional leisure for the millions of working people whose labor is being displaced. (Rifkin, 1995, p. 56)

- Part-time work will come to be even more important in the future. It is a clear indication that full-time full employment is no longer possible. Job insecurity is likely to rise despite the isolated attempts by some firms to find ways of reconciling competitiveness and security at work.

- Government attempts to create more jobs will continue by subsidizing work, creating jobs directly and increasing the pressure on the unemployed to accept any job in sight. Yet, not many believe that the rate at which this is being done will have spectacular effects on the employment situation.

Returning now to the question raised at the beginning of this chapter: can full-time full employment of the traditional kind return to the UK? Despite all the uncertainties, it is unlikely that unemployment will be abolished and employment for all in the traditional sense provided. Economic growth rates may be maintained and even improved, but this will be partly or largely jobless growth. Even the OECD, in its recent two-volume study of employment issues (OECD, 1994c), was undecided on whether full employment is a real possibility in the future. This was in marked contrast to its more confident outlook in many of its earlier documents.

But what are the prospects of a modern type of full employment, that is, with reduced hours of work, with sabbaticals, with work sharing and with a wider definition of work? At present these, too, appear bleak, primarily because of the prevailing ideologies concerning the nature of work, the purpose of employment, the incentives for work and the distribution of the economic benefits of work. It is difficult to see at present a government that will come forth with a radical programme of job creation along the lines envisaged by radical thinkers.

The more realistic scenario is that governments will carry on trying to reduce unemployment by using various mixtures of macro- and micro-economic policies. There is now more acceptance of the fact that neither a totally free market economy nor a centrally planned economy has any future. As Hain puts it, 'if the command economics of state socialism is obsolete, so too is free market capitalism' (Hain, 1995, p. 119). The experience of the Soviet Union and of Thatcherite policies provides the best evidence that what is needed is a mixed economy, the government playing a significant role in the strategic long-term planning of the economy and the private sector being responsible for most day-by-day economic activity.

There is also increasing agreement that both conventional and radical measures are needed in order to create a modern type of full employment. Radical thinkers acknowledge that 'we shall probably, in the end, muddle towards a compromise blend' of the various ways of creating and sharing jobs (Handy, 1984, p. 185). Governments and official bodies, too, are beginning to accept that some, although not all, of the proposals by radicals have merit and can be gradually implemented.

Challenges

Of the many challenges facing the future of work in Britain and other European countries, four stand out.

- Can conventional and radical ideas for the creation of a modern full employment society be blended? The choice facing industrial societies today is between two forms of work sharing: through the operations of the labour market in the form of part-time work, contract work, insecure work, early retirement and unemployment; through the methods outlined by radicals; or through a combination of the two. Can governments secure enough consensus to adopt such a policy?

- Providing jobs for all in the modern sense of full employment is only half the battle. Work needs also to be provided in ways that discourage discrimination, encourage upward mobility, pay a living wage to all and provide satisfaction to the maximum possible number of workers. The quality of work is just as important as its quantity. Should British society continue to concentrate on job creation almost irrespective of the quality of the work provided?

- Millions of women today interrupt or even abandon their careers in order to care for their children or look after elderly relatives. This work is largely ignored by governments. Is this a sensible policy, or should such work be recognized as equal to outside employment so that women are paid a wage and qualify for social security benefits, particularly retirement pensions?

- Government employment policies in the UK have to take into account regional and international factors. At the regional level, EU membership means that British governments play their part in the creation of a new Europe, but they also have to be bound by many of the policies introduced by the European Commission. At the international level, the forces of globalization provide both opportunities for and constraints on British industry. They limit, however, the freedom of any government to adopt the policies it wants. Regional and global factors raise the fundamental questions, what is the role of the UK in the new world of the twenty-first century, and how much freedom has the government to decide this role?

Further Reading

Journals

Economic and Industrial Democracy. Carries articles of both a conventional and a radical nature on issues of work. Of particular interest is the special issue 'The Challenge of Full Employment in the Global Economy', 1997, **18**(1).

International Labour Review. Publishes articles mainly of conventional ideology on issues of work and social security. Of particular interest is the special issue 'Perspectives on the Nature and Future of Work', 1996, **135**(6).

Books

Handy, C. (1984) *The Future of Work*, London, Blackwell. A very readable book examining the reasons why the author believes that there will not be enough jobs for all in the future and what needs to be done to redistribute work. A more recent book of this type is Rifkin, J. (1995) *The End of Work*, New York, Putnam's Sons.

Council of Churches for Britain and Ireland (1997) *Unemployment and the Future of Work*, London, CCBI. A well-researched and clearly written account of the problems faced by the unemployed and the various policy approaches advocated by different groups for the creation of full employment in the UK.

Philpott, J. (ed.) (1997) *Working for Full Employment*, London, Routledge. Contains chapters by experts on the various aspects of unemployment and the policies needed to increase employment.

3

The Family

If we really want to create a better society, we must value children and the families that nurture them far more highly than we do now. (Commission on Social Justice, 1994, p. 311)

I became increasingly convinced during the last two or three years of my time in office that though there were crucially important limits to what politicians could do in this area, we could only get to the root of crime and much else besides by concentrating on strengthening the traditional family. (Thatcher, 1993, p. 628)

Introduction

Although the family has its critics, its importance to society as the basic building block of social systems is a point of almost universal agreement between politicians, social scientists, moralists and the media. The 1997 Conservative Election Manifesto described the family as 'the most important institution in our lives' (Conservative Central Office, 1997, p. 15). The Labour Party was equally enthusiastic: 'Families are the core of our society... The breakdown of family life damages the fabric of our society' (Labour Party, 1997, p. 25). Jonathan Sacks, the Chief Rabbi, recently wrote of the devaluing of the family as 'the beginning of the end of a social system' (*The Times*, 26 February 1997). Establishing the precise nature of its importance and separating the grain of truth from the chaff of rhetoric is not, however, easy, but some points can be sorted out.

- Much is made of the role of the family in socializing the next generation, what the Finer Committee called 'the transmission of ethical and cultural values across the generations' (quoted in Brayshaw, 1980, pp. 64–5). In Berger's words, the family is 'the culture creating institution of modernity par excellence' (Berger, 1993, p. 9). Cicero saw it as 'the seedplot of the whole commonwealth' (quoted in Selbourne, 1994, p. 227).

- Much is made, too, of the importance of the family as a place where children learn about the need for self-restraint and give and take in social relationships. A government minister in 1996 spoke of the government's 'conviction that the family is the essential source of respect between individuals. It is the nursery school of their development as people and as members of society' (Bowis, 1996, p. 10). In Mrs. Thatcher's words, 'it's the place where each generation learns its responsibility to the rest of society' (quoted in Dean and Thompson, 1996, p. 145), as well as being 'the birthplace of the moral sense' (Sacks, 1995, p. 28), and 'an unending school for moral instruction' (Wilson, 1993, pp. 162–3).

- The family is important too as 'a safe place' for meeting the emotional needs of parents and children. Young people, in particular, argued *Something to Celebrate*, need to know that they matter to other people, because only if they are valued as people in their own right will they end up valuing themselves' (Church House, 1995, p. 67). Families are therefore seen as crucial to individual human happiness.

- The family is important as the basic caring unit in society. The bulk of care for children and dependent adults – young and old alike – takes place in the family. We need to experience care before we can, in turn, care for others. The role of public services is almost insignificant in comparison with care provided by families.

Families are seen as particularly important for men – particularly young men. Family responsibilities traditionally took young men into the labour market and held them there. As Helen Bosanquet put it as long ago as 1906, 'Nothing but the considered rights and responsibilities of family life will ever rouse the average man to his full degree of efficiency, and induce him to continue working after he has earned sufficient to meet his own personal needs' (quoted in Lewis, 1998, p. 8). Charles Murray wrote of 'young male barbarians for whom marriage... is an indispensable civilising force' (quoted in Hewitt, 1994, p. 174). Leaving aside the sexist assumptions in these views, the family has always helped to lock men into conventional patterns of behaviour, for example in relation to work.

There is, of course, a downside to this. The family has been a way of imprisoning women in dependent – and at times exploitative – relationships. It has trapped women in poverty. It has confined and constrained their lives. Equally, it has trapped some men, women and children in unfulfilling and destructive relationships. Societies, however, can ask and expect too much of families. There are vital prerequisites for successful families, for example adequate income, housing and employment. The good society depends on much more than strong families. They are a necessary but not sufficient condition of the sustainable society. The family, too, is an easy scapegoat. A broader crisis in society can easily be blamed on 'the family'.

What Has Been Happening?

The family, of course, is always changing. Many of the concerns that we outline below and which came to the fore in the 1980s and 90s were not new. Anderson reminds us that contemporary expressions of concern about a looming crisis in the family can be found for almost all periods in the last 500 years at least (Anderson, 1994, p. 1). Harris reports that, in the early 1900s, it was widely believed that mothering needed to be taught and learned like any other professional skill. Instinct and cultural transmission could not be relied upon to produce adequate mothering, and 'Bad mothering was no longer seen merely as a private failure, but as subversive of community, nation, Empire and race' (Harris, 1994, p. 80). It was such concerns that led Edwardian pressure groups to clamour for state intervention to preserve the family 'from moral, economic, demographic and racial collapse' (Harris, 1994, p. 61).

What was striking about the 1980s, however, was the speed of change – for example, the rapid increase in cohabitation and the number of extramarital births, and the almost doubling of the proportion of women with children under five in paid employment. Other changes reached critical landmark points. 1990, for example, was the first year in which the classic family household of a married couple with children was overtaken by the single person household as the most common household type. These changes followed half a century 'where family life probably showed more signs of conformity and outward stability than in any previous century for which records exist' (Anderson, 1994, p. 3).

There is now, however, a growing gap between the ideology of the family and reality. It is this gap which, in Gittins' view, accounts for the sense of a crisis in the family (Gittins, 1993, p. viii). There is really now no such thing as 'the family' – only families. Change since the 1960s, says Gauthier, 'has changed the reality of families' (Gauthier, 1996, p. 146). The family has now become, in Roll's words, a 'kaleidoscope' of living patterns (quoted in Harker, 1996, p. 3). Even though the majority of families are successfully doing what families have always done, and seven out of ten families with children are headed by both natural parents, families have become much more diverse in their patterns and structures. It is this which contributes to the sense of crisis.

What then are the key trends and developments that are so often interpreted as constituting imminent collapse?

A Decline in Marriage

Fox Harding describes the most striking change in family life in recent years as 'the increased wariness about formal marriage' (Fox Harding, 1996, p. 101). Figure 3.1 shows the change in marriage rates for the UK from 1968 to 1995. In the mid 1990s, the number of first marriages in England and Wales fell to the lowest level this century (Haskey, 1998, p. 21). Predictions about future marriage rates are, of course, always hazardous, but the Office of Population Censuses and Surveys predicts that while 5 per cent of young women aged sixteen in 1974 will not have married by the age of fifty, 25 per cent of young women who were sixteen in 1990 will not have been married by the same age (Maclean and Eekelaar, 1997, p. 17).

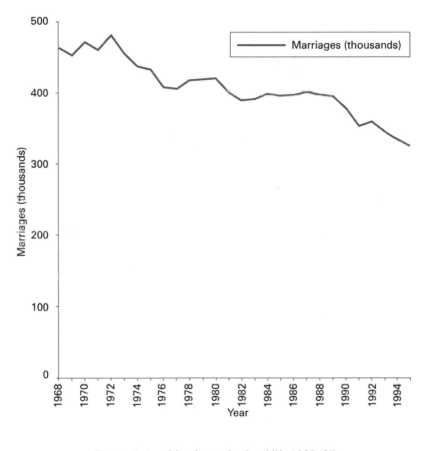

Figure 3.1   Marriages in the UK, 1968–95

Source: *Annual Abstract of Statistics* (various years), London, HMSO.

An Increase in Cohabitation

In the early 1970s, one in ten first marriages was preceded by cohabitation; in the early 1990s, the figure was seven in ten (Haskey, 1995, p. 5). In 1979, 11 per cent of women aged 18–49 were cohabiting, this figure doubling to 23 per cent by 1994 (*General Household Survey*, 1994, Table 2.24). The British Household Panel Study found that, by 1992, just under 50 per cent of the 1960s birth cohort – the average age then being 27 – had so far cohabited (Gershuny and Brice, 1994, p. 41). 'Few developments in family life', say Kiernan and Estaugh, 'have been quite as dramatic as the recent rise in unmarried cohabitation' (Kiernan and Estaugh, 1993, p. 5). Figure 3.2 shows the dramatic increase in recent years.

Attitudes towards cohabitation have also changed quite strikingly. Of those born pre-1930, more than a third think that cohabitation is always wrong compared with 7 per cent of those born between 1960 and 1976. Buck and

Figure 3.2   Percentage of women aged 18–49 cohabiting, Great Britain, 1979–94

Source: Results from the *1996 General Household Survey*, 1998, London HMSO.

Scott write of 'a massive breakdown of moral taboos against cohabitation' (Buck and Scott, 1994, p. 75). Cohabitation as a real alternative to marriage is still, however, an option chosen only by a minority. Although 64 per cent of respondents in the 1994 British Social Attitudes Survey thought it was 'alright for a couple to live together without intending to get married', 57 per cent thought that 'people who want to have children ought to get married' (quoted in Office for National Statistics, 1997a, p. 14). Fox Harding, however, suggests that we may look back to the 1980s as marking the transition to childbearing within cohabiting unions (Fox Harding, 1996, p. 83).

An Increase in Family Break-up

Over the whole of the post-industrial West, fewer than two thirds of parents who are legally married when their first child is born remain together until their youngest child leaves school (Leach, 1994, p. 9). Given the decline in marriage and the increase in cohabitation, divorce rates are less and less useful as an index of what is happening within families. What is plain, however, is that the divorce rate has increased sharply from 3.2 divorces per 1000 married couples in 1966 to 13.1 in 1996, and Britain now has one of the highest divorce rate in Europe – almost twice the EC average in 1993 – although the number of divorces fell slightly between 1993 and 1995.

Each year, around 165 000 children in England and Wales under the age of 16 experience their parents' divorce and divorces involving children under the age of sixteen have become more common in recent years, 70 per cent of involved children being under the age of sixteen. What is striking is that more than two and a half times as many divorces were granted to women as to men in the early 1990s. It is women who seem to be finding marriage unsatisfactory and are initiating the formal ending of marriage much more often than men.

An Increase in Lone Parent Families

The number of lone parent families trebled between 1971 and 1996 to more than 20 per cent of families with dependent children. Figure 3.4 shows the dramatic trend. The fastest growing group of lone parents in recent years has been never-married mothers – a corollary of the way in which cohabitation has increased at the expense of marriage. What is striking too – and this has increased the political visibility of lone parent families – is how the proportion dependent on social security benefits has grown from 44 per cent in the early 1970s to 70 per cent in the mid 1990s. Lone parents in Britain differ sharply in this benefit dependence from other countries in Europe where, in most countries, fewer than 40 per cent of lone parents are dependent on

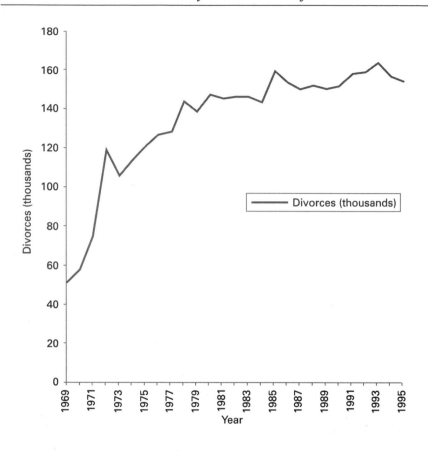

Figure 3.3   Number of divorces in England and Wales, 1969–95

Source: *Annual Abstract of Statistics* (various years), London, HMSO.

benefits. Also striking is the fact that whereas in 1979 half of all lone parents receiving state benefits were also receiving maintenance, by 1989 the figure was less than a quarter (Land, 1994, p. 92).

An Increase in Step-families

For the majority of lone parents, lone parenthood is an episode with half of divorced women and three quarters of divorced men remarrying within five years. In 1991, there were around half a million step-families with dependent children in Great Britain – one in fifteen of all such families (Haskey, 1994, p. 17). Around one in twelve dependent children – about one million alto-

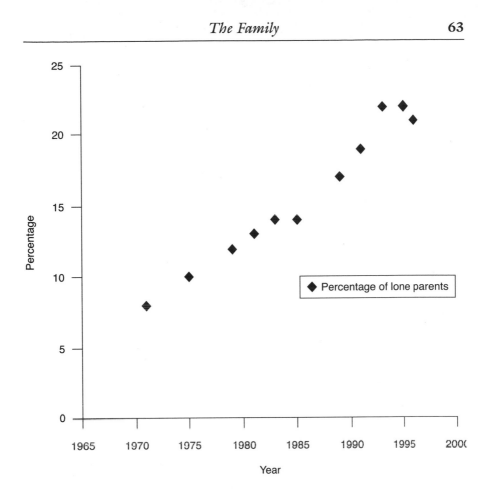

Figure 3.4   Lone parents as a percentage of all families
with dependent children, Great Britain

Source: Results from the *1996 General Household Survey*, London, 1998, ONS, HMSO.

gether – live in step-families. This is a direct result of the breakdown of marriages and cohabiting unions and the re-forming of families.

An Increase in Births Outside Marriage

The proportion of births taking place outside marriage doubled between 1961 and 1981 and then almost doubled again between 1981 and 1991, reaching 34 per cent in 1995 (Haskey, 1998, p. 19). Figure 3.5 shows the trend since 1971. What is so striking is the speed at which such a major

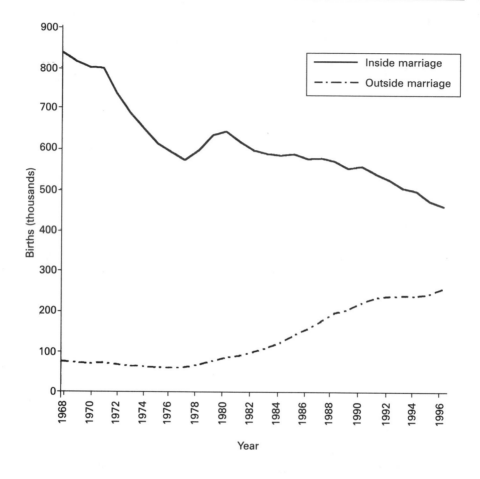

Figure 3.5 Births inside and outside marriage, Great Britain, 1968–96

Source: *Annual Abstract of Statistics*, various years, London, HMSO.

change in attitudes and behaviour took place in an area in which values and behaviour have historically changed extremely slowly. In Timms's study, fewer than half of the respondents disapproved of a woman having a child without a stable relationship with a man (Timms, 1992, p. 63). It should be noted, however, that, in 1993, three quarters of births outside marriage were jointly registered by both parents, and in 58 per cent of cases the parents were living at the same address – a sign of increased cohabitation and increased child-bearing – planned or unplanned – within cohabiting relationships (Haskey, 1998, p. 20). Thus, the majority of births outside marriage are to couples who are living together, even if not formally married.

A Decline in Fertility

In 1961, there were 90 births per 1000 women of child bearing age. By 1981, the figure had fallen sharply to 61.5, and it has remained at about that level. By the early 1990s, every country in the EC had a fertility rate below replacement level, which requires a fertility rate of around 2.1. In Britain by the early 1990s, the rate was around 1.8. In some countries in the EU, it had fallen as low as 1.3 – an unprecedentedly low level that will, in time, generate its own strains and stresses, for example in the family care of elderly people and in exacerbating unfavourable elderly dependency ratios.

Changes in Notions of Marriage and Motherhood

'Perhaps what is newest of all about the modern family', Anderson suggests, 'is the extent of moral and behavioural uncertainty which surrounds it' (Anderson, 1994, p. 18). Gittins suggests that perhaps the biggest recent change in families and family ideology is that more is now expected from marriage, childrearing and sexuality than in the past (Gittins, 1993, pp. 165–6) – a revolution of rising expectations. Various commentators have tried to capture what they see as a changing concept of marriage. The distinguished French legal sociologist Irene Thery has described the era that began to emerge in the 1960s as that of *demariage*. Thery uses the term, say Maclean and Eekelaar, to capture 'the intense social change from a time when marriage symbolised society's highest ideals to the present, when marriage has become a private matter, a subjective experience, to be entered or left as a matter of individual choice' (Maclean and Eekelaar, 1997, p. 8). So there has been a decline in the number of people embarking on marriage and a decline in the importance of marriage as a rite of passage and a social institution.

Morgan emphasizes the importance of the change to seeing marriage as a relationship rather than an institution. He comments that 'To treat marriage as an "institution" implies that the main points of reference for what constitutes appropriate marital statuses and roles comes from outside and "above"; to call it a "relationship" implies that the main points of reference come from within, from the parties themselves' (Morgan, 1985, p. 25). Hewitt reports a 1952 Gallup survey which found that a regular or adequate income was seen as just as important as 'mutual respect and appreciation' and 'understanding and tolerance' in making for a successful marriage. 'He's a good provider' was one of the highest tributes a woman could pay her husband. She contrasts this with the 1987 British Social Attitudes Survey, which reported that it was good personal relations between the parties which made the difference between a happy marriage and a divorce (Hewitt, 1994, p. 171).

Dennis and Erdos suggest that, before the 1960s, marriage was in reality child rather than spouse centred (Dennis and Erdos, 1993, p. 30). The decline in fertility, and the fact that childbearing and child rearing occupy relatively fewer years than in the past, must have altered the balance of emphasis in marriages. The fact that the majority of women no longer pursue motherhood as a full-time vocation is both a result of various broader trends and a result and a cause of changing patterns of marriage (Thompson, 1995, p. 61).

In the past, dependency in marriage – even if dressed up as partnership – was taken as a fact of the relationship and not seen as in any way problematic. Both partners, in fact, depended on each other for the survival and efficient management of the household, although the woman's dependency was more obvious. In a different world, one which stresses individuality and independence, dependence becomes problematic – actually or potentially.

An Increase in the Proportion of Married Women in Paid Employment

The proportion of women, particularly married women with children, in paid employment has increased steadily in the past forty years, as we saw in Chapter 2. By the early 1990s, 65 per cent of married women with children were in paid work. Between the late 1970s and the mid 1990s, the proportion of married women with children under five in paid work doubled – from 27 per cent to 54 per cent (Office for National Statistics, 1998a, p. 56). By the early 1990s, there were three times as many families in which both partners worked as families in which the man was the sole breadwinner. Figure 3.6 shows the rapid increase in two-earner families in the years since 1983. Attitudes have also changed strikingly rapidly. In 1984, 43 per cent of respondents in the British Social Attitudes Survey agreed with the statement that 'a husband's job is to earn money; a wife's job is to look after the home and family'. By 1994 the number taking this view had fallen to 24 per cent (reported in Office for National Statistics, 1997a, p. 30).

The dual-worker family has become the norm. Scott *et al.* see the rise in the proportion of women in paid work, especially women with young children, as 'perhaps the most potent force that has undermined traditional family arrangements' (Scott *et al.*, 1993, p. 25), clearly putting pressure on traditional roles. Walby argues that 'as women gain increasing access to paid employment, they will be less likely to live in marriage relations' (quoted in Fox Harding, 1996, p. 24) so the decline in marriage and the increase in cohabitation may well be linked to women's increased participation in the formal economy.

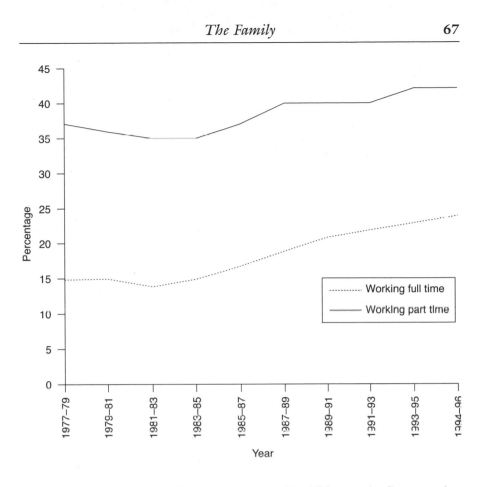

Figure 3.6   Percentage of married women with children under five years in paid employment, Great Britain, 1977/79–1994/95

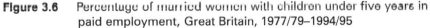

Source: Results from the *1996 General Household Survey*, 1998, London, HMSO.

An Increase in Family Poverty

In 1979 in Britain, as we discuss in more detail in Chapter 5, 1.4 million children – 10 per cent of all children, were living below 50 per cent of average income after housing costs, a rough and ready definition of poverty. By 1992–93, 4.3 million children – 33 per cent of all children – were living at this level (Oppenheim and Harker, 1996, p. 37). If we take an alternative measure of poverty – Income Support levels – then, in 1992, 3.7 million children – 29 per cent of all children – were living at or below income support levels, and 4.5 million children were living on incomes below 140 per cent of Income Support (Oppenheim and Harker, 1996, p. 30). The risk of poverty for families with children increased sharply in the 1980s. As Bradshaw put it for the years 1979–91, 'Britain has become a sharply more unequal society and the most common victims of this trend have been children' (Bradshaw, 1993b, p. xxi).

The family has been changing rapidly and radically. Many of these changes have been interpreted as marking the collapse of the family, but that would be to misinterpret the evidence. Family is still clearly of major importance in people's lives, but families have become much more diverse in their origins, nature and development. The British Household Panel Survey 1990–92, for example, asked people at the end of a long interview what had been important in their lives in the past year: 'The one overwhelming feature of the answers,' Scott and Perren concluded, 'is that they make clear that people are embedded in family life' (Scott and Perren, 1994, p. 265). Family events 'were far and away regarded as the most important aspect of people's lives over the last year... The fear that Britain is becoming less family centred and more individualistic is unfounded' (Scott and Perren, 1994, p. 263). 70 per cent of people in Britain in 1995 thought that 'People should keep in touch with close family members even if they don't have much in common.' Only 11 per cent said that they would rather spend time with friends than with their family and just 6 per cent said friends were more important than members of their family. (Office for National Statistics, 1998b, Table 2.12).

Most of the trends described above can be interpreted in different ways. Some are clearly negative, for example, the increase in family poverty. Some would be seen by many as positive. Many are clearly a matter of value judgement, for example whether it is good or bad that women are more able to escape from unsatisfactory relationships than in the past, or the increasing number of women in paid employment. Predictably, there is a long menu of competing – and conflicting – explanations. Fukuyama, for example, attributes what he calls 'The Great Disruption' to two key factors – the contracep-

---

What Has Been Happening?

- A decline in marriage
- An increase in cohabitation
- An increase in family break-up
- An increase in lone parent families
- An increase in step-families
- An increase in births outside marriage
- A decline in fertility
- Changes in notions of marriage and motherhood
- An increase in the proportion of married women in paid employment
- An increase in family poverty

tive pill and increased female participation in the labour force (Fukuyama, 1997, p. 45). Others see it as being rather more complicated. The decline in the birth rate shows women's (and men's!) increasing ability to choose whether or not to have children. What seem to be emerging are more egalitarian patterns of marriage relationships rather than relations of dominance and subordination, and people's greater willingness and ability to abandon unfulfilling relationships and look for alternative patterns. For most families, too, the years since 1945 have meant a rising standard of living and greater physical comfort.

Why Have Things Been Changing as they Have?

'Changes in family structures', Hewitt argues, 'are being driven not by some isolated (and by implication, reversible) "1960s permissiveness" but by profound economic and social forces' (Hewitt, 1994, p. 170). This is a vital starting point for analysis. Explanations for these major – and in some cases dramatic – changes can best be explored under three headings: economic changes, social and cultural changes and changes in government policy.

Economic changes have clearly played a major part. High unemployment has been an important factor in the increase in family poverty. The proportion of children living in workless families trebled in the 1980s and 90s from 7 per cent to 21 per cent (Straw, 1998). So has the relative decline in unskilled wages, which has meant that, if the breadwinner is unskilled, a second income is increasingly necessary to raise a family out of poverty – hence the need for women to take paid employment. Wilson writes of the USA that 'the labour market conditions which sustained the "male breadwinner family" have all but vanished' (Wilson, 1996, p. 105). The same is true of Britain.

Economic changes – the decline of manufacturing and the growth of a service economy, as well as the impact of the deregulation of the labour market – have increased the employment opportunities for women relative to men. These changes also help explain the increased number of women with children in paid employment.

Women's increased economic opportunities give them greater independence. They are more able to support themselves after divorce or separation and without marriage. Women's economic need for marriage and husbands has been reduced. Work (plus efficient contraception) is an alternative to childbearing. Childbearing, in fact, becomes a choice with very clear economic costs – which is surely a factor in the decline in fertility.

Social and cultural changes have also obviously played a part. Cohabitation, divorce, births outside marriage and lone parenthood have all become more acceptable in a more plural and secular society. Morality has become a matter of individual choice. That same individualism makes increasing demands on marriage, the main purpose of which is seen as being to increase the personal happiness of two individuals. There is obviously potential conflict between the ethic of individualism and individual satisfaction and the responsibilities of parenthood, which may well involve a subordination of individual desires to the family's collective good.

Changes in attitudes to the role of women in society have been both cause and result of the increase in the number of married women in paid employment. They have also contributed to the increase in family breakdown and to the decline in fertility. Women no longer see themselves as finding fulfilment solely in marriage and motherhood.

Government policies have also played a part in these changes – even though government has deplored many of them. Government economic and social policies have contributed to the increase in family poverty. Undoubtedly, the availability of social security benefits has made it possible for many lone parents to survive on their own. If there were no such provision, lone parenthood would simply cease to be an option for many such parents. There might then be fewer such families, but it could be that there would be more human misery if people were not able to escape from relationships that had, in fact, collapsed.

The absence of anything except very limited and residual support for families at a time of rapid change and therefore strain – for example, as partners seek to adapt to a new dual-career family model of marriage and combine work and the rearing of children – may well have contributed to the decline in fertility as well as to the increase in family break-up.

Government policies have also contributed to the decline of manufacturing employment and the rise of the service economy, and thus indirectly to the growth of employment opportunities for women.

What Has the Government Response Been to these Changes?

In 1978, Kamerman and Kahn classified countries into three groups in relation to their family policies – those countries with an explicit and comprehensive family policy, those where family policy was seen as a field covering various policies and those where family policy was implicit and reluctant. Britain was placed in the last category, along with Canada and the USA (Fox Harding, 1996, p. 205). Little has changed in the twenty years since 1978.

The Conservative government response to the changes we have set out above had six interconnected strands.

To assert and insist that the family is primarily a private rather than a social institution

This was a logical outcome of Conservative ideology, but such a view prevented the evolution of policies to bolster the model of the family that the government saw as under threat. When the Parliamentary Under Secretary of State at the Department of Health addressed a major Family Policy Studies Centre conference in 1996 on 'Families and Parenting', he put as the first responsibility of government 'the duty of government to acknowledge the integrity and the private nature of family life' (Bowis, 1996, p. 10).

The family is seen as a bulwark against the state. In Lady Thatcher's words, 'the independence of the family is... a powerful check on the authority of the state' (Thatcher, 1993, p. 630). It is also seen as an alternative to the state – the family can and should provide many of those services that the state has often come to provide. If left alone, it can and will do this. If the family is properly to be regarded as a private rather than a social institution, a personal rather than a political sphere, there is little case for a specific family policy.

To reaffirm the traditional model of the family and to reaffirm family responsibility

Finch and Mason speak of the 1980s as a period when the British government, along with many other Western governments, tried to redraw the boundary between state responsibilities and family responsibilities. Increasingly, they say, 'kin were seen as the first line of assistance for most people with the state playing a residual role' (Finch and Mason, 1993, p. 177).

The basis of this approach was both social and economic. Reasserting family responsibilities, it was believed, would teach people the true meaning of responsibility. In 1974, Sir Keith Joseph criticized socialists for allegedly trying 'to take away from the family and its members the responsibilities which give it cohesion' (quoted in Moroney, 1976, pp. 6–7). Family responsibility was reasserted in the 1980s and early 1990s in a wide range of policies. Social security provision for sixteen and seventeen-year-olds was virtually abolished to restore family responsibility. The Criminal Justice Act and the Criminal Justice and Public Order Act 1994 imposed new responsibilities on parents in relation to their children's offences. The Job Seeker's Allowance was reduced for the under-25s to push them back on their families. Student grants have been greatly reduced both to reduce public expenditure and to make students rely more on themselves and their families. Community care was redefined in the early 1980s as care *by* the community rather than care *in* the community. Care by family and friends was defined as the normal and desirable pattern, provision by the state being, as the Audit Commission put it, 'for those without assistance from friends and relatives' (quoted in Finch, 1989, p. 128).

Children Come First was an attempt both to reduce public expenditure and to reassert parents' – more specifically fathers' – financial responsibility for their children. Pascall sees the Child Support Act as aiming 'to put life back into the breadwinner-dependent form of family', an assertion of men's continuing financial responsibility for their children, of their role as provider (Pascall, 1996, pp. 223–4).

To reaffirm that provision of satisfactory child care is a private matter for parents

Edwina Currie summed up the government's approach in 1988. 'Our view', she said, 'is that it is for parents who go out to work to decide how best to care for their children. If they want or need help for this task, they should make the appropriate arrangements and meet the cost' (quoted in Brown, 1992, p. 164). Other ministers – and the Prime Minister – put forward the same arguments (see, for example, Moss, 1991, p. 133).

Part of this reaffirmation is the product of concern about the public expenditure implications of an acceptance of collective responsibility, but there is also a deep-seated and instinctive opposition to what Peter Lilley called on one occasion 'nationalizing parental responsibility' (quoted in Lister, 1996, p. 17).

To assert the costs and dangers of government intervention

Margaret Thatcher wrote of what she saw as the need 'to reduce the positive incentives to irresponsible conduct'. Young women, she argued, 'were tempted to become pregnant because that brought them a council flat and an income from the state' (Thatcher, 1993, p. 629).

It is the old issue of perverse incentives. Any services for special needs groups such as lone parent families can be seen as encouraging the behaviour to which those services seek to respond. Of course, there may be such incentives for a small minority. The issue is whether such possible effects of perverse incentives, which all the available evidence suggests are minor, should be allowed to stand in the way of provision for the needs of such groups. Some politicians stop short of answering this difficult dilemma but use the issue as a stick with which to beat such services.

Government has also laid great emphasis on the costs of provision of Income Support for lone parents, for example. Such groups are used to spearhead arguments about the burden that welfare imposes on the long suffering taxpayer and the costs in terms of economic competitiveness.

To deny any responsibility for the changes

The Conservative government's aim was to individualize responsibility. Lone parent families were defined as responsible for their plight; so were homeless families. Those men or women who simply cannot earn enough to keep their families out of poverty should seek other jobs – and accept that they are not poor, but simply not as well off as some other people. The government showed little or no sense that its economic policies, for example, were implicated in any way in the growth of family break-up and the increase in the number of lone parent families. It refused to accept that the ending of income support for sixteen and seventeen-year-olds was connected with the increase in youth homelessness. It accepted no responsibility for providing the caring services that those women whose labour is needed in the formal economy might find it more difficult to provide individually. It accepted that eight out of ten new jobs to be created in the 1990s would be filled by women but ignored the tensions that this would create for its policies of community care.

The government located the source of strains and stresses in the family in individual attitudes and behaviour rather than in economic and social changes. It could not be held responsible for many of those changes but it could be called to account for failing to try to alleviate some of the most damaging effects.

To deny any responsibility for forging a genuine family policy

This follows logically and inevitably from the earlier responses we have noted. Neglect is concealed by rhetoric. 'Families', Virginia Bottomley, Secretary for Health and Social Services, claimed in 1994, 'have taken their rightful place at the heart of the social policy agenda' (quoted in Jones and Millar, 1996, p. 1). At the World Summit on Children in New York in 1989, Mrs. Thatcher declared that 'The well being of children requires political action at the highest level. We make a solemn commitment to give priority to the rights of children' (quoted in Kumar, 1993, p. 197).

There have been bits and pieces of policy. The Conservative governments should be given credit for tax and benefit changes that try to take account of mothers' needs as both parents and workers, take some notice of child care costs and ease the poverty trap that has hindered women moving into paid employment.

However, the focus on lone parent families illustrates the residual nature of government policy in relation to the family. Gibbons broadens the argument. 'Over the last two decades', she writes, 'the balance in services for children and families has tilted away from the promotion of welfare and the development of effective family services towards the identification of children at risk and the development of procedures for their surveillance' (Gibbons, 1995, p. 97).

Mrs. Thatcher wrote after her retirement, maybe with all the wisdom of hindsight, that 'only the most myopic libertarian would regard it [the structure of the nation's families] as outside the purview of the state' (Thatcher,

1993, p. 631). That is fine but fine words do not create effective policies. All that recent Conservative governments accepted was a residual, reactive role. They denied and rejected – implicitly and explicitly – any broader responsibility for the health and well being of the family.

What Has the Government Response Been to these Changes?

- To assert that the family is a private institution
- To reaffirm the traditional model of the family and to reaffirm family responsibilty
- To reaffirm that the provision of satisfactory child care is a private matter
- To assert the costs and dangers of government intervention
- To deny any responsibility for the changes

What are the Broad Implications for Society?

In many cases, what has been happening is a matter of fact – more families, for example, have been breaking up, more women with young children have been entering paid employment. Assessing the implications of these 'facts' for society involves a range of judgements – about exactly what has been happening, about its importance, about which changes are worrying and which are not, about the ability of society to affect what has been happening, about the appropriateness of social action in relation to such developments, about the likely implications of such action.

An important judgement has to be made about whether the family is a private or a social institution and about what right – or need – society has to intervene in families. Commentators of all political persuasions stress the crucial role of the family for individual and social development. Where commentators differ is in their view of how the family can best be enabled to fulfill its private and social roles.

There is also debate about whether the objective should be to seek to restore the supposed traditional model of the family or whether it should embrace the present or the future. Should it design policies for the family as it is or for the family as it (supposedly) used to be or (supposedly) ought to be?

We see eight major implications for society in the changes outlined above.

The first is that society has to try to come to a judgement about what is happening to the family and in society. Gittins suggests that, when concern about the 'crisis in the family' becomes a recurrent theme, what is more probably being expressed is a fear that society itself is in a state of crisis (Gittins, 1993, p. 155). Her concern is that defining a range of problems as family problems conceals their real social, economic and ideological roots (Gittins, 1993, p. 165). Little is going to be achieved by focusing on the family if the real dislocation is in society. What looks like dislocation in the family may be a symptom rather than a cause of a wider social dislocation. Society must attempt to tease out what is happening as a prelude to any kind of action because 'the commitment to being a good parent in market societies is becoming more and more difficult' (Hutton, 1996, p. 304).

The second implication is that society has to make some important decisions about family–state responsibility. Cannan talks of 'a long British tradition of maintaining a high boundary between the family and the state' (Cannan, 1992, p. 1). There is a need, however, to resolve the historical 'deep ambivalence about the family and its relationship to the state' (Finch, 1989, p. 11). An accommodation has to be reached – one pragmatic rather than ideological. We have to rethink private and public responsibility, and the nature of the responsible state and the responsible family, in this very different world for the very simple reason that, as Rutter puts it, 'good parenting requires certain permitting circumstances' (quoted in Utting, 1995, p. 33).

Third, society has to resolve a series of key questions about what we have loosely called 'family policy'. The essential issues are to do with its nature and focus. Should policy seek to respond to families as they are today – the approach of the Church of England report *Something to Celebrate* (Church House, 1995, p. 160) – or should policy seek to reassert and re-establish a past family form on the basis of its supposed superiority? Another problem is that many strong supporters of action to support families are deeply anxious about what some types of 'family policy' might mean, for example for non-traditional families or families affected by the kind of ill-conceived 'family policy' embedded in the Child Support Act.

It may be that what we need is not a family policy as such but rather 'redistributive social policies for families' (Bradshaw, 1997, p. 2). Or maybe the focus should be not on families but on children. It may be that, when we talk about 'the family', our basic concern should be less with the structure of the institution and more with the 'functions' it performs – or fails to perform. These are some of the issues that require resolution.

Fourth, there are the sharp implications of the massive amount of family and child poverty. Families with children were the most rapidly growing group in poverty in the UK in the 1980s, and one third of children are now being brought up in poverty. There is a mass of evidence about what poverty means to children and how it damages their future development – physical, intellectual and emotional (see, for example, Kumar, 1993). Any society concerned for its future must confront the issue of the redistribution of resources towards families with children given the levels of child poverty currently prevailing in Britain.

Fifth, there are issues and implications for society in terms of the effectiveness of the new emerging diverse family forms in achieving the socialization of children. Etzioni has suggested that half of American families are no longer discharging this duty satisfactorily (*Guardian*, 15 July 1994). Are dual-earner families, lone parent families and step-families as capable of fulfilling this ever more complex task as the traditional two-parent family?

The answer, of course, is that it depends on a range of factors – past experience, adequacy of income, the availability of employment and housing, parents' ability to deal with the problems that inevitably face re-formed families. What has very clearly happened in recent years is that 'the family' has become the scapegoat for a range of troubling ills – increases in crime and vandalism, the seeming lack of discipline in schools, the lack of respect for authority, increased violence and so on – and deviant family forms come in for particular blame. They both become the victims of social changes and are stigmatized as the cause of other social ills.

There is clearly a problem in today's world in making the individual do what he or she has to do, and it is a much more complex problem than in the past. Changes in the family are both the product of that more complex world and a contribution to its complexity. The implication of this complexity is that society cannot afford simply to leave responsibility to the family. It has to explore new patterns and methods of support for the family and the action required effectively to socialize the next generation.

Sixth, the demographic and family changes that are currently taking place in Britain mean that the state will have to play a larger role in caring. The question about whether families are less willing to look after their elderly relatives than in the past is, as Finch points out, meaningless. Most people's sense of obligation was simply not put to the test in a world where fewer people survived into extreme old age with high levels of dependency (Finch, 1989, p. 81).

There is – effectively – a new caring situation, and many trends are militating against family care – the fact that currently one third of elderly people have no surviving relatives, the smaller size of families, the decline in the number of never-married women (the traditional reservoir of carers), the rising proportion of women in paid employment, the seemingly increased reluctance of elderly people to be a burden on their families. We do not yet know the effect of increased divorce, family break-up and cohabitation on kin relations but, as Dennis and Erdos emphasize, it is marriage that creates extended families (Dennis and Erdos, 1993, p. 70). Radical changes in family patterns raise profound questions about caring.

Seventh, there are the implications of a world in which dual-earner couples are becoming the norm. One approach is to say that how couples respond to this trend is a private matter and no concern of the state unless they fail to provide legally acceptable standards of care for their children. A more mature approach is surely for society to accept a measure of responsibility for the situation and to seek to assist parents to make satisfactory arrangements because the care of children is too important an issue to be left to parents. Society must be concerned with more than simply pursuing parents who fail to provide a very basic minimum standard of care.

State responsibility does not necessarily mean the state provision of day care. There are a range of possible options in terms of financing, source and types of provision. The central issue is for society to review the implications of the trends in women's employment, deemed by the majority to be economically necessary and socially desirable, and carry out the appropriate reconsideration of public responsibility for families and children in the light of this new dual-earner family model.

Finally, changes in families imply and require changes in the law. Divorce law has to respond to changing views about, and patterns of, marriage. The spread and acceptance of cohabitation requires a rethinking of the law on a variety of issues, for example, rights to social security benefits, rights to a share of a partner's occupational pension and fathers' acquisition of 'parental responsibility'. The increased paid employment of married women and the spread of part-time employment also require a reconsideration of tax and social security law to bring it into line with current patterns of activity.

Few would argue that the major and accelerating changes in families in recent decades have no implications for society. The issue is the degree to which the changes are accepted and the implications are thought through and recognized as having implications for policy, and the extent to which new policies are developed. Ideologies, values and costs are at issue. So is the quality of life of families – and in particular that of women and children.

What Proposals for Action Have Been Made by Conventional Sources?

The conventional response can be summarised under five headings.

Governments should give families a more significant place in policy and policy making

One obvious way is the creation of a Minister for the Family – tried briefly in the UK in the early 1990s. Whether that is the best way is a matter for debate. Hill's view is that separate departments for family affairs have tended to be weak, lacking resources, status and a clearly defined area of responsibility (Hill, 1995, p. 23).

An alternative to a Minister for the Family is a Minister for Children, as proposed, for example, in a Labour Party consultation document prior to the 1997 election. The Minister was to have a coordinating role and ensure that each department of government reviewed its policies and practices, current and proposed, in terms of the probable impact on children: 'As a catalyst for change and a policy coordinator, Labour's Minister for Children will be central to a new government approach to family policy' (Labour Party, undated, p. 5).

Another possibility, although fuelled by the same concerns, is the idea of some kind of Family Commission of high and independent status with responsibility for acting as catalyst, initiator and watchdog on behalf of the family (Brayshaw, 1980, p. 68). The Commission would be required to examine all government policies and proposals likely to affect families and to comment on policies in the light of experience of their impact on families. Such a Commission could, for example, insist that government departments submitted Family Impact Statements on policies likely to have an impact on families and Family Impact Analyses on the actual impact that the policies had been found to have on families.

All these instruments have possibilities, but they depend on government (1) having a commitment to families (2) creating the appropriate machinery to achieve those goals and (3) being prepared, if necessary, to commit to expenditure. Without such clarity, Ministers and Commissions and Statements and Analyses will achieve little.

Children's Services Plans at the local level could be given a new status

A mandatory duty has been laid upon social services departments to produce Children's Services Plans in collaboration with local education and health authorities. Joint planning is clearly an advance from separate, uncoordinated incrementalism, but to be effective, it will depend on working out agreed priorities, securing the necessary resources and ensuring that agreed policies can, and will, be implemented.

In the view of Packman and Jordan, the 1989 Children Act 'takes a quantum leap from the old restricted notions of prevention to a more positive outreaching duty of "support for children and families"' (Packman and Jordan, 1991, p. 323). Utting's review, however, suggests that 'instead of spreading their preventive umbrella, authorities appear to be targeting services towards their traditional responsibility of protecting children at risk of harm or neglect' (Utting, 1995, p. 66) – a product of the constraints imposed by cash limits. There is clearly scope for an extension of co-ordinated planning of children's services.

Family poverty must be tackled

The most conventional government cannot but see this as a central issue. The extent and degree of poverty among families and children is unacceptable and socially and economically dysfunctional. As Utting puts it, 'living on low income in a rundown neighbourhood does not make it impossible to be the affectionate, authoritative parent of healthy, sociable children. But it does, undeniably, make it more difficult' (Utting, 1995, p. 40). In Leach's view, the effects of poverty 'undermine the possibilities, restrict the choices and over-power the practices of good parenting' (Leach, 1994, p. 225).

There are a range of proposals within the 'conventional' paradigm for finding the resources to tackle family poverty – for example, phasing out the married man's tax allowance – and for how best to tackle the problem via, for example, changes in child benefit (compare this with Chapter 5).

More support should be available for lone parent families

Two characteristics distinguish lone parent families in the UK from those in other countries – the higher percentage in poverty and the smaller percentage in paid employment. In Bradshaw *et al.*'s study of the employment of lone parents in twenty countries, the UK had the lowest proportion of lone parents in full-time work (Bradshaw *et al.*, 1996, p. 9).

McKay and Marsh concluded that, among British low-income families, lone parents were strikingly worse off than couples – almost twice as likely to meet the authors' criterion of severe hardship (McKay and Marsh, 1994, p. 47). Ninety per cent of lone parent families are in the lowest 25 per cent of the family income distribution (McKay and Marsh, 1994, p. 2). In 1996, 33 per cent of families headed by a lone mother and 27 per cent of those headed by a lone father had a gross weekly income of £100 or less per week compared with 3 per cent of married couples and 6 per cent of cohabiting couples (Office for National Statistics, 1998a, p. 12).

Lone parents would obviously benefit from any policies aimed at tackling family poverty. They also need targeted help, because of the extra relative costs of children in one parent families (Social Policy Research findings, December 1995), for example, through a one parent addition to Child Benefit or an increase in Child Benefit for the first child. Lone parents also need policies to help them to return to paid work because it is being able to engage in paid work that is the best route out of poverty.

Here, Family Credit can be a crucial bridge into work for lone parent families. It is claimed by one in three lone working parents – compared with one in fourteen of couples with dependent children. The crucial factor in the expansion of Family Credit seems to have been the reduction of working hours for eligibility to sixteen, which enables many more parents to return to part-time work and claim Family Credit to supplement their limited part-time earnings. Very important, too, is the fact that child care costs may be set against earnings in some benefit claims.

There should be an expansion of nursery education

Nursery education should be seen as a way of enriching children's lives and supporting parents and families. It is immensely popular. By European standards, provision is sadly lacking, only around a quarter of four-year-olds attending nursery schools and classes. The National Commission on Education set a target for the year 2005 of 85 per cent of three-year-olds and 95 per cent of four-year-olds in pre-school education (Commission on Social Justice, 1994, p. 129) at the modest cost of considerably less than one penny in the pound on income tax.

In a 'realistic' strategy, the target may be seen as too demanding, but, even so, the case for an expansion of nursery education, possibly targeted on particular areas, is overwhelming.

What Proposals for Action Have Been Made by Conventional Sources?

- Government must give families a more significant place in policy making
- Children's Service Plans must be given a new status
- Family poverty must be tackled
- More support should be available for lone parent families
- There should be an expansion of nursery education

What Proposals for Action Have Been Made by Radicals?

As pointed out earlier, classifying proposals as conventional or radical involves value judgements. This section sets out proposals that are radical in relation to contemporary political discourse in Britain but are well within the capacity of an affluent late twentieth century society. They do, however, depend on a change in ideas and approach.

Diversity and divergence must be accepted

Recent Liberal Democrat proposals for helping families and family life begin with the statement that 'Liberal Democrats recognize and relish the diversity of family life in Britain today' (Liberal Democratic Party, 1994, p. 16). Any policies concerned for families, radicals argue, have to start from there and go on to explore how different kinds of family can be helped to be the settings that enrich the lives of their members and provide an environment in which children can be reared to be good citizens. Policy making has to begin from reality, and reality is diversity and pluralism. The focus must be on functioning – how can families be supported and helped in the roles and functions that society requires of them? – rather than on structure – how can a particular model of the family be restored or reinforced? 'Anyone who would really restore the nuclear family in the forms of the fifties', says Beck, 'must turn back the clock of modernization' (Beck, 1992, p. 121). That quite simply cannot be done.

A new relationship between the state and families has to be forged as necessary for building a sustainable society

This involves the end of the 'stand-off' relationship that has characterized state–family relations in Britain, and an acceptance of the mutual dependency of state and families. Radicals argue that society has to put the family back at the centre of economic, political and social policy. For generations, Novak argues, political, economic and social theorists have focused on the individual, the state and the market, and have 'systematically neglected the social vitality of the family' (Novak, 1991, p. 159).

The ability of families to perform the tasks and functions that they have historically undertaken can no longer be taken for granted. Families need institutional underpinning if they are to function effectively. The personal is inescapably political because of the importance of families to society and because of the pressures that contemporary changes have put on families and what that means to society. As Etzioni puts it, 'parents have a moral responsibility to the community to invest themselves in the proper upbringing of their children, and communities – to enable parents to so dedicate themselves' (Etzioni, 1995, p. 54).

Recognition of the mutual dependence of state and family leads to a preventive, proactive, institutional strategy. The state will be concerned with actively promoting the health and well being of all families and not simply with propping up or regulating failing or struggling families. It will be concerned with families in all their diverse forms rather than just with 'the family' – that is a particular traditional model.

The state will be concerned with supporting parents in their parental responsibilities. It will also be concerned to support the family in its broad caring responsibilities, responsibilities increased by demography and government policy in recent decades. Care as an activity shared between families, communities and the state will be a central element in this mutual dependence.

What is involved is the acceptance of the social and public nature of families and of the need for state and family to share responsibilities and be mutually supportive. Parenting has to be seen as a shared responsibility – as must caring more generally. A new relationship has to be forged. Above all, it means government funds to finance services provided by either private, voluntary or public sources. In September 1997, the British Prime Minister set up a Ministerial Group on the Family, to be chaired by the Home Secretary to work out 'the construction of a modern policy which goes with the grain of our society' (Straw, 1998).

Children must be put first

That means a major redrawing of social and political priorities. As Leach puts it 'establishing a moral priority for children's known needs and the political will to meet them as of right is the difficult part of what needs to be done for children' (Leach, 1994, p. 173). Radicals argue for a new stronger commitment to children by society. The focus of public policy must be on what is needed to ensure that children flourish. The Commission on Social Justice put as its first objective for a government that was serious about children ensuring 'that all our children grow up in surroundings which enable their needs – physical, emotional, intellectual – to be met' (Commission on Social Justice, 1994, p. 313). That does not seem an extravagant objective.

Putting children first has obvious implications. Radicals see it as involving the redistribution of income in favour of families with dependent children. The kind of redistribution required demands an attack on unemployment and underemployment, and the establishment of a national minimum wage as a move towards re-establishing the 'family wage'. A less radical approach requires large increases in Child Benefit – certainly for all children but also with higher rates for children below the age of five, whose parents are less likely both to be in paid employment, and for teenage children because of the greater costs they involve.

Putting children first requires government to make a clear statement of how it defines its responsibilities, of targets for service provision, of strategies to achieve such levels and of the machinery required to ensure a coordinated strategy that is need led rather than service or department led. The 1997 Labour government made a start on this in *Meeting the Child Care Challenge*, which set out a national child care strategy (Department for Education and Employment, 1998). The corollary is an official index of childhood well being constructed by independent experts and published annually.

There are, of course, many groups of children with particular needs. Children in lone parent families, however, stand out in terms of their number, material deprivation and diminished life chances. They need extra help, and the focus of policy must be on their needs; they must be the primary concern. There is a good case for providing additional financial support for lone parent families dependent on Income Support and for providing extra help – for example income disregards for child care costs and bridging support for return to paid employment. What is quite unacceptable in a Children First strategy is that children suffer because of their particular family situation.

Policies must be developed to help parents to reconcile work and family life

This is vital to avoid what Etzioni has called a 'parenting deficit' (quoted in Hewitt, 1994, p. 176). The problems are essentially threefold: the lack of good-quality, affordable day care; the limited availability of flexible, family-friendly employment; and the failure of fathers to assume shared responsibility for reconciling work and family responsibilities. What is required are policies that enable parents to put family first and work second at key periods in their lives. Ditch and his colleagues see measures that help parents to reconcile the demands of work and family life as being 'at the heart of social policy' (Ditch *et al.*, 1995, p. 41).

Various policies are needed to create family-friendly employment. Policies for maternity and paternity leave and policies to establish a right to parental leave are obviously crucial. The Commission on Social Justice suggests as an 'aspiration' that either parent should be able to take (or share) leave for at least 12 months after the ending of paid maternity leave (Commission on Social Justice, 1994, p. 190) to be funded from a new social insurance scheme.

In 1995, the 'social chapter' gave working parents in the EU the right to a minimum of three months unpaid leave after the birth or adoption of a child. At the time, Britain opted out – on the basis that the issue was one for employers and not a matter for legislation (*Guardian*, 7 November 1995).

Also important, obviously, is a greater flexibility in the choice of working hours. The heavy work commitments of the fathers they researched, say Ferri and Smith, 'represented an obstacle to equal parenting and, as such, a source of conflicting pressure' (Ferri and Smith, 1996, p. 48). The authors describe this as 'an issue requiring urgent consideration' (Ferri and Smith, 1996, p. 50). What is needed, too, is an extension of rights for part-time workers. The long-term costs of part-time work deter many parents who might prefer part-time to full-time work from going part time in their children's early years.

A development of caring services is obviously vital – accessible, publicly provided and affordable child care as well as before and after school care services. The need is well known. It is estimated that one in five children aged 5–10 is left alone at home during the school holidays and one in six comes home at the end of each day to an empty house (Leach, 1994, p. 247). What are lacking are commitment and resources, but family-friendly employment demands a rethink of the needs of the children of working parents as well as of the parents' needs. The 1997 Labour government has made a start on this with its White Paper *Fairness at Work* (Department of Trade and Industry, 1998).

Policies must be developed to give women – and men – a real choice in the early years of a child's life

Policies designed to enable women to engage in paid employment are only part of the answer. 'Does it really make sense', ask Kiernan and Wicks, 'that both parents should be fully active in the labour market when they are also responsible for the care of very young children?' (Kiernan and Wicks, 1990,

p. 38). What is at issue is parents' right to care for their children themselves if they so wish. The most desirable policies for some women will be those which enable them to stay in, or return to, paid employment when their children are still young by providing caring services for very young children. Hewitt and Leach, however, argue that 'enabling women to see as little of their children as men have traditionally done and are doing seems to us a poor aim for reformers' (Hewitt and Leach, 1993, p. 24). One of the aims of a families' policy must be to re-establish the status of parenthood and thus the financial viability of full-time parenting for parents who want to stay at home and care for their young children themselves.

There are clearly financial implications. Many women's paid work is what keeps their families out of poverty. A genuine choice depends on making it financially possible for women or men to choose to stay at home, for example by a higher rate of Child Benefit when there is only one earner in the family, or for children under school age, or by providing 'wages for housework' or developing a social security system that affords equal status to paid and unpaid work.

There is evidence that circumstances force women into courses of action they do not want to take. One study found that a quarter of women who wanted to stay at home after having a baby ended up returning to paid employment to maintain family income, while the same proportion who stayed at home would have preferred to be in a job (Commission on Social Justice, 1994, p. 184).

There is a need for a national reconciliation/mediation service

A national reconciliation/mediation service, radicals argue, could be a very good investment – one perhaps on the lines of National Family Mediation, which coordinates the work of local services offering help to couples about to separate or divorce (Office for National Statistics, 1997, pp. 20–1). Divorce and separation are often a tragedy for those most directly involved and for their children. Preventive-type services are very underdeveloped. Holtermann speaks of Relate (formerly the National Marriage Guidance Council) receiving some £2.2 million from public funds, while the estimated cost of separation and divorce to the public sector is £1.3 billion (Holtermann, 1995, p. 21).

How the divorce process is actually handled seems important to the outcome for children. How the process is managed will certainly be important to whether absent parents continue to maintain contact with their children – and that is crucial. Cockett and Tripp's conclusion from the Exeter Family Study was that the most important association with adverse outcome for children after family break-up was the loss of parenting figures from the child's life (Cockett and Tripp, 1994, p. 61). What we do know is that half of all absent parents lose touch with their children after divorce.

Research shows how little divorcing parents know about the divorce process, about possible sources of information, advice and support, and about their need for help. A reconciliation/mediation service might help to prevent some divorces actually happening. It might also affect the divorce process, thus easing the pain for all parties, particularly any children involved, and so helping to maintain contacts with absent parents.

There is need for a national families, children and young people's service

Such a service, radicals envisage, would focus on families and their needs. It would embrace the coherent policy for the under-fives discussed above but would also provide a range of other supportive, advice and information services and opportunities for families, children and young people.

The aim would be preventive and promotional in the sense of seeking to improve the quality of life of families. It would obviously have close links with other services – for example schools – but it would represent one important face of the new relationship between family and state and a recognition of collective responsibility for families, children and young people.

The Youth Service in Britain has always been a Cinderella service, taken seriously by hardly anyone, yet a reformed and expanded service could obviously play a major role in improving the quality of life of children, young people and families. If society is genuinely concerned about families and young people, services aimed at their needs are an important area for experiment and investment.

A radical policy will give a new importance to fathers and fatherhood

Fathers have been neglected by social policy in Britain. They must be reestablished as central to thriving families – as all the evidence shows that they are. Their right to paternity leave and to a share in parental leave without damage to their working lives must be firmly established, as must a right to work part time during their children's early years and not to work the excessive hours that clearly damage family life (Ferri and Smith, 1996).

Hewitt sees the so-called 'parenting deficit' as largely a fathering rather than a parenting deficit (Hewitt, 1994, p. 176). Children clearly need shared parenting, and public policy must seek to make this possible. The conflicts and tensions that women face in the new world are better recognized than those facing men, but the conflicts that men face are real and need attention.

A 1997 MORI Poll found that one in five children living with their fathers could not remember doing anything with him in the previous week. Only 37 per cent had done things round the house or garden with him compared with 63 per cent who had done so with their mothers (*Guardian*, 10 April 1997). This suggests that fathers are playing less than an equal part in the rearing of their children.

There is a strong case, too, for research to establish how and why it is that so many fathers lose touch with their children after the breakdown of relationships and what could be done to remedy what research shows to be clearly damaging to children.

What Proposals for Action Have Been Made by Radicals?

- Diversity and divergence must be accepted
- A new relationship between state and family must be forged
- Children must be put first
- Policies must be developed to help parents reconcile work and family life
- Women and men must be given a real choice in a child's early years
- There is a need for a national reconciliation and mediation service
- A national families, children and young people's service should be set up
- A new importance should be given to fathers and fatherhood

Conclusions

The past two or three decades have been a period of unprecedented change in 'the family'. We set out the key changes at the beginning of this chapter, but they can usefully be summarised under four headings.

First, there is the increase in family and marriage breakdown, with the corollary of more one parent families and more step-families. The result is disruption to families and to children's lives, increasing diversity in family forms and an increased reactive involvement of the state with families in relation to, for example, divorce and social security provision for lone parents.

Second are the changes in notions of marriage and motherhood and the spread of cohabitation as an accepted prelude – or even alternative – to marriage. Accordingly, there is an increase in the number of births outside marriage. Marriage is no longer seen as the only route to success and satisfaction for women. Expectations and aspirations of, and for, marriage are high. Equally, motherhood is now a lifestyle choice – and seen by many people as an expensive one.

Third, increasing numbers of married women with children have moved into, or remained in, paid employment. In recent years, there has been a sharp increase in the number of women with very young children in paid work. This is a sign of a new conception of women's role and is both evidence of a desire for increased independence and an important element in asserting and maintaining it. However, women's double shift has obvious implications for marriage and families, putting both under greater pressure.

Fourth, there has been a sharp increase in family and child deprivation, one third of children now being brought up in poverty. Poverty makes good parenting much more difficult and has a deep, permanent and socially costly effect on children's life chances.

These changes have had profound effects on families. The most obvious change – the increase in family break-up and rising numbers of lone parent families – is the one seized on by the media, politicians and pundits. However, other changes – the increased diversity of family forms, the increase in dual-earner households, women's changing expectations and the increase in family poverty – are equally significant in their impact on families.

What has been happening to families has clear implications for society for two main reasons:

1. The family unit in all its diverse contemporary manifestations is a public as well as a private institution. Of course, families' privacy must be protected, but the personal and familial is also the political. Families are central to the socialization and opportunities of the next generation and to the care of a range of dependent groups. Families' successful functioning is central to social well being and the sustainability of society. In this sense, the state of the family is a public issue and a matter for public policy.
2. There are things that government can and should do to support families in their core tasks. As the 1997 Labour Party Election Manifesto put it, 'families cannot flourish unless government plays its distinctive role... Society, through government, must assist families to achieve collectively what no family can achieve alone' (Labour Party, 1997, p. 25).

We have reviewed what we categorized as conventional and radical approaches and proposals. What conclusions can be drawn about ways of easing the strains that face contemporary families, supporting them in their roles and functions, and enhancing their contribution to human flourishing and social stability? The conclusion has six main points.

The first general point to emerge from this review of changes and policy proposals has to be about the need to work through the nature of possible policy responses and proposals. Anne Helene Gauthier's study of state–family relationships in twenty-two countries brings out how deep seated is the publicly expressed concern for families. From the 1970s, many countries set out to explore the changes that were taking place in families, and possible policy responses. In 1989, for example, the EC set up its Observatory on National Family Policies and identified a broad area for Community action (Gauthier, 1996, p. 148).

Policy responses are shaped by definitions and perceptions of the nature of the changes taking place in families, by judgements about their assumed significance and by underlying values and beliefs about the role of government and the social and moral significance of 'the family' to individuals and society.

There are those who see only the weakening or supposed collapse of a particular model of the family – the lifelong, male breadwinner model. There are those who focus on the emergence of more diverse patterns of family life and whose concern is not to support a particular model of the family but instead to focus on families' functioning rather than family structure.

There is a major difference of approach here – not normally as starkly clear in reality as on paper – but it has to be faced and resolved by government. The traditional model of the family seems to be linked with order and stability and the sustainability of societies, yet it is clearly changing. What is most obvious is its weakening. As Morgan puts it, expressing one approach, 'What we are witnessing now, is not the formalisation of other "family structures" but the de-regulation of the conjugal nuclear family which we have known for centuries' (Morgan, 1998, p. 71).

One response to that situation is to seek to buttress the type of family that seems to be crumbling because of its assumed essential and irreplaceable contribution to individual and societal well being. The other response, deriving from historical and sociological judgement and in some cases fed by ideology and hope is to welcome – or at least endorse – the weakening of the traditional family model and seek to adapt policies to new forms of family. The centre of attention here is the 'functions' of the family rather than family structure, and the aim is to support families in what are seen as their essential roles and tasks – raising and socializing the next generation, caring for the dependent and enriching the lives of their members.

The choice, crudely, is between idealism, the idealization of a particular historical form, and realism, the acceptance of what now is, or seems to be, emergent. The choice involves sociological judgements about what has been happening and is likely to happen to families. It also involves judgements about the significance of what has been happening to individuals and to society. It is a classic dilemma for public policy at a time of economic and social change – seek to restore the past, or embrace and seek to sustain what seems to be the future.

Experience of social change suggests that there is no going back to the traditional lifetime, self-sufficient male breadwinner model as the universal family form. There is little point in policies that seek to advantage that model and penalize other kinds of family. That would be pointless – and it would be the children who suffered. The only realistic approach for public policy seems to be to accept the changes and the new diversity and seek to respond positively and creatively to the current needs of families, although the issue has to be worked through and resolved.

Second, families, children and caring must be placed at the forefront of public and social policy. The case for doing this rests on three assumptions – the central importance of families to societal well being and sustainability;

the way in which changes in society and families are making it more difficult for many families to perform their traditional functions successfully;
and the belief that there are ways in which public policy can sustain and
support families.

There is a need to recover a sense that children belong to society as well as
to their parents, that children are a social investment rather than a private
good. In Britain, the situation suggests that we need to break with the view
that the state's responsibility is purely residual and exists only in relation to
children and families in need. Gauthier contrasts French and British responses
to changes in families. The French response is to increase general support to
families; the British reaction is to concentrate efforts and resources on the
families in greatest need (Gauthier, 1996, p. 2). Morgan makes the point in a
slightly different way, complaining about 'the way in which provisions for
families are now understood and developed with almost exclusive reference to
lone parents' rather than to support traditional families (Morgan,
1998, p. 71).

What is needed is a broader and clearer acceptance of public responsibility
for families in all their current varied manifestations and responsibilities, and
for children. In 1994, the British government took a tentative shuffle in this
direction with the appointment of the Secretary for Health as coordinator of
family policy. Individual departments were still left with responsibility for
policy making in their particular areas, but the Health Secretary had some
scope for influencing their agendas. Gauthier sees this move as 'highly significant. Not only was the term "family policy" used for the first time in British
politics but this action also went against the restricted way the government
had so far viewed its responsibility towards the family' (Gauthier, 1996,
p. 161). No significant effects, however, resulted from the change. It was
symbolic politics in terms of tangible outcomes.

There are obvious dilemmas that governments have to resolve in any
commitment to policies for families. One is the issue of perverse incentives.
If government provides more support for families whatever their form or
nature, the critics argue, then (1) families will do less to help themselves,
which is ultimately bad for them and for society, and (2) the traditional family
will be further weakened. Fears may be strong about such outcomes, but the
evidence suggests that that they are not well founded (see, for example, Finch,
1989). Families, in general, prefer to be self-helpful rather than dependent.
The traditional family is being weakened by the gales of economic and social
change. Policies supportive of other family forms have only a minor influence
on what is happening.

There are three other specific dilemmas that face governments wishing to
support families and children. Should policies focus on 'the family', on children or on parenthood? If the focus is on 'the family', there is the risk that
non-traditional types of family will be left out in the cold – to their overall
detriment and particularly to the detriment of the children involved. A focus

on children may avoid that dilemma, but while children are a central concern in any family policy, the concern must also be to support and facilitate good parenting. Kiernan suggests that 'parenthood' rather than marriage should be the primary policy focus and that parenthood rather than marriage should be seen as underpinning family relations (Kiernan, 1998, p. 64). The focus of policy need not and cannot be exclusive, but it is helpful to be clear about the possible tensions of focus and their implications.

Once the principle of an active, universalist families/children/parenthood policy has been accepted, it has to be operationalized. This means generating Family Impact Statements and Family Impact Analyses for all relevant policies and programmes. A Minister or Commission for Families and Children is necessary but not sufficient. Either could be a catalyst keeping family or children's issues at the forefront of government's agenda, but unless there is a prior commitment by government to the importance of families, children and parenthood, little will be achieved.

Governments must be sensitive not only to families' responsibilities for caring for children, but also to the responsibilities that families assume for caring for their elderly members. Many families find it much more difficult than in the past to carry out these responsibilities because of the changed pattern of their lives. Public policy has to be sensitive to these difficulties and to the need to work in partnership with caring families.

The third conclusion is of the overriding necessity for an attack on family and child poverty, as proposed in Chapter 5. It is striking that the recent decades that have been characterized by such widespread concern about the state of 'the family' have been years that have seen a seemingly remorseless increase in the number and percentage of children in the UK being brought up in poverty.

An adequate income does not, of course, necessarily guarantee successful parenting, but there is a mass of evidence (see, for example, Kumar, 1993) showing how poverty makes effective parenting much more difficult and is strongly associated with a wide range of childhood disadvantages. The long-term economic and social costs of allowing a third of all children to be brought up in poverty are dangerously high.

What is required are policies that radically redistribute resources to families and children, and ensure them an adequate income. Given the way in which successive UK governments have allowed the problem of child poverty to grow, solutions will not be cheap, but the costs of inaction are also heavy. An effective assault on family poverty requires a mix of at least four elements – a national minimum wage set at a realistic level, selective increases in Child Benefit, an increase in the level of Income Support and an attack on unemployment and underemployment.

The fourth conclusion to be drawn from any review of trends and changes in family patterns is the need for the development of a network of locally based supportive services to be available not just for families deemed to be 'at risk' but for all families. What is plain is that, for a variety of reasons, bringing up children has become much more difficult and demanding than it was in the past. The expectations of both parents and children are higher. There is less agreement among parents and society generally about what constitutes good parenting and how to achieve it. There are more lone parent families and step-families. Adolescence has been prolonged as more young people stay on longer in full-time education. There is a greater sense of the need for, and value of, support from other parents and experts.

Family centres have clearly shown their potential as a focus for relevant services and a way of supporting and empowering parents and children (Holman, 1988). Schools are another possible and acceptable basis for such services. What seems to be needed is the development of locally based, coordinated services for families and children within the context of the development of a families, children, youth and leisure service offering a range of services and opportunities for families of all kinds at all stages of their development. As a society, Britain has invested extraordinarily little in services to support, sustain and enrich 'normal' families. It has also failed to invest significantly in a range of services and facilities for young people while bewailing their propensity for law-breaking behaviour. That situation lacks any kind of logic.

Fifth, there is compelling evidence that lone parents need more support from society. One quarter of all children spend some of their childhood in single parent families, and the deprivations and disadvantages that many of them face are all too plain (see, for example, Rodgers and Pryor, 1998). Policy has been bedevilled by conflicts of ideology and aims. If too much is done for lone parent families, it is argued, more two-parent families will decide to become lone parent families – the problem of perverse incentives. If more is done for single parent families, this would be unfair to those two-parent families who face similar problems. Thus, inaction is justified by arguments that leave children suffering acute disadvantages.

There has been a failure to decide whether lone mothers should be treated as mothers or as paid workers (Lewis, 1998). If treated primarily as mothers, there is a risk of creating a dependency culture and a dependent class. If they are treated as workers, this is in conflict with traditional dominant British norms of motherhood (Edwards and Duncan, 1997, p. 30) and seems to deny the importance of child care as 'work' (Lewis, 1998, p. 10).

The way to cut through the tangle of these dilemmas is to focus on the needs of the children and how to secure them the best possible parenting rather than on any possible broader social implications. That means, above all, ensuring that the family has an adequate income – adequate in terms of contemporary norms and patterns of living whether or not the caring parent engages in paid work. Second, it means policies that encourage and enable the caring parents to return to work as and when they feel ready and able to do so. The line between encouragement and unacceptable pressure is obviously at times difficult to draw, and an overenthusiasm to press single parents into work if and when they see the need to be full-time mothers or fathers has to be guarded against. Such policies will, of course, require an individually tailored mix of elements – subsidized day care for younger children, tax allowances to set against the costs of child care, opportunities for training, payments to complement low pay or part-time work and so on.

One element in a policy of providing more support for one parent families must obviously be to ensure that absent parents – usually fathers – make an appropriate financial contribution. In the 1980s, a trend developed for fathers of broken relationships or marriages 'to leave the support of the children of their first families to the state benefit system' (Land, 1994, p. 92) – what the then Secretary of State for Social Security described in 1993 as 'the nationalization of fatherhood' (quoted in Land, 1994, p. 93). The principle is unexceptional, but implementing it is less straightforward. Many fathers subsequently acquire other family responsibilities and cannot adequately support two families. If the children are not to suffer from public and political ambivalence about 'whose children' they ultimately are, the state has to balance fathers' responsibilities for past and current families and try to secure what is best and fair for all parties. The bottom line – which has not been drawn with sufficient vigour or clarity – is that the children must be properly provided for in ways that encourage rather than discourage the absent parent's involvement with their future. Children's well being must not be sacrificed on the altar of abstract concepts of fathers' responsibility to support their children if that responsibility is not, or cannot be, fulfilled.

A sixth conclusion that can be drawn from a contemporary analysis of the issues is that helping parents to reconcile the competing demands of work and family life must be accepted as a central public responsibility. It is too difficult and important a task to be left solely to individuals. The Conservative government's reiteration that this was a private matter and that it was up to parents to make arrangements they saw as appropriate ignores the practical problems that parents face and the costs that can fall on the children.

Two principles emerge as central to policy in this area. The first is that parents should have a choice about the balance of their commitment to work and family while their children are young – say under school age. The second principle is that the necessary services should be provided to make a genuine choice possible. That is to say, if both parents choose to work full time, affordable day care services – and later on appropriate after school and holiday care – should be available to make this practicable. If parents prefer to work less than full time, the law will then guarantee parental leave and will ensure that they are not disadvantaged at work and that their right to return to full-time work is guaranteed.

What the evidence makes plain is that, in the EC generally in 1990, if men and women were given a free choice, 80 per cent of women and 40 per cent of men would prefer not to work full time when their children were under school age (Kiernan, 1998, p. 63). Parents are very aware of the problems of combining full-time work and quality parenting.

A wide range of policies, some of a radical nature is required to help parents in this task of reconciling conflicting demands and pressures. These policies will run from improving the availability and affordability of day care, allowing parents to share the right to what is currently classified as maternity leave and instituting a right to a given number of days of parental leave per year to be used for family/parenting purposes, to providing a level of Child Benefit that makes it practicable for parents who so wish to remain at home as full-time carers in a child's early years.

Combining full-time work and the care of young children puts family life and relationships under strain. With an adequate structure of support services, it may be possible, but many parents lack access to such services. They and the children then suffer. It is in the best interests of society to enable people to choose and to help them to make their choices workable.

Conclusions
There is a need to work through possible policy responses
Families, children and caring must be placed at the forefront of public policy
An attack must be made on family and child poverty
A network of local supportive services is necessary
Lone parents need more support
Parents need help to reconcile the competing claims of work and family life

Challenges

What are the key challenges that face government in the search for a family policy for a sustainable society? Essentially these are as follows:

- How should government come to terms with diversity and difference? The traditional lifetime male breadwinner model that embedded itself so firmly in public consciousness is now almost extinct, and the new diversity of family forms has to be accepted as the basis for policy. What are the implications?
- Must government accept the need for a more active policy towards families because of (1) the central importance of families to the sustainable society, and (2) the way it has become more difficult for families successfully to perform their traditional functions?

- How can society secure for all families an adequate income so that families with children are not disadvantaged in comparison with families without children or in comparison with different types of families?
- What pattern of support services is best suited to supporting families and promoting family flourishing?

Further Reading

David, M.E. (ed.) (1998) *The Fragmenting Family: Does it Matter?*, London, Institute of Economic Affairs. A good mix of up-to-date data and strong opinions.

Gittins, D. (1993) *The Family in Question*, London, Macmillan. A very useful basic text.

Office for National Statistics (1997) *Social Focus on Families*, London, Stationery Office. All the facts you need to know and lots of very pretty graphs.

Utting D. (1995) *Family and Parenthood*, York, Joseph Rowntree Foundation. An authoritative overview.

For up-to-date reports and commentary, look at publications from the Family Policy Studies Centre, 231 Baker Street, London, NW1 6XE. The Centre also produces a very useful newsletter.

4

The Environment

We have a moral duty to look after our planet and to hand it on in good order to future generations. (HMSO, 1990, p. 10)

The air we breathe, the water we drink, the land we inhabit, the countryside we enjoy: these are fundamental issues that affect us all. At heart, the fate of the environment is about the well-being of people. (Labour Party Policy Commission on the Environment, 1994, p. 7)

Introduction

This chapter is concerned not only with the traditional problems of the environment, but also with many of the issues surrounding the concept of sustainable development. The two overlap, but the latter are broader in scope and are also of more recent origin. Debates on sustainable development first became prominent during the early 1970s with the UN Conference on the Human Environment in Stockholm in 1972 and the publication of two influential reports around the issue of 'limits to growth' – the fear that the environment could not survive the modern-day lifestyle of continued production and consumption (Goldsmith *et al.*, 1972; Meadows *et al.*, 1972).

Definitions of sustainable development differ depending on the ideological perspective of the author (Basiago, 1995). They range from the shallow green or consumerist pro-growth perspectives, which require very minor changes to the existing system of production, consumption and environmental protection, to the deep ecological approaches that see current rates and forms of economic growth as fundamentally incompatible with the protection of the environment.

Despite the inevitable plethora of definitions, it is the definition of the World Commission on Environment and Development (in the Brundtland Report) that has gained general acceptance by official bodies at national and international levels as the basis for policies designed to protect and improve the environment:

95

Sustainable development is development that meets the needs of the present without compromising the ability of future generations to meet their own needs. (World Commission on Environment and Development, 1987, p. 43)

The focus of the chapter is necessarily more global than that of the other chapters simply because environmental issues are global in character. The consequences of such problems as air pollution, deforestation and the annihilation of animal and plant species respect no national boundaries and affect the whole globe irrespective of the part of the world in which they occur. It is partly for this reason that several international conferences have been held and treaties signed under the auspices of the United Nations. Despite this international character of environmental issues, it is important to understand what has been happening to the environment in Britain.

What Has Been Happening in the UK?

Unlike the other issues that we discuss in this book, data on environmental trends are scarce, patchy, unreliable and only of recent origin. All that can be done in this section is to present the current situation with pointers to the past and the future wherever possible. It is not usually possible to establish clear and valid trends over the years.

Housing, Health and the Environment

Housing is the most essential part of the environment as it is in our housing that we spend most of our lives. Trying to interest people who live in grossly inadequate housing in the problems of the stratosphere is largely pointless and, to some extent, unethical.

In the past, the housing literature concentrated mostly on the direct ill-effects that inadequate housing can have on people's physical and mental health. Recently, however, the focus of attention has been widened to include the effects of housing on the ecological environment and, through that, on the welfare of not only individual residents, but also the general population. From this perspective, 'global warming, ozone depletion, depletion of non-renewable resources, as well as human health and well being are influenced by the particular way in which housing in Britain is provided, managed and used' (Bhatti *et al.*, 1994, p. 6).

The direct ill-effects of inadequate housing on people's welfare are well known. To begin with, successive studies have documented the association between damp, cold and mouldy housing with poor health:

Wheezing, breathlessness, cough, phlegm, meningococcal infection, respiratory diseases, and a wide range of symptoms in children have been implicated. The association of damp and mould with childhood asthma has been repeatedly studied. (Ineichen, 1993, pp. 38–9)

There is ample evidence that good sanitation is vital to health; that inadequate housing conditions can be the cause of many fires and accidents at home; that noise resulting from thin walls is common in many types of housing; that overcrowding or living in high-rise apartment blocks can affect people's emotional health; that badly lit housing can cause tension headaches and precipitate accidents; and that cramped housing restricts opportunities for child development and educational achievement. Inadequate housing conditions are obviously associated with low income, with the result that their ill-effects exacerbate and compound one another.

Housing conditions have improved over the years, although there is still a minority of households living in inadequate conditions and who may be also homeless. Table 4.1 shows both the improvement that has taken place since 1971 and the size of the housing problem in the early 1990s. As the next chapter will show, these housing problems are more acute among some ethnic minority groups.

Table 4.1   Housing amenities and conditions in England, 1971 and 1991

	1971	*1991*
Per cent of dwellings lacking basic amenities	16.4	1.0
Per cent of dwellings without central heating	69.9	16.0
Per cent of dwellings classified as unfit	7.5	4.1

Source: Department of the Environment, 1993.

There is also solid evidence regarding the possible ill-effects of the immediate environment on housing and through that on people's health. A good example is the exposure of people to radon that gets into their housing from building materials, ground water and, mostly, from soil gas – a particular risk in some parts of the country, for example Cornwall and Devon. It is estimated that 'one in 20 cases of lung cancer in Britain may be caused by domestic exposure to radon' (Lowry, 1991, p. 28). Such building materials as asbestos, lead and formaldehyde can cause sickness. Modern methods of double glazing and draughtproofing can also increase health risks by raising the level of radon or formaldehyde in the house.

A more contested issue is the relationship between childhood leukaemia and electromagnetic fields induced by power lines. The findings of studies in the UK, USA and Sweden have been differently interpreted, but the disagreement is over the level of magnetism that can cause child leukaemia (Knight, 1997, p. 20) rather than over the question of causation itself. While this may be a legitimate bone of contention among scientists, it is of no comfort to parents whose houses are situated close to power lines.

What is perhaps less well known is the influence of housing on environmental pollution. The way in which houses are constructed, furnished and heated affects the degree to which they use up energy and emit gases that pollute the air and thus lead to global warming, ozone depletion and acid rain. In the past, and to a lesser extent today, houses were constructed with little thought being given to energy conservation; they relied on coal for heating, either directly or indirectly through electricity from coal-fired power stations; they used building materials that could be dangerous to health; and they were furnished with certain models of refrigerator that contributed to ozone depletion. All these factors contribute to atmospheric pollution through the emission of greenhouse gases (Bhatti, 1996). The domestic use of energy is responsible for 22 per cent of black smoke, 15 per cent of carbon dioxide, 3 per cent of nitrogen and 3 per cent of sulphur dioxide emissions.

It is, however, important to note the beneficial effects on the environment of some of the recent technological changes. The changes in heating methods – moving from coal to gas – the newer methods of construction and the new regulations concerning fridges have all reduced the polluting effects of housing on the environment in recent years.

Transport and the Environment

Modern methods of transport are 'a major cause of environmental degradation' in the UK (Button, 1995, p. 17). As Table 4.2 shows, road transport is responsible for 53 per cent of the UK's emissions of nitrogen oxides – a major reason for acid rain; 40 per cent of volatile organic compounds, which under certain conditions can exacerbate respiratory illnesses; 90 per cent of monoxide, which can be lethal; 25 per cent of carbon dioxide, which contributes to global warming and ozone depletion; and other pollutants that can affect both people and buildings.

There is general agreement that it is road – rather than rail – transport that is the main polluter. Most passengers travel by car, and most freight goes by road; more car journeys per driver are made today than in the past, and each journey covers a longer distance. Walking and cycling have declined over the years in both absolute and relative terms. The result is that road pollution is the only type of pollution that has not declined substantially on a national scale, having in fact risen in many congested urban areas. It is also generally acknowledged that the positive effects of catalytic converters on gas emissions will be more than overtaken in the future through the increase in car usage.

The figures in Table 4.2 refer to the national situation, although they obviously vary from one locality to another, emissions being particularly high in congested urban areas. Their ill health effects are also more severe among certain groups – pregnant women, the elderly, children and people suffering from respiratory and heart conditions. Some of the pollutant emissions – nitrogen monoxide, carbon monoxide and benzene – are higher for vehicle occupants than people outside, while cyclists in congested areas are more exposed to nitrogen dioxide than are the car drivers themselves.

Table 4.2   Share of total UK emissions derived
from road transport, 1994

Type of emission	*Per cent of total emissions*
Nitrogen oxides	53
Carbon monoxides	90
Carbon dioxides	25
Volatile organic compounds	40
Lead	58
Black smoke	58
Particulates	25

Source: British Medical Association, 1997, Table 7, p. 32.

It is also important to refer, even if only briefly, to the ill-effects of road transport in terms of noise, road accidents, the increased use of land for road building, the impact on biodiversity ill effects and the gradual depletion of non-renewable resources. Whichever way one looks at the issue, the car is a major polluter, and methods must be found to make it environmentally more friendly and reduce the excessive public reliance upon it.

The only encouraging aspect of road transport has been its improved safety, as Table 4.3 shows. Despite all the problems involved in comparing statistics over the years, road deaths and serious accidents have declined considerably, while non-serious accidents have increased slightly in number. Indeed, the picture is even more favourable if one looks at the accident rate per million vehicle kilometres: this declined for all types of accident from 75 in 1986 to 53 in 1996. Obviously, safer car design, better roads, more careful driving and legislation concerning speed limits and alcohol consumption have all played their part in this improvement. Having said all this, it needs to be stressed that ten persons are killed per day as a result of accidents on the roads in Britain, and the number is higher if one takes into account deaths that occur more than 30 days after the accident.

Table 4.3   Road accident casualties by road user and severity, Great Britain, 1986 and 1996

Road user and Severity	1986	1996
Child pedestrians and child pedal cyclists		
Killed	337	185
Killed or seriously injured	8,102	5,363
All severities	32,025	26,725
Adult pedestrians and adult pedal cyclists		
Killed	1,773	1,006
Killed or seriously injured	15,982	9,810
All severities	53,515	42,512
Car drivers and passengers		
Killed	2,231	1,806
Killed or severely injured	29,686	24,045
All severities	159,178	205,277
Motor cyclists and passengers		
Killed	762	440
Killed or seriously injured	16,466	6,193
All severities	52,280	23,044
Others		
Killed	279	161
Killed or severely injured	3,898	2,660
All severities	24,453	22,744
ALL ROAD USERS		
Killed	5,382	3,598
Killed or severely injured	74,134	48,071
All severities	321,451	320,302

Killed refers to number of deaths less than 30 days after the accident.
Source: Department of the Environment, 1997a, Table 4.15, p. 75.

Industry and the Environment

Industrial pollution has changed in both volume and nature in the UK. The days when factories discharged their effluent straight into the sea or rivers and when factory chimneys belched black smoke over the countryside are almost – but not quite – over. Manufacturing has been made safer and cleaner, and has also shrunk considerably in size, having been replaced by service industry, which is less polluting, as the major employer in the country.

New industrial risks, however, have emerged, for example, chemical fertilizers that have been proved to have, or are suspected of having, detrimental effects on the soil, agricultural workers, agricultural products and hence consumers. The real possibility that some agricultural fertilizers and pesticides may gradually seep into water supplies has already caused a good deal of government and public concern (Pearce, 1993, Chapter 8). Nuclear power stations and the recycling of radioactive nuclear wastes pose unquantified degrees of risk both now and in the future to those directly involved, to local communities and to the country (Blowers, 1995). Industry may have been made cleaner over the years, but it is still a major source of pollution.

Government statistics on trends in the emission of pollutants show that domestic and industrial sources of pollution declined between 1970 and 1993, while road transport gained in importance because of 'the continuing growth in road traffic' (House of Lords, 1996, p. 10).

Forests and the Environment

Forests perform many economic, leisure and ecological functions nationally and world wide that are not always appreciated:

> Forests create soil, moderate climate, control floods, and store water against drought. They cushion the erosive effects of rainfall, hold soil on slopes, and keep rivers and sea coasts free from silt. They harbour and support most of the earth's species of life... Forests take in and hold a great stock of carbon, which helps balance the stock of carbon dioxide in the atmosphere and thus combats the greenhouse effect. (Meadows *et al.*, 1992, p. 63)

Forest cover in the UK totalled only ten per cent of all land in 1992, the third lowest figure within the EC after Ireland and the Netherlands, compared with an EC average of 25 per cent (Pearce, 1993, p. 132). Even this low figure represents a success story since the Forestry Commission has managed to double the forest area since 1919.

The government's decision, however, to sell large areas of forest land to private developers may not augur well for the future since private developers may be less likely to bear the public good in mind despite the conditions attached to the forest sales. Private owners are more likely to be interested in using forests for sheep and deer, and for sport and shooting, than for conservation.

There are also forest problems arising out of acid rain, and again the future does not look promising since government targets for controlling acid emissions have not been met.

The UK imports 90 per cent of its wood requirements and, as such, is a major contributor to deforestation in Third World countries, with all the well-known adverse effects on the world atmosphere and biodiversity. Both affluence and poverty contribute to the degradation of the environment, albeit for different reasons. The seriousness of the problem is illustrated by the fact that in Brazil, which hosted the Earth Summit Conference in 1992, 'forest loss is said to have increased by more than a third in the past five years' (Nuttall, 1997, p. 12). It is one of many examples where decisions taken at international conferences on the environment are directly and indirectly ignored by both the developing and the developed countries, although their motives differ.

Water and the Environment

The quality of drinking water has improved over the years, with more than 99 per cent of tested drinking water samples in Britain meeting the official quality targets. River and canal quality, however, is more mixed, 'with five per cent of rivers and canals classified as poor or bad quality in 1990' (House of Lords, 1995, p. 27). In contrast, the figures given by another government publication for poor or bad river and canal quality are much higher, illustrating the unreliability of environmental statistics. They show that, for 1992–94, the assessment of river and canal quality in England and Wales resulted in the following ratings: good (59 per cent), fair (32 per cent), poor (8 per cent) and bad (1 per cent) (Central Statistical Office, 1996, p. 195). Despite these high ratings of the quality of water, there are still public doubts and fears as a result of the evidence that chemicals used in industry and agriculture are infiltrating water supplies and that water contamination results also from many landfill sites.

At the national level, there are no serious problems with the quantity of water in the UK today, although there are shortages at regional and local levels. Demand is rising fast, however, and there may well be problems in the future, particularly in view of the possible climatic changes discussed below.

The quality of beaches for bathing may have improved in recent years, although many remain unsafe. The proportion of beaches considered to be unsafe for bathing varies depending on the criteria used. A survey of 755 beaches in 1998 by the Marine Conservation Society found that 122, or 16 per cent of the total, failed to reach the EC mandatory standards, but many more – 525, or 70 per cent of the total – failed to reach the society's own more stringent standards (Jenkins, 1998, p. 7).

The Air, the Atmosphere and the Environment

Unlike the case with water, air quality is affected by global factors beyond the control of any one government. It is this which currently makes air pollution the most serious of all forms of environmental pollution. This is not to suggest that there is nothing that national governments can do but rather to stress the importance of international action in this area.

Global warming, ozone layer depletion and acid rain are all the result of increased air pollution on a national and global scale. Global warming results from the increased warming effect of rising gas emissions in the atmosphere – the so-called greenhouse effect. At moderate levels these emissions perform the useful role of keeping the earth warm, but at high levels they accelerate the warming effect, with possible disastrous consequences in the future. The main gases are carbon dioxide, contributing probably half the emissions, with methane and nitrous oxide accounting for another quarter. There are many causes for the rise in these emissions (Pearce, 1995, p. 11), but the burning of fossil fuels (coal, oil and gas) is by far the most significant, particularly in relation to carbon dioxide emissions.

The most recent estimates suggest that the temperature of the earth's surface will rise by an average of $0.25°$ C per decade so that, by the end of the twenty-first century, it will be about $2.5°$ higher than it was at the end of this century. The warming effect will be higher in the northern hemisphere, with its greater land mass, and lower in the southern hemisphere. These estimates are slightly lower than earlier ones but not so significantly as to require any important revisions in the predicted effects. It is important to remember that global warming is cumulative and that its effects will be felt more in the distant than in the near future.

Although there is no general agreement on the detailed effects of global warming, there is broad agreement on its overall effect. The Department of the Environment concludes as follows:

> Increased atmospheric concentration of greenhouse gases originating from human activity is expected to change the earth's climate markedly over a 25–100 year timescale, with potential wide ranging consequences. (Department of the Environment, 1997b, p. 1)

The more detailed picture is that as Arctic ice caps begin to melt and ocean temperatures rise, sea levels will also rise increasing the risk of flooding; as temperatures rise, deserts will spread in some parts of the world; and crops will be variously affected. The exact health effects are equally difficult to predict, but they are likely to be important. High temperatures contribute to morbidity, particularly among the elderly, in certain parts of the world; they increase the risk of food poisoning; and, if the incidence of floods increases, more deaths can be expected in low-lying areas of the Third World where protection against such weather hazards is minimal. Although the details of these adverse effects cannot possibly be known at this stage, the degree of risk to future generations is high enough to warrant government action.

The ozone layer in the earth's stratosphere acts as a shield protecting the earth against ultraviolet radiation from the sun. Scientific observations have shown that this layer has been getting thinner in recent years, with the result that more ultraviolet radiation gets through to the earth. The discovery that a huge hole had appeared in the ozone layer over Antarctica and that it was getting larger added a chilling dimension to the whole debate. The approximate area of this Antarctic ozone hole in million square miles was estimated at 1.4 in 1982, 6.7 in 1990 and 8.5 in 1996 (Department of the Environment, 1997b, p. 13). Although the same does not apply to the Arctic, very high concentrations of ozone-destroying chemicals have been found in the Arctic stratosphere, which may lead to severe ozone thinning in the future.

The main cause of the ozone depletion is the emission of chlorofluorocarbons (CFCs) from such domestic appliances as fridges and freezers and from cosmetic hair sprayers. Despite the fact that their production and use have been curbed in the affluent countries in recent years, 'it is expected that concentrations of these substances in the stratosphere will continue to rise into the next century' (Bentham, 1994, p. 36). In the UK, there has been a substantial decline in the emission of CFCs but a significant rise in the related HCFCs from 1985 to 1995 (Department of the Environment, 1997b, p. 15).

Skin cancers have been increasing over the years, but it is difficult to determine the precise extent to which this is the result of new leisure activities involving sun tanning or of the thinning of the ozone layer. Fair skinned people, particularly in the southern hemisphere, are more likely to be affected than other people. Most of the skin cancer cases are of the minor type that can be treated (non-melanoma), but some are of the more serious type (melanoma), which is more difficult to treat. Ultraviolet radiation has also been linked with cataracts and, possibly, with the increasing incidence of infectious diseases. Although there are still many question marks in this area, the evidence is 'overwhelming that UV exposure is a major factor in non-melanoma skin cancer' and that 'it is prudent to assume' that it is also a factor in the more severe melanoma cancers (Bentham, 1994, pp. 37–8).

Ozone depletion may also be a potential risk to the ecosystem. Ultraviolet radiation appears to affect the sea plankton and, through that, fish stocks; similarly, it seems to affect the growth of certain agricultural plants – cotton, peas, beans, melons and cabbage – and thus food chain systems and public diets.

Acid rain results primarily from the oxidization in the air of sulphur dioxide and nitrous oxide emissions, mainly from cars and the generation of electricity through fossil fuels. The ill-effects of acid rain depend on the amount of rainfall and on the type of soil. Northern Ireland and the Scottish Highlands are particularly vulnerable for both these reasons. There is no evidence, however, that acid rain has any direct adverse effects on human health.

Acid rain is yet another of those pollutants that respects no national boundaries. Unlike global warming and ozone depletion, however, its reach is
regional rather than global. It can damage forests, lakes and buildings not
only in the country of origin, but also in other neighbouring countries
depending on the air currents. For this reason, acid rain can have political
implications as well, 'due to the fact that acid-producing nations are not
always those that suffer the greatest damage' (Mannion, 1992, p. 182). Thus,
the Scandinavian countries with the best record on gas emissions suffer most
from acid rain because of wind currents from other European countries,
including the UK. Similarly, Japan suffers from acid rain as a result of industrial pollution in China.

The total annual emission of gases for the UK appears to have declined, as
Table 4.4 shows. There are, of course, regional and local variations with the
result that there has been some reduction in some air pollutants in some parts
of the country but there has also been some increase in other air pollutants in
other parts of the country (Royal Commission on Environmental Pollution,
1997, p. 39). This reduction has taken place as a result of the substantial
reduction in the use of coal in power stations, homes, and so on. The replacement of coal, however, by nuclear power poses other environmental problems. The risks of radioactive contamination arise not only from accidents and
breakdowns at power plants but also 'during the processes of mining radioactive fuels, preparing fuel for reactors, operating reactors and dealing with
waste and reprocessing' (Huby, 1998, p. 82).

Table 4.4   Estimated emissions of different gases in the UK (thousand
tonnes), 1970 and 1995

Gases	1970	1995
Sulphur dioxide (SO^2)	6434	2365
Black smoke	1072	356
Black smoke (PM10)	531	232
Nitrogen oxides (NOx)	2382	2295
Carbon dioxide (CO)	6502	5478
Volatile organic compounds (VOCs)	2266	2337

Source: Department of the Environment, 1997b, Tables 2.3, p. 32; 2.7, p. 36; 2.8, p. 36; 2.11,
p. 38; 2.14, p. 42; and 2.21, p. 48

The three main sources of gas emissions are transport, industry and power
stations, as seen in Table 4.5. Although the importance of each of these three
sources varies from one kind of gas emission to another, transport is the major
source for most of them.

Table 4.5 Estimated emissions of different gases by source as a percentage of the total, UK, 1995

	SO^2	Black smoke	PM10	NOx	CO	VOCs
Road transport	2	50	26	46	75	30
Other transport	2	9	3	13	13	6
Industrial and refineries	22	5	46	15	2	14
Power stations	67	5	15	22	4	–
Domestic	3	19	9	3	4	–
Commercial and public services	2	1	2	2	–	–
Other	–	12*	–	–	–	47*

* For black smoke, it refers to the extraction and distribution of fossil fuel; for VOCs, it refers to solvent uses.
Source: as for Table 4.4.

Biological Diversity and the Environment

Biological diversity is seen by all commentators as crucial to the survival of the planet. 'The maintenance of biological diversity', declared the United Nations, 'is a precondition for sustainable development' (United Nations Organization, 1990, p. 95). It is a precondition in economic, ethical and cultural terms. The British government's White Paper expresses very crisply the cultural value of biodiversity to human life:

> Biodiversity is strongly linked to cultural diversity and identity. Human cultures are shaped to a large degree by the natural environment. Historically, biological resources have played an important part in local folklore and traditions. Plants form an integral part of many customs and rituals, and may be the source of superstitions. They have been celebrated in literature and in song, and are used frequently as a source of decoration for arts and crafts. (HMSO, 1994b, p. 109)

Yet the extinction of species at a global scale is taking place at a fast and accelerating rate, 'possibly 1000 times greater than the background or natural rate and these losses are almost all human induced' (Pearce, 1993, p. 98). The loss is not just economic: it is aesthetic, cultural and moral as well.

Biodiversity destruction today is far more serious in developing countries simply because affluent countries have long ago destroyed most of their woodlands and forests. In the UK, there has been an improvement in recent years as the government has shown more commitment to this aspect of the environment than to many others. It is also an area in which campaigning pressure groups are stronger than those tackling other environmental issues, although they are far less powerful than the long established business lobby. Despite the improvement, it is officially conceded that 'there is a continual threat to both plants and wildlife' in the UK (Central Statistical Office, 1996, p. 192).

Why Have Things Been Changing as they Have?

As with other complex problems, explanations possess different levels of significance. At the most basic level, one might say that changes are the result of the failure of governments to implement fully the various United Nations Conventions on the environment; the failure, particularly of affluent countries, to provide the necessary financial assistance to developing countries in order to help them to implement environmentally friendly policies; the implementation of mistaken policies in agriculture or irrigation; the weakness of government regulatory measures on industrial production; and so on. This is a policy failure explanation, and while it has some merit in explaining specific failures to prevent further environmental destruction, it does not really explain why the process started, why it gained such momentum and why it is proving so difficult to control, let alone reverse.

At a slightly higher level of significance are those approaches which single out one major factor – monocausal explanations. There are those who blame it all on rapid population growth; on technology that takes little or no account of the protection or conservation of the environment; on poverty that drives people and governments to pursue actions and policies that they would not otherwise have pursued; or on affluence that leads to overconsumption, which in turn feeds into the activities of the industrial system. Again, each of these explanations has something useful to say, but no one explanation by itself can account for the entire complex process of environmental damage.

At a third level of significance are those explanations which use a number of broad interacting factors and core values. Meadows *et al.*, in their two books, used a model of global environmental destruction based on the interactions of four factors: rapid population growth, industrial technology, food consumption and the depletion of non-renewable resources (Meadows *et al.*, 1972, 1992). Hempel uses an explanatory model that involves eight interacting factors: anthropocentrism, contempocentrism (concern with the present and a consequent neglect of the future), technological advance, human population growth, poverty, affluence, market failure and failure to recognize the economic price of ecological resources or services (Hempel, 1996, p. 60).

The explanation proposed here is based on four core interacting social values that have shaped the beliefs and the actions of individuals, enterprises and governments for generations now: industrialism, consumerism, individualism and anthropocentrism.

Industrialism refers not simply to the process of industrialization but also to its accompanying beliefs that profit and inequality are necessary driving forces for increased economic growth; that technology can find answers to all environmental problems; and that when the demands of economic growth are in conflict with those of the environment, the former should be given priority.

Consumerism, whether induced by industrialism or jointly with other factors, stands on its own as a driving force. It encourages increased volumes and types of consumption, and it knows no boundaries as many 'needs' are artificially created to ensure continued production, profit and perhaps employment. It dominates the lives of people in affluent societies, and it is the way of life to which people in developing societies aspire.

Individualism places the interests of the individual above the welfare of the community. This can inevitably lead to both extreme affluence and abject poverty, each of which, for different reasons, tends to lead to disregard for the environment. It can result in the use of cars on a colossal scale, to the detriment of transport on trains or buses. Individualism is closely linked to consumerism as the ultimate goal of industrial societies is the satisfaction of material needs according to the ability of the individual to pay. The satisfaction of basic needs for all is often sacrificed on the altar of individual consumerism. The combination of industrialism, consumerism and individualism creates a powerful force that boosts economic growth but at the same time generates destructive effects on the environment.

Anthropocentrism is the belief that human beings are superior to all other species on the planet. Resources must be exploited to satisfy human demands irrespective of any effects on other living organisms. Any consideration for other living beings is wholly or largely pragmatic – to promote human welfare either directly or indirectly. Any conflict between the welfare of the two should be resolved to the satisfaction of the human world.

Why Have Things Been Changing as they Have?

Because of:

- The failure of government policies
- Population growth
- Technology
- Poverty
- Affluence
- Industrialization
- Consumerism
- Individualism
- Anthropocentrism

These four central values dominate, in varying degrees, the actions of the public and the policies of governments the world over. It is this dominance that makes the fulfilment of the four Brundtland principles of sustainable development outlined later in the chapter so difficult. For the same reason, progress towards a sustainable environment will at best be slow, gradual and full of disappointments.

Government Policies on the Environment

The environment has never been a central issue in British party politics, let alone in government policy. There have been isolated pieces of effective legislation dealing with specific issues during the postwar period (the 1956 Clean Air Act, passed in response to the killer smog of 1952, is a good example), but there has never been an environmental policy in the sense of an employment or health or education or foreign policy. The oil crisis of the early 1970s raised the issue of energy consumption most starkly and created some government interest in an energy policy, but this faded during the 1980s as a result of the discovery of new oil deposits in Europe and elsewhere. Even after the first White Paper in 1990, the environment remained 'a relatively minor issue on the British political agenda' (McCormick, 1991, p. 7). Nothing that has happened during the 1990s justifies changing this observation.

The causes of environmental destruction run deep, as the section above has shown, and progress towards sustainable development is bound to be slow even under the most committed of governments. What has made the situation worse in the UK is the fact that a sustainable environmental policy was in conflict with the market philosophy of successive Conservative governments. The major thrust of government policy in the 1980s was towards maximum economic growth, achieved through the free operation of the market and the rolling back of the frontiers of the state. Sustained economic growth was not interpreted to mean concern for sustainable development. Even policies protecting the physical environment, let alone those advancing the causes of sustainable development, were often seen by the government and the business community as standing in the way of rapid economic growth.

The emphasis on the private market meant the introduction of privatization and deregulation measures that were either contrary or, at best, neutral to environmental causes. The privatization of many utilities – electricity, gas, water – meant that the dominant policy concern became how to encourage maximum consumption in order to boost profits rather than to save energy or water. The deregulation of road and rail transport signified an emphasis on private enterprise criteria rather than environmental protection. The general belief in deregulation resulted in the government placing excessive emphasis

on economic incentives rather than regulatory measures for promoting environmental causes.

Added to all this is the basic political fact that many environmental groups
are weaker than long established groups whose immediate private interests
can be adversely affected by environmental measures. The overall effect of this
is that environmental groups may have won a few battles, but they have lost
many more to the long established groups in business and agriculture. As
McCormick points out, the Control of Pollution Act 1974 'was essentially
shaped by industry and local government', while the Countryside and Wildlife
Act 1981 was the outcome of 'powerful farming and land owning lobbies'
(McCormick, 1991, p. 12), despite the lively campaigning and lobbying by
environmental groups.

The White Paper in 1990 was an unexpected but welcome document as it
seemed to espouse the language of the Brundtland report. As Cullingworth
and Nadin point out, however, it did not 'resolve the dilemma faced by the
Conservative Government: how to reconcile its enterprise philosophy with a
concern for good environmental management' (Cullingworth and Nadin,
1994, p. 139). Inevitably, the White Paper was high on rhetoric and low on
specifics. The *Financial Times* aptly summed up its contents:

> It dwells mainly on proposals previously enacted or announced; when it comes to
> plans for the future the best that can be said is that it is a compendium of muted
> declarations of hesitant intent. (*Financial Times*, 26 September 1990, quoted in
> Anderson, 1993, p. 52)

It is beyond the scope of this section to examine the details of government
environmental policies during the past twenty years. All that can be attempted
is to assess the extent to which the Brundtland principles discussed later in the
chapter were supported and promoted.

Beginning with the first principle, the elimination of poverty, government
policies throughout the 1980s and 90s exacerbated rather than ameliorated
the extent and depth of poverty in the UK, as Chapter 5 will show. As for
poverty in the Third World, the amount of aid, both bilateral and multilat-
eral, granted by the UK government as a proportion of gross national
product (GNP) has declined over the years. In 1980, overseas development
assistance amounted to 0.5 per cent of GNP; it declined to 0.34 per cent in
1983, dropping further to 0.31 per cent in 1994 and then to 0.25 per cent –
the lowest figure ever recorded for the UK – before a planned rise back to
0.30 over the years 1997–2000, this still being one of the lowest figures
among EC countries.

The second principle, generational equity, can only be assessed as a result
of what happens in relation to the third and fourth principles.

The third principle, the improvement of the physical environment, is the
most crucial as well as the most complex. In general, governments have used

five main types of measure in the hope of achieving this aim: advertising, the price mechanism, taxes, regulations and grants. Housing and transport are briefly discussed here in order to illustrate the record of successive Conservative governments during the 1980s and 90s.

All five types of measure were used in varying degrees in the case of the housing environment. There have been intermittent government publicity campaigns exhorting consumers to change their ways, improve their housing, save energy. The evidence suggests that the impact of such publicity campaigns was minimal and that 'saving energy is still a low priority for many people' (Bhatti, 1996, p. 163). Prices of energy were allowed to rise, and taxes on electricity were increased. This may well have reduced energy consumption among the low paid, but it also increased the problem of 'fuel poverty' – the inability of low-income groups to consume adequate amounts of fuel or pay for their fuel bills.

Building regulations were revised several times in order to improve the thermal and environmental quality of housing, but these regulations were either voluntary or applied only to new housing. Since about two thirds of housing was built prior to these regulations, they could affect only a minority of housing. Grants to cover part of the cost of house insulation have long been paid, but there have never been enough and, on most occasions, they have been means tested and very difficult to obtain. Expenditure on them was low and declined over the years as governments tried to reduce public expenditure.

The overall conclusion must be that government policy on improving the environmental quality of housing was always half-hearted and dominated by market principles, with the result that it achieved very little. Indeed, the reduction in expenditure on home improvement and new public housing may have accentuated housing shortages and made the environmental quality of many houses worse, thus creating a major housing problem for the future.

Government and local authorities have tried in a rather incoherent way to encourage the recycling of household waste, but with very little success. In 1995/96, only 7.1 per cent of municipal solid waste was recycled. The remaining 83.3 per cent was emptied into landfill sites or incinerated – 8.7 per cent – or was used to manufacture fuel – 0.9 per cent. The UK's record on recycling is very disappointing by the standards of advanced industrial countries, as Table 4.6 shows.

Government policies on transport during the 1980s and early 1990s were designed to accommodate the demands of rising car ownership. New roads were built and old ones widened, a great deal of green land and much habitat being destroyed in the process. At the same time, rail services, which are environmentally far more friendly, were allowed to decline and were then privatized. The deregulation of buses has meant a plethora of services on the profitable routes and a neglect of services elsewhere. Leaving the economic issues aside, these policies could not have been of much help to the quality of the environment.

Table 4.6   Percentage of household wastage recycled

Country	Percentage
Switzerland	42
Finland	30
Canada	29
Netherlands	28
Denmark	25
USA	24
Sweden	19
Germany	18
UK	6
Belgium	3

Source: Bowcott, 1998, p. 15.

Government hopes for reducing traffic air pollution were based primarily on the policy of raising taxes on petrol, but such taxes have proved a blunt instrument since they can be afforded by most people and are passed on to the consumer by business. Indeed, over the years, motoring has become cheaper both in real terms and in relation to public transport:

> Between 1974 and 1994 rail and bus fares increased by 50–70% in real terms, slightly faster than the growth in disposable incomes. The cost of private motoring, on the other hand, has fallen by 2% in real terms. (Royal Commission on Environmental Pollution, 1997, p. 7)

The only significant government measure with clear positive effects on the environment was the legislation that, as from 1992, all new cars would have to be fitted with catalytic converters that reduce gas emissions. This, coupled with the lower prices for unleaded petrol, are the two environmentally successful measures of this period. Apart from these two measures, government transport policies have had either an adverse or a neutral effect on the environment. It is difficult not to agree with Pearce's comment that 'Transport is one sector of the UK economy in which almost everything has gone wrong' (Pearce, 1993, p. 150).

Even in such areas as the protection of wildlife, in which the UK has a long history, Young's assessment of policies during the years of Conservative government is enigmatically negative:

> By 1994 conservation interests had won some victories, and opened up new issues. But many groups remained depressed both by the scale of the tasks confronting them and by long-term trends not being amenable to government

action. Making progress was like trying to run up a long escalator that goes down. (Young, 1995, p. 249)

There is no coherent policy on biodiversity even though there are various bodies each trying to protect its own particular type of species or patch of land. As Pearce argues, the term 'biodiversity' is not a regular term in government policy documents. Instead, 'Biodiversity is something that tropical countries have; in Britain the emphasis is on "nature conservation"' (Pearce, 1993, p. 113).

'The "greening" of business represents both the greatest challenge and the best hope for sustainable development' as work is so central to society and to the environment (Clark *et al.*, 1993, p. 132). Although the Brundtland report acknowledged this centrality of business to human welfare, it also argued that industrial activities should be sustainable. It set out the principles to be borne in mind by governments and enterprises. In the case of renewable resources, the rate of use should be 'within the limits of regeneration and natural growth' (World Commission on Environment and Development, 1987, p. 45). For non-renewable resources, 'the rate of depletion should take into account the criticality of that resource, the availability of technologies for minimizing depletion, and the likelihood for substitutes being available' (World Commission on Environment and Development, 1987, p. 46).

It would be wrong to even claim that these considerations have ever been on the government or business industrial agenda in the UK, let alone pursued vigorously. There is, of course, a fine balancing act to be struck between the pursuit of economic growth and the protection of the environment. Although the government accepted the so-called precautionary principle, it interpreted it so strictly that the interests of economic growth dominated environmental concerns. Thus, the government felt that the precautionary principle should only be invoked 'if the balance of likely costs and benefits justifies it' (HMSO, 1994, p. 242). More explicitly, the principle 'is not justified for any action regardless of cost: the expected benefit to the environment of any action must be proportionate to the cost of the action' (HMSO, 1995, p. 3). Bearing in mind the complex and difficult problems involved in deciding costs and benefits, the government mostly acted according to its neo-liberal market philosophy.

A few general conclusions can be drawn from the above review of government policies in the UK during the past 20 years or so:

● The environment was a peripheral issue in government policy despite the rhetoric of the early 1990s. On the positive side, it could be said that environmental issues featured more in the public domain than at any time before in the postwar period.

- Some positive steps were taken – the encouragement of recycling, catalytic converters for new cars, water purification and so on – some agencies were abolished, set up or amalgamated but this did not amount to an environmental policy. As Pearce puts it, what the country experienced was 'a sectorised and tangled pattern of agencies and departments; a pattern which ill-suits the holistic and connected operation of environmental systems' (Pearce, 1993, p. 192).

- On the whole, the environment is in no better shape as we enter the twenty-first century than it was twenty years ago. Even carbon emissions from fossil fuel burning during 1990–94, the years following the government's White Paper on the environment and the legislation on catalytic converters from cars, declined by only 0.3 per cent (Flavin, 1996, p. 30). Air pollution on a worldwide basis worsened, and, as argued earlier, it respects no national boundaries.

- The deregulation of many public services, whatever their other consequences, has made the development of a coherent national policy on the environment less likely or even impossible. This is particularly the case with water and transport. Water privatization has made national planning more difficult since some regions of the country have an abundance of rain while others experience shortages. Transport privatization has meant more reliance on cars, excessive public transport in some areas and a reduction in services in others, reflecting commercial rather than environmental criteria.

- There is, however, substantial public awareness that the environment is precious and that some action to protect it is necessary. Reviewing public opinion studies, Young concludes that the change in public opinion in favour of the environment 'is almost beyond doubt' (Young, 1991, p. 113). Similarly, Green consumerism, although still weak, at least exists and may become stronger in the future. Equally important, public awareness that environmental hazards can result in individual health hazards is greater than before. People are beginning to realize that 'self-interest and a common interest in survival converge', and this can only be good for future campaigns on the environment (Blowers, 1993, p. 18). Despite all these favourable changes, it is important not to draw overoptimistic conclusions for, as Norris has warned, 'public attitudes towards the environment are divided' (Norris, 1997, p. 339). Those who support, say, the cleansing of the rivers or the lakes may not support the campaigns against nuclear power, and so on.

● The general verdict on the performance of Conservative governments during the 1980s and 90s is that they should and could have done much better. The acceptance of the principle of sustainable development was an important step forward, but the strategy to translate principle into reality 'can only be described as marginal in terms of public investment' (Christie, 1994, p. 18). A good indication of the scope of the failure is the refusal of successive governments to set firm targets that committed them to specific action. Instead, what one finds is a long list of indicative targets, which, as the government itself concedes, 'are not binding' (HMSO, 1997b, p. 18).

Government Policies on the Environment

Trying to reconcile the tensions between a free enterprise philosophy and
  sustainable development:
  ▨ Changing public opinion/advertising
  ▨ Use of the price mechanism
  ▨ Through taxation
  ▨ By regulation
  ▨ By grants to encourage environmentally desirable behaviour

---

What are the Broad Implications for Society?

Although the implications of environmental trends for society were discussed throughout the above section, it is worth summarising them here before proceeding further.

First, there are the direct dangers to human life, some of which are agreed and quantifiable while others are disputed and more difficult to quantify:

● Deaths and injuries resulting from car accidents are the most obvious and most publicized ill-effect of transport on humans. As shown earlier, there does seem to have been a decline in the number of fatal accidents and in serious injuries occurring on the roads, although the number of slight injuries has increased.

   Some of the accidents involve pedestrians and cyclists. The trends in road accidents might, therefore, give the impression that walking and cycling have become safer. This is far from being the case bearing in mind the even higher decline in both of these two forms of activity.

- Several illnesses are connected, or believed by many researchers to be connected, with emissions from cars. Benzene emissions from cars are connected with leukaemia deaths; diesel particulates can aggravate respiratory diseases such as asthma and bronchitis; professional drivers run a higher risk of bladder cancer, kidney cancer and non-Hodgkin's lymphoma; and drivers, car occupants and cyclists in urban areas are exposed to high risks of gas emission poisoning (British Medical Association, 1997, p. 33).
- There are possible increased risks to child health for families living close to electricity pylons or to nuclear power stations, to which we referred earlier.
- Gas emissions from transport, industry and housing affect global warming and ozone layer depletion, with all the possible health risks for humans both now and in the future, which was discussed above.

Second, there are the indirect dangers to human health resulting primarily from the increased dependency on cars. People walk and cycle far less than they used to, preferring the comfort of their cars. The average mileage walked yearly per person declined from 239 in 1972 to 199 in 1992 – 'an overall decrease of 20%' (British Medical Association, 1997, p. 17). Similarly, the number of kilometres cycled declined fourfold between 1951 and 1991 so that 'cycling now only accounts for 4% of all journeys undertaken' (British Medical Association, 1997, p. 19). This is despite the constant reminders that both walking and cycling improve health and reduce the incidence of illness, particularly of heart diseases, obesity and hypertension (British Medical Association, 1997, pp. 16–21). This is part of the wider medical conclusion that sedentary lifestyles are linked to ill health, while physical activity is the best type of preventive medicine.

Third, heavy traffic increases noise, increases risks and lowers the quality of life for people living nearby. All this can have adverse effects on their physical and emotional health and can disrupt their social networks.

Fourth, as we have already referred to, are dangers posed to agriculture, forests and plant life from global warming, ozone depletion and acid rain.

Fifth, the total or near annihilation of many species is a most serious problem when one sees life on the earth as dependent on the proper functioning of the total system of interrelationships between all its species. The problem is at its most acute in developing countries, but it is still serious enough in affluent countries, including the UK.

Sixth, the threat of total or near depletion of some of the earth's non-renewable resources may have been abated in the past couple of decades because of discoveries of new energy sources, but, in the long run, there must be limits to such energy resources. It may well be that new discoveries of non-renewable resources and technological inventions will cope with this problem, but this is only a possibility and not a certainty. As part of the affluent world, the UK must bear part of the responsibility and may suffer some of the consequences.

Finally, the implications of the various environmental trends in the UK should be seen in relation to the rest of the world. Affluent countries comprise a small proportion of the world's population, consume most of the world resources and produce most of the polluting emissions. In 1996, the USA comprised 4.7 per cent of the world's population but was responsible for 25.0 per cent of the world's carbon dioxide emission, which is responsible for global warming; the figures for the UK were 1.0 per cent and 2.5 per cent respectively; for Japan, 2.2 and 5.6; for Australia, 0.3 and 1.3; for Canada, 0.5 and 2.1; and for the whole of Europe, 9.0 and 19.6 respectively. In contrast, the figures for the two most populous countries, China and India, with 21.5 and 16.3 per cent of world population respectively, were responsible for 13.5 per cent and 3.6 per cent of world carbon dioxide emission (Brown, 1997, p. 17). It is this combination of conspicuous consumption and overwhelming pollution by the affluent world that some feel 'must be greatly curtailed if environmental catastrophe is to be avoided' (Blowers, 1993, p. 1).

What Proposals for Action Have Been Made by Conventional Sources?

Environmental policy agendas inevitably vary as they reflect different ideological positions. They have been classified in a variety of ways (Schnaiberg and Gould, 1994, p. 158) but fundamentally range from the conventional Light Green to the radical Dark Green positions. Conventional approaches underestimate the seriousness of environmental problems and overestimate the ability of technology to deal with these problems. Radical approaches differ a great deal in the solutions they propose, but they all agree on the seriousness of the problems.

Light Greenism

Acceptance of high rates of economic growth and rising consumption levels achieved through ever-increasing technological sophistication is the hallmark of this approach. Light Greenism acknowledges the importance of the environment but firmly believes that technology can deal with the problems. Moreover, in the final analysis, it places more emphasis on economic growth than environmental protection. It is an environmental agenda that goes down well with voters as it does not force them to make any difficult choices. Indeed, they are promised the best of both worlds – higher consumption and a better environment.

Both major political parties in the UK support this approach to varying degrees. Where they differ is that the Labour Party, in opposition, appeared to be more prepared to commit resources and introduce policies and regulations in order to rectify some of the environmental consequences of this policy. The Labour Party's paper *In Trust for Tomorrow* is a much bolder document than the Conservative party's leaflet *The Environment: Principles and Policies*. After two years in office, however, the Labour government policies on the environment show no significant differences from those of the Conservative governments. It remains to be seen whether this will change in the remaining years of its term of office.

The Anti-poverty, Pro-growth Approach

The anti-poverty, pro-growth approach is a left-wing offshoot of the Light Green position. It considers environmental and sustainable development prescriptions to be a middle-class pursuit. It accepts that there are some environmental problems but believes that these are not all that serious and can be easily dealt with by government action and new technologies. Government policy should concentrate on the more important issues of increasing economic growth, raising living standards and abolishing poverty.

As early as 1971, Crosland, who later became Secretary of State for the Environment in the Labour government of 1974, dubbed the anti-growth environmentalists a bunch of affluent, 'often kindly and dedicated people', who, while 'being militant about threats to rural peace and wildlife and well loved beauty spots... are little concerned with the far more desperate problem of the urban environment in which 80 per cent of our fellow citizens live' (Crosland, 1971, p. 5).

It is, however, Beckerman's work that best exemplifies this position. He saw the anti-growth movement of the early 1970s as 'largely a middle class movement in the more affluent countries' (Beckerman, 1995, p. 124). The limits to growth argument reflected a middle-class fear that working-class people were beginning to buy cars, go on holidays and so on, thus threatening to spoil hitherto exclusive middle-class pastimes! Such problems as the greenhouse effect, he argued, had been grossly exaggerated, and there was no justification 'for panic action and for the hasty implementation of draconian measures to slow down economic growth' (Beckerman, 1995, p. 128).

Economic growth and environmental quality, it is argued by this approach, go hand in hand rather than being in conflict, as 'the limits to growth' writers claimed. In the early stages of industrialization, the environment will suffer, but there is no doubt that, 'in the longer run, the best way to get a clean environment is to be rich' (Beckerman, 1995, p. 138). Affluent countries have both the financial and technological resources to deal with environmental problems, whereas poor countries do not. So go for growth.

Despite its laudable concern with raising living standards and reducing poverty, this approach suffers from three main weaknesses. First, it underestimates the degree of environmental damage, both actual and potential; second, it overestimates the ability of technology to deal with environmental problems without creating serious side-effects; and third, it ignores the political obstacles involved in government policies to protect the environment or rectify environmental destruction.

The Pro-business, Pro-growth Approach

The pro-business, pro-growth position sees no inherent contradiction between the pursuit of economic growth by private business and the improvement of the quality of the environment. Elkington, the main proponent of this position, in fact argues that the 'most "excellent" companies now include environmental quality objectives among their core values' (Elkington, 1987, p. 16). Good business leaders are just as concerned about the environment as environmentalist campaigners, although they, of course, differ on the role of economic growth.

Like the previous position, economic growth and technological advance are seen as essential to achieving environmental improvements. They provide the finances and the know-how for environmental improvements. Moreover, there is no reason 'why private enterprise should be any more environmentally damaging than public or state enterprise' (Elkington, 1987, p. 17). It may be true that, in the past, private industry was part of the problem of environmental destruction, but it is now increasingly part of the solution. We witness today the 'emergence of a new breed of "green" capitalists and "environmental entrepreneurs" ' (Elkington, 1987, p. 23).

With the demise of centrally planned socialism in Europe, argues Elkington, the world belongs to capitalism, and the only debate remaining is what kind of capitalism is best suited to today's world. Capitalism comes in many colours, and Elkington's choice is 'the green dimension', which is 'the kind of capitalism we must have if there is to be a planet worth having for our children to inherit' (Elkington, 1987, p. 252).

The pro-business, pro-growth agenda is built around the activities of a few industries and a few industrialists. It ignores the polluting effects of most of industry and underestimates the effects of the unrelenting drive for profit on the environment. Like the previous approach, it overestimates the ability of technology to solve environmental problems and underestimates the political obstacles to environmentally friendly policies. Its positive side is that it may act as an encouragement to industry to pursue profitability in environmentally friendly ways.

What Proposals for Action Have Been Made by Conventional Sources?

Light Greenism
- Growth and technology will save us

The anti-poverty, pro-growth approach
- Economic growth and a high-quality environment go together

The pro-business, pro-growth approach
- Green capitalism is the answer

What Proposals for Action Have Been Made by Radicals?

The various proposals by radicals can be roughly placed into two groups, depending on whether they accept or reject current levels and types of industrialization and hence the centrality of continued economic growth to human welfare. The deep ecology movement rejects, while the Brundtland approach accepts, the necessity of continued industrialization and economic growth, albeit with adequate safeguards.

The Deep Ecology, Anti-growth Approach

All three of the conventional positions on the environment are reactions to the deep ecological ideology on the environment. There are numerous, often conflicting, strands to this ideology, which are beyond the scope of this section. Basically, one can identify at least five common themes in the deep ecology approach.

1. There is the common belief that the ecosystem does not simply consist of a number of parts but instead must be seen as a whole, with the result that damaging one part of it damages the whole system. This will be accepted by many other environmentalists without necessarily subscribing to the rest of the deep ecology ideology. Thus Taylor, writing from a Labour Party perspective, concludes that the global environment 'is not a collection of separate parts, it is a highly complex whole, a system' (Taylor, 1992, p. 6). However, her suggestions for environmental improvement are in stark contrast to the deep ecology proposals.

2. A broad type of intrinsic equality is believed to exist between all the living organisms inhabiting the planet. Humans are not superior to other living organisms, and this should be reflected in human activities. Biocentrism – equality of the species – rather than anthropocentrism – superiority of the humans – is the value that should govern relationships between the various species. Despite this general support of biocentrism, there are disagreements on how the phrase 'broad equality' should be interpreted and what its policy implications are. Biocentrism, in the strong sense, is rejected by the other approaches discussed here because they see the non-human world as a means of improving the living standards of the human race.

3. There are limits to growth that cannot be solved by ever-increasing complex technology. A reduction in consumption is the only solution, and this implies reduced rates of economic growth. Failure to act will have catastrophic consequences for the whole planet. Meadows *et al.* have been the strongest exponents of the 'limits to growth' thesis over the years. Having set it out in 1972, they repeated their thesis in equally strong terms in 1992. All the resources used by the economy have limits in terms of both resource exhaustion and the pollution that they cause. Today, they claim, we have reached the limits in many areas in both senses:

    > Human use of many essential resources and generation of many kinds of pollutants have already surpassed rates that are physically sustainable. Without significant reductions in material and energy flows, there will be in the coming decades an uncontrolled decline in per capita food output, energy use, and industrial production. (Meadows *et al.*, 1992, pp. xv–xvi)

4. Population growth rates are too high and need to be substantially reduced in order to bring about a reduction in the overall size of world population. Without such a reduction, many of the other efforts to 'save the planet' are redundant. Many others have supported policies for population control without necessarily subscribing to the other tenets of the deep ecology. The government of China, for example, has for decades pursued a population control policy by insisting on only one child per family, but, at the same time, it has encouraged rapid industrialization in the belief that it will improve the welfare of its people.

5. Schumacher's concept of 'small is beautiful' finds resonance among most deep ecologists in a variety of ways: industry should be reduced to manageable size; large urban living should be abandoned in favour of smaller human habitats; there should be more self-sufficiency and less reliance on international trade; and, generally, there should be a rejection of the modern technological way of life because it is against the spirit of

living in harmony with the environment and is thus anti-human. Using modern methods of intensive farming as an example, Bunyard and Morgan-Grenville write:

> In modern farming, the farm worker is increasingly isolated from the soil he is tilling; he sits encased in his tractor cab, either with ear muffs to shut out the noise or with radio blaring, and what goes on behind the tractor has more to do with the wonders of technology than with the wisdom of countless generations of his predecessors. (Bunyard and Morgan-Grenville, 1987, p. 71)

The deep ecology perspective entails such a fundamental shift from contemporary ways of thinking and living that even Green parties have had to trim it when appealing to the electorate. As Dobson rightly points out, ecologism is so different from capitalism and socialism that it cannot be absorbed by them, whereas Light Greenism can easily be incorporated by these two political systems (Dobson, 1995, p. 7).

The two fundamental flaws of deep ecology are, first, its belief that all economic growth based on modern technology is inevitably polluting, and second, the demand that economic growth should cease. The claim that a sustainable environment requires a 'zero growth' economy as a precondition is, as Jacobs has pointed out, faulted in logic:

> Because current patterns of economic growth are environmentally damaging, it does not follow that the solution to environmental problems is no growth. (Jacobs, 1991, p. 54)

Modern technology can be both polluting and non-polluting, depending on its kind and its use. Without it, it would be difficult to deal with some of the current accumulated pollution, and it would also be difficult to raise living standards in the Third World. Indeed, several leaders of Third World countries have described the deep ecology advocacy of reduced rates of economic growth as a form of cultural neo-colonialism – an attempt to convince Third World people that the benefits enjoyed in the affluent world should not spread to them.

Second, there is no reason to believe that a 'no-growth' policy is inherently environmentally friendly. Many parts of sub-Saharan Africa have, in recent years, witnessed both a stagnation in their economies and a deterioration in their environments.

The Brundtland Approach

The Brundtland definition of sustainable development mentioned at the beginning of this chapter represents a compromise 'in the debate between the advocates of continued growth and the advocates of non-growth' (Anderson, 1991, p. 12). It is, however, more than a compromise: it is an attempt to understand the issues of the environment in a broad perspective not only in physical, but also in policy terms and hence to put forward recommendations that reflect this position. It combines the concern for the environment with concern for social equity.

Five central values are subsumed in the Brundtland definition of sustainable development: the satisfaction of basic needs for all, generational equity, conservation of the environment, sustainable economic growth, and an international approach to resources and problems.

First, such basic social needs as food, clothing, shelter, employment, health and education should be satisfied for all, not only in the affluent, but in the developing countries as well. This is not simply a moral imperative, important though that is, but a social, economic and ecological one. The poor suffer more than the rich from environmental problems in both the affluent and the non-affluent countries. Poverty is both the cause and the consequence of environmental degradation. For all these reasons, the alleviation of poverty is a central objective of sustainable development.

Second, the present generation has a duty to use the planet in such a way that it delivers it to future generations in a good condition. This is a novel contribution to environmental debates that has now been generally accepted, even by the Thatcher government in its White Paper in 1990. The implementation of the principle necessitates, among other things, some sacrifices on behalf of the present generation as well as refraining from actions such as dumping radioactive material in the sea that may not pollute at present but may do so in the future.

Third, the report was clear that economic growth was a necessary part of sustainable development. Without economic growth, the needs of millions of people could not be met, but economic growth should be pursued in environmentally friendly terms. It, therefore, acknowledged that industry 'has the power to enhance or degrade the environment; it invariably does both' (World Commission on Environment and Development, 1987, p. 206) and argued for economic policies that do not degrade the environment. The principle clearly implies both a high degree of social responsibility on the part of private enterprise and active government policies to ensure the kind of economic growth that is sustainable.

Fourth, the conservation of the environment is necessary not only for the benefit of the human race, now and in the future, but also for that of other species. The report rejected the simple anthropocentric view of development but neither did it espouse the deep ecological biocentric position of species equality. Although this may appear a convenient compromise, the report argued that the relationship between the human species and other animal life is so complex that no simple solution can do it justice. For example, although cruelty to animals is to be condemned, this does not necessarily mean a rejection of meat consumption, or that the relationship between humans and dogs is necessarily different from that between humans and spiders and so on.

Fifth, only an international cooperative approach to the utilization of resources and the solution to environmental problems stands a chance of succeeding. Thus, rain forests in developing countries are global assets that are worth preserving, to the benefit of all mankind. This implies, however, that 'the resources in developed nations are the property of the global community, and as such must be handled in a way that benefits everyone fairly' (Luper-Foy, 1992, p. 61). Global equity is just as important as generational equity for environmental protection.

There are inevitably problems of defining and reconciling these five principles, but these difficulties pale into insignificance when compared with the problems of deciding what policies are necessary and how and by whom they should be implemented on a national and international scale. For this reason, sustainable development is an ideal that individuals and nations should strive for even though they may never achieve it in full. Like other important social values, it is 'never completely attainable but always worth fighting for' (Pearce, 1993, p. 183).

Conclusions

There is now general agreement between the political parties and among the public that the quality of the environment is important to human welfare and that government policies should endeavour to bring about an improvement in the quality of the environment. Opinions differ, however, on the kinds of policy that are needed to preserve and improve the environment. The deep ecology approach is so vehemently hostile to the industrial consumerist way of life and demands such fundamental changes in society that it receives little support from either the public or the political parties, other than Green parties. Not unexpectedly, government policies have been mostly of the Light Green type.

Government policies on the environment have been uncoordinated and mostly of the permissive kind. They have involved very low levels of public expenditure and have achieved far less than they promised. So far, the government response has established mechanisms and procedures in several fields in relation to the environment, but it 'has produced little in the way of policy realignment and new administrative cultures' that are essential for real progress towards sustainable development (Voissey and O'Riordan, 1997, p. 24).

Many aspects of the environment are in no better a shape today than they were twenty or so years ago, bearing in mind that environmental pollution knows no national boundaries. International agreements on the environment have achieved little, partly because poor countries want to put as a priority policies that increase economic growth, partly because the rich countries have been unwilling to provide the financial aid that is necessary to pursue environmentally friendly development policies and partly because multinational companies have put profit making above environmental considerations.

All the evidence suggests that unbridled economic growth is detrimental to the environment. The Brundtland view that it is possible to combine economic growth with the preservation of the environment is now generally accepted. Conflicts between the demands of economic growth and the demands to protect the environment should be resolved by applying the precautionary principle, that is, that action should be taken to protect the environment 'where there are good grounds for judging either that action taken promptly at comparatively low cost may avoid more costly damage later, or that irreversible effects may follow if action is delayed' (HMSO, 1990, p. 11). It is the interpretation of the principle rather than the principle itself that is proving controversial.

Although combining industrial and business profitability with environmental care and green production is difficult (Clark *et al.*, 1993), it would be a mistake to underestimate the opposition of industry to some of the necessary measures. The failure of the US government to agree to the targets put forward by the EC on the reduction of gas emissions has been attributed to the power of the 'industry lobby which fears action on global warming will put up taxes and cost them business' (Brown, 1997, p. 17). Fears that a strong environmental policy will cost jobs is not substantiated by existing evidence. The recent OECD study has shown that 'the net impact of environmental policy on employment in OECD countries to date appears to have been beneficial, though small' (Long, 1997, p. 17).

Agricultural productivity has risen enormously over the years, largely because of technological innovations. At the same time, however, the excessive use of fertilizers and pesticides has created several environmental problems that, on present evidence, can only be addressed satisfactorily through a reduction in intensive farming and a greater reliance on traditional farming. The use of fertilizers and pesticides has had an adverse effect on the quality of water and has destroyed many species of plants, birds and animals.

It is now generally accepted that the current transport policy of extending and widening roads in order to accommodate the ever-increasing number of cars while at the same time neglecting the public transport system cannot continue, for a variety of good reasons: air pollution will not be substantially reduced; a higher proportion of land will be taken up by roads; more harm will be done to the nation's ecosystem; traffic congestion will worsen; health hazards will intensify; and deaths and injuries on the roads will continue. Within towns and cities, it is accepted that ways must be found whereby residents can reclaim their streets: more traffic-free areas, better facilities for pedestrians, extending the system of bus lanes, enforcing speed limits, providing cycle path facilities and encouraging people to walk short distances.

Such a transport policy, together with the 'greening' of the car through the use of catalytic converters or some technological innovation, will reduce the consumption of non-renewable resources and make for a healthier, safer and more enjoyable way of living without any adverse effects on economic growth. To get maximum advantage, however, all these measures 'would need to be implemented in concert to have any significant effect' (Gossop and Webb, 1993, p. 130).

Environmental degradation affects us all, but none more so than those on low incomes. Rich people and affluent nations are the greatest polluters but can avoid many of the environmental hazards. Poor people have little option but to live with and experience most environmental problems. Environmental anxieties about the ozone layer, global warming or the Amazon rainforests seem irrelevant to many low-income people, as well as nations, as there are more pressing personal issues to be solved.

Adequate housing in an acceptable environment is a basic need for all. Despite the improvements over the years, nothing can justify the current extent of homelessness, overcrowding, physically unfit housing and degrading environments in an affluent society. The knowledge and technology for greener housing is also available. It is quite possible to construct new housing that is weather tight and to make existing housing highly insulated so that housing becomes much more energy efficient and far less polluting than it is now. Brown *et al.* refer to some of the superinsulated homes in Saskatchewan, Canada, which 'use one third as much energy as modern Swedish homes do, or one tenth the U.S. average' (Brown *et al.*, 1990, p. 180).

Energy consumption has risen considerably and will continue to do so in the future. Energy conservation is one way of dealing with the problem, but by itself it will not be sufficient. Hence, many environmentalists claim that a greater reliance on solar, wind and water energy is necessary. It is less polluting than fossil or nuclear energy, it is renewable and, with technological advances, it will be no more expensive than conventional fossil or nuclear energy. So long as traditional sources of energy remain in ample supply, the pressure to utilize the sun, wind and water as sources of energy will remain weak. However, this cannot last for ever, and, with the public concern over the risks of nuclear energy, it is inevitable that the new sources of energy will eventually take over. Brown *et al.* rightly refer to the late twentieth century as 'the dawn of the solar age' (Brown *et al.*, 1990, p. 176).

Scientists are also hopeful that it will soon be possible for solar power 'captured in outer space and beamed to earth' to be sold 'at prices equal to – or even lower than – ground-based alternatives' in order to solve the looming energy crisis of the twenty-first century (Eadie, 1997, p. 10).

The Deep Green fears that current consumption levels in affluent societies are unsustainable may well be exaggerated but they cannot be ignored altogether, particularly if one wants consumption levels in the developing world to improve. Although it is difficult to reverse consumerist trends, it is possible to reduce, even if only slightly, the consumption of energy and materials. New ways of house building, greater emphasis on energy-saving domestic appliances, more attention to the energy use and durability of cars, and so on, will do a great deal to reduce the consumption of non-renewable resources.

Another way in which resource consumption can be reduced in a socially acceptable way is through the greater application of recycling techniques. As mentioned earlier, much more can be done because most materials are used only once and then thrown away into landfill sites. Recycling not only reduces waste but is also less polluting than current methods of waste disposal. The re-education of the public is central to the success of a recycling policy – 'only if the throwaway mentality is replaced by a recycling ethic' will this type of policy succeed (Brown *et al.*, 1990, p. 182).

Governments so far have largely refused to set legally binding environmental targets. It is true that it is sometimes not possible to set targets because we do not know enough about the issue in question. More often than not, however, failure to set targets reveals either the government's lack of commitment or its unwillingness to face up to entrenched interests. In such a sensitive area, progress will inevitably be slow, but, if it is to be achieved, it does seem that government will have to play a stronger part than it has done so far. Writing about industry and the environment, Taylor is justified in insisting that:

> The case for making regular audits of environmental performance a mandatory requirement is now overwhelming, at least for all large and medium-sized industries. (Taylor, 1992, p. 168)

The arrival of a green and sustainable society depends to a large extent on the public acceptance of a new set of values. Both fear and hope will play a part in the creation of an environmental ethic. When people come to realize that, unless they change their attitudes and behaviour towards the environment, they and their families will suffer, when manufacturers and consumers realize that energy-saving goods do not threaten their way of life and can in fact enhance it, only then their attitudes and values will begin to change, making the possibility of a sustainable society more of a reality.

Taylor quite correctly argues that plans for a sustainable society should be made 'in a spirit of hope and determination, not in a spirit of despair' (Taylor, 1992, p. 1). Many of the changes needed to move towards sustainability are fairly easy and have general support – recycling, the use of solar power, protection of the animal and plant world and so on. Other changes – a reduction in consumption and dealing with poverty at the national and global level for example – are more difficult and perhaps impossible in the short run.

Challenges

- First, despite the fact that this chapter is based on the belief that there are no 'limits to growth', this belief is based as much on hope as on scientific evidence. The depletion of the stocks of non-renewable resources, the disposal of waste, the ability of technology to contribute to human welfare without excessive pollution and the rise of new human demands or needs are complex issues that cannot be measured accurately now, let alone at some time in the future. Thus, although the 'limits to growth' argument seems at present to have been rejected by most, should not prudent students of the environment keep an open mind on this issue?
- Second, sustainable development is only possible on a worldwide basis. The way in which one nation treats its environment and the way in which multinational companies exploit the environment of all countries have worldwide implications. Does this not mean that affluent countries, out of self-interest as well as out of a moral duty, should provide the necessary financial aid to poor countries to enable them to move closer to sustainability? In the same way that the forests of the Amazon are an international environmental resource, should not the GDP of affluent countries be an international resource?
- Third, there are some situations in which the pursuit of economic growth and the preservation of the environment are in conflict. So far, the interests of economic growth have taken precedence over environmental issues in Britain. Should a more balanced view be taken so that economic growth might suffer at times? Would this not benefit from the setting of firm environmental targets wherever possible? And should we start measuring individual and societal welfare not only in economic and social, but also in environmental terms?

Fourth, an essential part of sustainability is the eradication of poverty at both a national and an international level. Bearing in mind the failure of successive governments to abolish poverty in this country, what hope is there for the abolition, or at least the reduction, of poverty in developing countries?

Further Reading

Journals

Environmental Ethics, a quarterly journal for those interested in ethical discussions on environmental issues.

Environmental Politics, a quarterly journal for those wishing to read about political discussions on environmental issues.

Books

Dobson, A. (1995) *Green Political Thought* (2nd edn), London, Routledge. Perhaps the best book on the conceptual debates between different schools of thought in the Green movement. Bearing in mind the nature of the theoretical issues, the book is remarkably clear and easy to follow.

Huby, M. (1998) *Social Policy and the Environment*, Buckingham, Open University Press. A very readable account of the implications of sustainable development for policies in relation to water, food, housing, energy, travel and recreation.

Pearce, D. (1993) *Blueprint 3: Measuring Sustainable Development*, London, Earthscan. A very good documentation and discussion of the state of the environment in the UK, together with a critical review of government policies by one of the foremost writers on these issues.

5
Social Divisions

It is the mark of a civilised society to aim at eliminating such inequalities as have their source, not in individual differences, but in its own organisation. (Tawney, 1931, p. 57)

[The] translation of a want or need into a right is one of the most widespread and dangerous of modern heresies. (Powell, 1972, p. 12)

Introduction

Social divisions are an integral part of all advanced industrial societies, the UK being no exception to this. Divisions by wealth, income, occupation, education, housing and so on are obvious enough for all to see. What is unique about the UK is the speed at which these divisions have intensified in the past twenty years. They have now reached a degree that threatens the social cohesion of society and, many would argue, the economic fortunes of the country as well. This chapter concentrates primarily on two manifestations of these divisions – income inequality and poverty – and only briefly on other divisions.

Inequality of income and wealth is an endemic feature of any capitalist society since the various aspects of the economic system operate on the principle that people must be rewarded unequally if efficiency, risk taking and hard work are to be encouraged. The dominant view is that an inequality of pay and reward is an essential component of the engine that powers the economic system. Inequalities in the economic domain inevitably spill over into the social and political fields; the result is a divided society.

Critics of class inequalities are not against all forms and degrees of inequality. They are in essence opponents of excessive inequalities, particularly of the inherited kind. Debates about class inequality represent, therefore, divisions of opinion about the types and degrees of inequality that ought to exist in a capitalist society rather than about whether they should or should not exist.

Despite the centrality of class to debates on inequality, it is important to acknowledge that class is a less coherent and unifying concept today than in the past. There are serious divisions and conflicts of interest within all three

130

classes – capitalist, middle and working class – as well as uncertainties over where to draw the boundaries between the three classes. Moreover, statistics are normally provided according to socio-economic groups rather than these three broad classes, reflecting a Weberian rather than Marxist conception of class, and it is these groupings that will be used in this chapter.

Inequalities of class are, however, only one of several types of division in advanced industrial societies. Gender inequality is another very significant type, but there are differences of opinion over whether or not this is a necessary ingredient of a capitalist society. While capitalism cannot by definition exist without class inequality, it is a matter of debate whether the same applies to gender inequality. Theoretically, one could conceive of a capitalist system where gender inequalities were non-existent or at least minimal.

Ethnicity or race is the third major dimension of inequality. All capitalist societies exhibit inequalities that hinge on a person's ethnicity and that cannot always be reduced to or attributed to class or gender. As with gender, there are unresolved debates on whether ethnic inequalities are an inherent part of a capitalist society.

Spatial divisions constitute the fourth major dimension of inequality – within cities, between urban and rural, within the rural areas, between regions and so on. As we shall show later, all spatial inequalities are significant, although some are more so than others.

Although these are the major cleavages within contemporary Britain, they are supplemented, reinforced or contradicted by others of comparatively lesser significance. Age is fast becoming a characteristic that affects people's life chances and will do so even more in the future as the proportion of the retired and the very old in the population increases. Gay or lesbian groups claim that their life chances are affected as much, and sometimes more, by their sexual categorization as their class, gender, race or region. Persons with disabilities insist that disability is as important as any of the other dimensions as, in many instances, it affects their lives irrespective of other social categorizations.

The four major dimensions of inequality are interdependent and tend to reinforce each another. Divisions of gender, race and locality 'are related to – but are not reducible to – those of class, but they are not necessary in the same structural sense as those of class' (Hudson and Williams, 1995, p. xiv). Class is the central, most important dimension on most occasions and in most situations. There are, however, issues in which the other dimensions assume supremacy. Knowledge of a person's ethnicity will provide more information regarding the risk of experiencing prejudice and discrimination than will knowledge of a person's class. Similarly, despite the real differences in life chances between upper class women and unskilled women, there are certain issues – abortion, rape and so on – that unite women and in which class is almost an irrelevance.

What Has Been Happening?

The aim of this section is not to provide a detailed account of trends but instead to bring out their salient features and their implications for British society.

Inequalities of Wealth

There are serious difficulties in estimating the distribution of wealth at any one time and even more so in mapping trends over time in any country, let alone between countries. Definitions of wealth vary, the units of wealth ownership can be different, some studies are based on the data published by the Inland Revenue while others are based on other estimates, and the data refer sometimes to the UK and on other occasions to Great Britain. These methodological problems do not negate the trends shown in Table 5.1, although they may affect them at the margin.

Table 5.1 Distribution of wealth, GB/UK (percentage of wealth), 1960–1994

Quintile group	1954	1960	1970	1975	1981	1994
Top 1 per cent	43.0	38.2	29.0	23.2	18.0	19.0 (28)*
Top 5 per cent	71.0	64.3	56.3	46.5	36.0	38.0 (52)
Top 10 per cent	79.0	76.7	70.1	62.4	50.0	51.0 (65)
Top 20 per cent		89.8	89.0	81.8		
Top 25 per cent					73.0	73.0 (82)
Top 50 per cent				92.0	92.0	93.0 (94)

Figures for 1960, 1970 and 1975 refer to Great Britain, those for 1981 and 1994 to the UK. Other data suggest that there is little difference between the UK and Great Britain.
*Figures in brackets for 1994 refer to the distribution of wealth that does not include the net value of dwellings.
Sources: For 1954, 1960, 1970 and 1975: Royal Commission on the Distribution of Income and Wealth, 1977, Table 33, p. 76. For 1981 and 1994: Central Statistical Office, 1998, Table 5.26, p. 104.

Several important conclusions flow from Table 5.1:

- The distribution of wealth is less concentrated today than it was forty years ago, although there may be legitimate differences of opinion on the exact extent.

- This trend towards redistribution appears to have been halted, although not reversed, in the early 1980s.
- It is unclear how much of the registered redistribution is real and how much is, in fact, between different members of the same family or household in an attempt to evade tax liability. It would be most unusual if part of the redistribution was not of this kind.
- All the redistribution of wealth appears to be within the top half of the population. In other words, the bottom half of the population has always owned very little wealth – about 8 per cent from the mid 1970s onwards.
- Despite all the redistribution, the richest 5 per cent of the population still own either one third or one half of the nation's wealth, depending on the exclusion or inclusion of housing in the statistics. The proportions are even higher if one refers only to the ownership of land, stocks and shares.
- It is more than likely that the concentration of wealth is gendered, with the result that women may not own as much as men. The situation may be different in old age as women outlive their partners.
- Most of the seeming redistribution of wealth is accounted for by the spread of house ownership. If the net value of housing is excluded from the data, wealth concentration becomes steeper, as the data in brackets for 1994 indicate. Thus, the top 10 per cent of the adult population owned 51 per cent of wealth when the net value of housing was included in the statistics, but they owned a staggering 65 per cent if housing was excluded.

Recent debates about the definition of wealth revolve not so much around housing but around the inclusion or exclusion of state and occupational pension rights in the measurement of wealth distribution. If pensions are included, wealth becomes slightly less concentrated, as Table 5.2 shows. It is highly questionable, however, whether pension rights constitute wealth because, unlike other forms of wealth, pension rights cannot be sold by their owner. Including pension rights in the estimation of wealth serves to devalue the power that wealth confers on its holders and thus confuses political debates on wealth policies.

Inequalities of Income

Although income and wealth are separate concepts, they are obviously inter-related. Those with high incomes almost inevitably possess modest or significant amounts of wealth, and vice versa in that the very wealthy are likely to be found among the high-income groups.

People's incomes can derive from various sources: earnings from work, social security benefits, profits, interest from savings, rent and so on. Clearly, those with very low incomes tend to rely primarily on either benefits or earnings from work; those with high incomes tend to have more sources of income.

Table 5.2   Distribution of wealth among adults, UK (percentage), 1994

Quintile group	Marketable wealth	Marketable wealth plus occupational pensions	Marketable wealth plus occupational pensions plus state pensions
Top 1 per cent	19	14	11
Top 5 per cent	38	31	25
Top 10 per cent	51	43	36
Top 25 per cent	73	66	58
Top 50 per cent	93	90	83

Source: Government Statistical Service, 1997, Tables 13.5, 13.6 and 13.7, pp. 135, 136 and 137.

Irrespective of which method of income measurement one uses or whether one refers to income before or after taking into account housing costs, the direction of the trends in income inequality is very similar – toward less concentration up to 1980 and increased concentration since then.

The Gini coefficient for the years 1961, 1970, 1979 and 1991 for income before housing costs was 0.260, 0.255, 0.248 and 0.337 respectively. The trend was the same for income after taking into account housing costs, although inequalities were consistently higher: 0.269, 0.265, 0.257 and 0.365 respectively. The general conclusion from using the Gini coefficient measurement is that income inequality declined between 1961 and 1980 but rose in the subsequent period to 1991 (Goodman and Webb, 1994, Table A.2).

The same picture emerges if one uses the distribution of income between the various decile groups as the measurement of income inequality in society. The turning point is again 1979, when the Conservative government under Mrs Thatcher took office. Whereas income inequality declined consistently between 1961 and 1979, it rose during the 1980s and 90s, although it may have peaked at about 1992.

The contrasting fortunes of the poorest and the richest sections of the population are striking. Whereas the bottom 20 per cent of income earners received 9.3 per cent of total national income before housing costs in 1961, and 9.9 in 1979, their share dropped to 7.8 per cent in 1996. On the other hand, the corresponding share of the top 20 per cent of income earners dropped from 37 per cent in 1961 to 35 per cent in 1979, although it rose sharply to reach 41 per cent in 1996. It was only the top three deciles of income earners who saw their fortunes improve, and this was at the expense of not only the low-income, but also the middle-income groups.

The distribution of income after 1979 became even more unequal if one takes into account housing costs. Thus, the income share of the bottom decile declined from 4 per cent to 2.0 per cent, and the income of the bottom two deciles dropped from 9.6 per cent to 6.2 per cent. At the other extreme, the income share of the top decile rose from 21 to 28 per cent, while the income of the two top deciles increased from 35 to 43 per cent.

Table 5.3   Income share by decile group (percentage), 1961–1996/97

	1961	1979		1993/94		1996/97	
	(A)	(A)	(B)	(A)	(B)	(A)	(B)
Bottom decile	4.2	4.2	4.0	3.1	2.1	3.1	2.0
Second decile	5.1	5.7	5.6	4.6	4.1	4.7	4.0
Third decile	5.9	7.1	6.4	5.3	4.8	5.2	5.0
Fourth decile	7.0	7.0	8.0	7.0	7.0	7.0	6.0
Fifth decile	8.2	9.0	8.0	8.0	7.0	8.0	8.0
Sixth decile	9.6	9.0	10.0	9.0	9.0	9.0	9.0
Seventh decile	10.9	11.0	10.0	10.0	11.0	10.0	10.0
Eighth decile	12.1	12.0	13.0	12.0	12.0	12.0	13.0
Ninth decile	15.0	14.0	14.0	15.0	15.0	15.0	15.0
Top decile	22.0	21.0	21.0	26.0	28.0	26.0	28.0
Total	**100.0**	**100.0**	**100.0**	**100.0**	**100.0**	**100.0**	**100.0**

(A) Income before housing costs. (B) Income after housing costs.

Source: For 1961, Goodman and Webb, 1994, Table A3. For 1979 and 1993/94, Department of Social Security, 1997, Table A.3, p. 117. For 1996/97, Department of Social Security, 1998, *Households Below Averge Income, 1979–1996/7*, Government Statistical Service, Table A.3, p. 150.

The rise in income inequality during the 1980s and 90s took place despite the improvement in real average incomes, which indicates that a rise in national economic prosperity does not necessarily benefit all income groups. Which income groups get most out of rising economic growth will depend on government policies. The claim that a rise in national prosperity inevitably benefits all citizens more or less alike – the so-called 'trickle-down effect' – is not supported by the evidence from this country.

In brief, the UK remains a very unequal society in terms of both income and wealth distribution. This inequality occurs not only by social class, but also by gender and ethnicity. While some progess has been made in gender terms, ethnic inequalities appear to be more persistent. Examining the fortunes of first- and second-generation immigrants in terms of obtaining positions in the top two socio-economic groups, Heath and Mcmahon conclude that, for both men and women, 'the second generation experience the same pattern and magnitude of ethnic penalties in the British labour market as did the first generation' (Heath and Mcmahon, 1997, p. 108). Moreover, these 'ethnic penalties' occurred even after taking educational qualifications into account. Their data from the 1991 census showed that of those aged 25–29 with graduate qualifications, 82 per cent of whites were to be found in the top two socio-economic groups compared with only 63 per cent of the black African with the remaining in both cases found in lower classes.

Poverty in Britain

> The simple question of how much or how little money is enough to lift a person out of poverty subsumes three interrelated questions: how many of a person's requirements should be met; the quantity of each of these requirements that is necessary; and the quality of each of these requirements. (George and Howards, 1991, p. 2)

> A family is poor if it cannot afford to eat. It is not poor if it cannot afford endless smokes and it does not become poor by the mere fact that other people can afford them. (Joseph and Sumption, 1979, p. 27)

> People are in poverty 'when they lack the resources to obtain the types of diet, participate in the activities and have the living conditions and amenities which are customary, or at least widely encouraged or approved in the societies in which they belong'. (Townsend, 1979, p. 31)

The way in which poverty is defined has obvious implications for its measured extent and depth in society as well as for the policies that are needed to deal with it. This is why there is no agreement on how to define poverty and why poverty debates are essentially political in nature. The three opposing definitions listed above are good illustrations of a minimal and a maximal approach to poverty issues.

Poverty is a fact of life in contemporary Britain, however, irrespective of whether it is defined in minimal or maximal terms: in terms of hunger, basic needs, social coping, social participation, as a form of social exclusion or as a type of social oppression. The refusal of successive governments, both Conservative and Labour, to lay down an official poverty line has been due more to their lack of commitment to eradicating poverty than, as they claimed, to the methodological difficulties involved in constructing such a line.

During the postwar period, government statistics have documented poverty in two ways: in terms of studies relating to low-income families and to households with below-average income. The first group was composed of those families whose income was below, on or just above their assistance entitlement levels; the second comprised those households whose incomes were below 60, 50 or 40 per cent of the average income. Both series of statistics exclude those who live in institutions and those who are homeless, with the result that they both underestimate the extent of poverty.

Table 5.4 shows that, even by the most stringent of poverty definitions, in those whose incomes are lower than the amount of assistance benefit to which they are entitled, poverty is high, rising from 6 per cent of the population to 8 per cent between 1979 and 1992 that is, from 3 170 000 to 4 740 000 persons. A great deal of evidence, however, suggests that the amount of the assistance benefit is insufficient for basic daily needs. Defining poverty in terms of those on and below assistance level is a modest and more realistic approach. It shows that the proportion of people in poverty rose from 14 to 24 per cent of the population, that is, from 7 740 000 to 13 680 000 persons between 1979 and 1992. The figure may well be higher today as most of the poverty risks have intensified in the 1990s. However, even without this, one quarter of the country's population have incomes that are either below or only equivalent to the generally acknowledged stringent assistance benefit level.

Table 5.4   Percentage of the population in poverty by the assistance method, UK, 1979 and 1992

	1979	1992
Below the assistance level	6	8
Below and on assistance level	14	24
Below, on and up to 140% of assistance level	24	33

Source: Oppenheim and Harker, 1996, Figure 2.1, p. 28.

It is even more uncertain which benchmark one should use as the poverty line in terms of the second approach that relates poverty to some proportion of average national income. The EU uses 50 per cent of the national average income as the dividing line, while other countries adopt either the more stringent approach of 40 per cent or the more generous 60 per cent as the benchmark. Whichever benchmark one uses, however, the trend is the same: a decline in low incomes and hence of poverty during the 1960s and 70s, and a rise in the post-1979 period. As expected, the proportion of people in poverty rose even more after taking housing costs into account during the 1980s and 90s.

The figures in Tables 5.4 and 5.5 are snapshots of the numbers of people in poverty at any one time. It does not mean that the same individuals remained in poverty throughout the period as some people move out of poverty while others join the ranks of the poor. The number of people who experience poverty over a period of years is naturally much greater than that shown in the tables here. Despite all that has been said, however, about the withering away of class as a useful concept in social policy debates, it is more than likely that most of those who move in and out of poverty are, in terms of occupation, working-class individuals. The risks of poverty remain sharply class related in contemporary Britain.

Table 5.5   Percentage of the population below 40, 50 and 60 per cent of mean income

	Before housing costs			After housing costs (UK)		
	40%	50%	60%	40%	50%	60%
1961	5.3	10.5	17.6	6.1	11.1	18.8
1970	3.2	9.4	17.4	3.8	10.9	18.3
1979	2.0	8.0	18.0	3.0	9.0	19.0
1994/95	8.0	18.0	28.0	13.0	23.0	32.0
1996/97	8.0	19.0	29.0	15.0	25.0	33.0

Source: For 1961 and 1970: Goodman and Webb, 1994, Table A13. For 1979 and 1994/95: Department of Social Security, 1997, Table F2, pp. 155–8. For 1996/97: Department of Social Security *Households Below Average Income, 1979–1996/7*, Government Statistical Service, 1998 Table F2 pp. 174–177.

Table 5.6 shows that, by family status, the largest group among the poor in 1994 consisted of families with children (39 per cent), while single pensioners comprised the smallest group (10 per cent). By economic status, those in full-time work were the smallest poverty group, accounting for only 8 per cent of the poor, despite the fact that they are the largest group in society. On the other hand, those with the head or spouse aged 60 or over were the largest poverty group, accounting for 23 per cent of the poor.

It is important to distinguish between the composition of the poor and the risk of poverty. The former refers to which groups make up the poverty population, while the latter refers to the degree of risk that any one population group runs of being in poverty. Thus, a large population group may also be a large poverty group, but this does not necessarily mean that it runs a high risk of being in poverty. Conversely, a small population group such as the unemployed may also be a small group among the poor but may run a very high risk of being in poverty. Thus, Table 5.7 shows a different picture from that of Table 5.6.

Table 5.6   The composition of the poor population, that is, those whose incomes were below 50 per cent of average income after housing costs, UK, 1994/95

Population group	Percentage in poverty
I. By family status	
– pensioner, couple	11
– pensioner, single	10
– couple with children	39
– couple without child	11
– single with children	13
– single without children	15
ALL family types	**100**
II. By economic status	
– self-employed	9
– single or couple, all in full time work	8
– one in full-time work, one in part-time work	10
– one in full-time work, one not working	13
– one or more in part-time work	9
– head or spouse aged 60 or over	23
– head or spouse unemployed	11
– other	17
ALL economic types	**100**

Source: Department of Social Security, 1997, Table D1, p. 130; Table D2, p. 134.

The importance of earnings from work as a safeguard against poverty is supported by the data of Table 5.7. Families in which both parents are at work run the lowest risk of being in poverty; the risk rises for families in which only one parent works; and the unemployed run the highest risk of all – three quarters of them were in poverty in 1994 in terms of incomes below 50 per cent of mean income after housing costs. Similarly, the retired are more likely to be in poverty than those in full-time work.

Table 5.7 The risk of poverty: proportion of each group whose income was below 50 per cent of average income after housing costs, UK, 1994/95

Group	Percentage in poverty
I. By family status	
– pensioner, couple	24
– pensioner, single	32
– couple with children	22
– couple without children	10
– single with children	60
– single without children	22
ALL family types	23
II. By economic status	
– self-employed	22
– single or couple, all in full-time work	2
– one in full-time work, one in part-time work	3
– one in full-time work, one not working	17
– one or more in part-time work	33
– head or spouse aged 60 or over	29
– head or spouse unemployed	74
– other	61
ALL economic types	23

Source: Department of Social Security, 1997, Table F1, p. 153; F2, p. 157.

Family status is another indicator of the risk of poverty, as Table 5.7 shows. Lone parents run the highest risk of all family types – almost two thirds of them were in poverty in 1994, as defined above. Elderly women on their own run the second highest risk, partly as a result of their age and the gender discriminations that exist in both the work situation and social security provisions.

The presence and number of children in the family understandably increases the risk of poverty, bearing in mind the inadequacy of Child Benefit. At a general level, families with children are almost twice as likely to be in poverty as those without. The presence of children and the absence of earnings from work creates the highest risk situation for poverty, with the result that about three quarters of children in lone parent families and in two-parent families with no wage earner exist in poverty, as defined above. Two-parent families with one or both parents at work and with three or more children ran three times the risk of being in poverty as similar families with one or two children. It is a sad reflection on society when the risk of poverty is higher among children than among adults – one third of them were in poverty compared with one quarter of the whole population. If children are the nation's future, they deserve better.

The Feminization of Poverty

Although the social science concept of the feminization of poverty is new (Scott, 1984), 'the assumption that the feminisation of poverty is recent is misplaced. The simple fact is that throughout the last century women have always been much poorer than men' (Lewis and Piachaud, 1987, p. 28). The majority of the poor have always been women, for obvious economic, demographic, social and legislative reasons. Women's pay at work is still well below that of men despite equal pay legislation; women are less likely to be covered by generous occupational pension schemes than men; the majority of the retired, particularly the very elderly, when financial resources diminish, are women; nine tenths of all lone parent families are headed by women; and the, until recently, inability of divorced wives to benefit from their ex-husbands' occupational pensions made women far more vulnerable than men to poverty in old age. To all this must be added the fact that the distribution of income within the family is unequal, to the detriment of women, so that even in families with adequate incomes women may be economically disadvantaged.

The feminization of poverty is applicable to all countries in varying degrees. Some recent evidence, however, suggests that the poverty risk among women of working age is becoming similar to that of men in some countries. In the case of Italy, the two rates were the same, while in the case of Sweden in the mid 1980s, working age women were less likely to be in poverty than men – the proportion of women aged 18–57 in poverty was 8.8 per cent compared with 9.6 per cent for men (Casper and McLanahan, 1994, p. 597).

Despite the general relative improvement of women's position in employment, as described in Chapter 2, gender inequalities are still substantial with regard to income and in relation to the higher positions in society. In 1992/93, there was no woman Chief Constable in Britain; only 2 per cent of the top managers were women; only 10 per cent of university professors were women; only 20 per cent of head teachers of secondary schools were women; and, similarly, only 20 per cent of senior executive officers in the civil service were women (Equal Opportunities Commission, 1993, pp. 25–32).

Ethnicity and Poverty

The risk of poverty among ethnic minority groups is higher than among the rest of the population (Amin, with Oppenheim, 1992). They suffer a higher risk of unemployment and low pay than do the rest of the population (Department of Employment, 1995; Sly, 1995), and a lower eligibility for social security benefits. Thus, the Joseph Rowntree Foundation report noted that 'Whereas only 18 per cent of the (white) population was in the poorest fifth of the whole population, more than a third of the non-white population was in the poorest fifth' (Joseph Rowntree Foundation, 1995, p. 28).

If one extends the definition of poverty beyond income to cover housing, then most ethnic groups suffer from inadequate housing conditions more often than do the white population, as Table 5.8 shows. It is also clear that there are wide housing inequalities between the various ethnic groups, the Chinese arguably doing best.

Table 5.8   Ethnicity and inadequate housing, Great Britain, 1991

Ethnic group	Lacking or sharing bath/WC	No central heating	Seriously overcrowded	Overcrowded
White	1%	19%	*	1%
Black Caribbean	1	17	1	3
Black African	5	16	6	9
Indian	1	12	3	10
Pakistani	2	34	8	22
Bangladeshi	2	24	19	28
Chinese	3	16	3	7

* Figure of less than 0.5%.
Serious overcrowding means over 1.5 persons per room; overcrowding means over 1 and up to 1.5 persons per room.
Source: Ratcliffe, 1997, Table 7.5, p. 142.

Geographical Distribution of Poverty

The geography of poverty is as important as it is complicated (Philo, 1995). The public image of rural bliss and affluence is a caricature of the true situation. To begin with, fewer than 8 per cent of the rural workforce are now agricultural or forestry workers, while the service sector absorbs more than two thirds. Poverty is higher in some rural areas than in many urban areas, the elderly being the most vulnerable group (Shucksmith, 1997). Rural areas can also be more disadvantaged than urban areas in terms of the provision of schools, libraries, employment, transport and many other social indicators. Rural poverty is more invisible than urban poverty and, as such, it tends to perpetuate a myth of rural tranquillity and prosperity. Inequalities of health also vary considerably by location. Dorling's work shows that, in nearly 30 areas in Britain, ranging from the old industrial towns to the inner city areas and some rural areas, mortality rates increased during the 1980s (Dorling, 1997).

It is worth remembering that what happens in a locality can affect the rest of the country. Writing of the situation in the USA, Wilson comments:

> The growing concentration of poverty and social isolation of the inner cities has implications not just for the quality of life and social interaction in impoverished urban neighbourhoods, but for the larger environment as well. (Wilson, 1991, p. 476)

All these dimensions of poverty interact in myriad ways, a good example being the concentration of ethnic minorities in wards with high levels of deprivation. Thus, in 1991, 'more than 60 per cent of the whole ethnic minority population were living in neighbourhoods (wards) which were in the worst fifth by unemployment nationally' (Joseph Rowntree Foundation, 1995, p. 28).

Finally, the claim that poverty is temporary because the financial circumstances of the poor change so quickly is incorrect. Most of the movement in and out of poverty is within very limited boundaries: some of those on benefits move out into low-paid jobs, and others may rise and fall within the bottom half of the income distribution. There is no major upward income mobility. As Walker and Walker put it, the poor 'remain economically insecure even though the severity of this insecurity may rise or fall slightly' (Walker and Walker, 1997, p. 281).

What Has Been Happening?

- Redistribution of wealth among the top half of the population only
- Less concentration of wealth than in the past
- Redistribution halted in the 1980s
- Inequalities of income increased after 1979
- Poverty has increased
- Unemployed people are at the greatest risk of poverty
- Single parent families run greater risk of poverty than two-parent families
- Families with children are the largest group in poverty
- Women are at greater risk of poverty than men
- Ethnic minorities are at greater risk of poverty than the native population

Why Have Things Been Changing as they Have?

The rise in poverty and inequality during the 1980s and 90s was the result of an array of factors, some within and others largely beyond the control of governments. The increased globalization of industry and trade, as well as technological developments, had a great deal to do with the rise in poverty in the UK, as in other countries. Imports of goods from low-wage countries have had an adverse effect on both employment prospects and wage levels, particularly those of the unskilled. Technological developments always lead to unemployment, at least in the short term, and this was as true of the 1980s as of any other time. There were also the obvious demographic factors associated with an increase in the number of the retired as well as a sharp rise in the number of one-parent families – both groups being very poverty prone.

These trends, however, do not account for all of the growth of poverty and inequality in the UK. Government policies on social security and taxation, as well as the deregulation of the labour market, must also be held responsible. Indeed, the argument here is that they bear the lion's share of responsibility as the rise in poverty in the UK was far greater than that in any other member country of the EU. Only the USA, with similar neo-liberal policies, experienced comparable increased rates of poverty.

The change in the indexation of benefits from wage rises to price rises in the early 1980s meant that the incomes of those not at work fell even more behind the incomes of those at work. This was particularly significant during this period, when unemployment reached unprecedented high postwar levels. The reduction in the level of benefit paid to the unemployed, the changes in the benefit schemes for the sick and disabled, the disqualification of many people from Housing Benefit, the freezing of Child Benefit for several years, the introduction of the Social Fund paying out loans to those in need rather than grants, the changes in school meals qualification rules, the rise in prescription, dental and optician charges – these and many other changes in social security have increased inequality and the risk of poverty among those relying on benefits.

Changes in taxation rates had a bonanza effect on the incomes of the top groups in society. Reviewing the impact of tax changes during the years 1985–95, Giles and Johnson show that, while the annual cost of the tax changes to the Exchequer was £5.3 billion, the benefits fell very unevenly: 'the richer the decile the higher the gain, with the poorer four deciles actually losing on average as a result of the changes' (Giles and Johnson, 1994, p. 11). It was, in fact, the top decile that got the lion's share of the tax benefits.

The deregulation of the labour market that enabled employers to pay lower wages, which reduced workers' protection against redundancies, and did away with wages councils, meant that insecurity at work, the risk of low pay and the incidence of poverty increased.

In brief, while some of the increase in poverty and inequality was beyond the control of the government, most of the rise was of its own making. It was the result of the zealous application of a series of inegalitarian policies based on a resurgent neo-liberal philosophy that considered inequality to be necessary to encourage incentives and hence raise rates of economic growth, which would benefit all through the trickle-down effect. We have already seen that the belief in the trickle-down effect proved grossly mistaken because poverty rose considerably during the period. But what of the belief that inequality is necessary in order to encourage efficiency and hence improve rates of economic growth?

There are two areas where empirical evidence could be examined to test the validity of the thesis: first, the rates of economic growth in Britain during the 1980s and 90s compared with previous postwar decades, and second, the rates of economic growth in countries with different degrees of inequality. All the evidence shows that rates of economic growth in the UK were in fact lower than those in some of the earlier postwar decades. The average rate of growth during the 1960s and 70s was 3.1 and 2.4 per cent respectively while for the 1980s it was only 2.1 per cent (George and Miller, 1994, p. 23).

Second, the evidence concerning rates of economic growth and inequality in different countries is either inconclusive or points to the opposite conclusion, in relation to advanced industrial societies, from that assumed by neo-liberals (Corry and Glyn, 1994). Indeed, the World Bank's conclusion from the evidence from all countries – affluent and non-affluent – totally contradicts the neo-liberal claim. In its 1991 report the Bank concluded that 'there is no evidence that saving is positively related to income inequality or that income inequality leads to higher growth. If anything, it seems that inequality is associated with slower growth' (World Bank, 1991, p. 137). In brief, it is both simplistic and erroneous to claim that there is a direct and robust relationship between inequality and economic growth.

High levels of poverty and inequality can exact both a social and an economic price and can, as a result, be detrimental to economic growth. We shall be reviewing the social effects of poverty and inequality in the following section. Suffice it to say here that social ill-effects have economic costs. Rises in crime, ill health, marital breakdown and so on, which can result from high levels of poverty, have economic implications in both direct and indirect ways. The direct costs relate to the increased levels of expenditure on health, the penal services, social work and so on that become necessary. The indirect costs stem from the loss of production that results from people being unable to work because of ill health, crime and so on. It is one of the reasons why egalitarians view the reduction of inequality to moderate levels and the abolition of poverty as conducive to both the social and the economic good of the nation. Such a situation helps to create a socially cohesive society whose members are less strife-ridden and more able to work together to achieve common goals, including economic growth. In brief, equity and economic growth are seen as complementary rather than contradictory.

Why Have Things Been Changing as they Have?

- Factors outside the control of government
- Government policies
- Changes in social security policy
- Taxation
- Deregulation of the labour market

What Are the Broad Implications for Society?

The implications of poverty and inequality for individuals, families, communities and the whole of society are serious and manifold.

Inadequate Diets

There is now abundant evidence that families with incomes around the assistance benefit level have to cut down on many essentials of life, including food. Those on low incomes for long periods of time run a serious risk of undernutrition and malnutrition. Their incomes are never sufficient to purchase enough food all the time, let alone nutritious food. Buying nutritious food and fruit becomes particularly impossible when they have to meet an unexpected or even expected bill for the replacement of a cooker, fridge or washing machine, for example. (Dobson *et al.*, 1994; Morris and Ritchie, 1994). Choice in diet is an impossibility, and going without food is not unknown. Using two indicators of food insufficiency – 'inadequate intake of nutrients and limited food variety' – Craig and Dowler conclude from their analysis of government and other data that hunger is still a fact of life in the UK (Craig and Dowler, 1997, p. 121) The National Children's Home found that, because of lack of money, one in ten children and one in five parents, mostly mothers, in 345 families with low incomes had gone without food some time during the month previous to the study (National Children's Home, 1991). As Cooper puts it:

> No system of food distribution is morally justifiable if it excludes a significant sector of the population. (Cooper, 1994, p. 7)

Continuous Debt

The constant struggle to manage on restricted budgets, particularly over long periods of time, inevitably leads many families into debt, which they find it hard or impossible to pay off. In a consumer society, most people are in debt, but the debt of low-income people is of a different kind. It is mostly debt to secure the necessities of life rather than the purchase of consumer goods. As a study in the UK pointed out:

> low income led to indebtedness through the week-to-week budgeting problems it caused, rather than because poor people persisted in buying consumer goods they could not afford. (Berthoud and Kempson, 1992, p. 179)

For people on benefits, debt must be the only way out of the constant struggle to square the circle of income and expenditure. The practice of deducting benefit at source to pay for debt arrears may seem a sensible way of budgeting to professionals, but for families in debt, it means that they have either to live on incomes well below subsistence level or borrow from money lenders at exorbitant interest rates and get further into debt (National Association of Citizens Advice Bureaux, 1993). It is not surprising that a government study found that only 40 per cent of families with deductions for debts felt that they had enough money left to manage, 26 per cent had not quite enough and 32 per cent were definitely unable to cope (Mannion *et al.*, 1994).

Debt for basic necessities is one of the severest manifestations of deprivation and mental anguish. Not being able to see a way out must cause constant strain and anxiety, particularly to mothers in lone parent families, as well as feelings of guilt and shame in a society where being financially independent is highly valued. A study of families in debt found that 71 per cent of respondents felt depressed and 50 per cent could not sleep (National Children's Home, 1992). Professional help to budget and to cope with stress may be useful, but only after the level of benefits is raised to cover adequately daily needs. Without adequate income levels, such professional help is oppressive and a form of policing of the poor. It does nothing about the basic problem.

Homelessness

There has been a noticeable growth in homelessness during the past two decades even though the official statistics cover only part of this rise. Apart from those who are rehoused by local authorities, there are those who live in temporary accommodation, those who live in privately owned grossly overcrowded and unhealthy accommodation and those who sleep rough on the streets of London and other cities. Yet government statistics on poverty exclude most of these, some of the poorest people in the country. Temporary accommodation ranges from bed and breakfast places, hostels and women's refuges to private sector housing and so on. Conditions in most of these places are well below acceptable levels. One study of bed and breakfast places in London found that 95 per cent of families had nowhere to lock their possessions in their rooms, 97 per cent of bedrooms had unsafe electric sockets, 90 per cent provided no safe areas for children to play, and 30 per cent of families complained of vermin in their rooms (Carter, 1995). A study of private sector leased housing for the homeless showed a very similar picture (Edwards and Tritter, 1993).

Effects on Schooling

It comes as no surprise that the schooling of children in poor families and poor neighbourhoods suffers. This has been well documented over the years by several government reports, particularly by the Plowden Report as far back as 1967 (Central Advisory Council for Education, 1967). The situation is more serious for homeless children or children living in bed and breakfast accommodation for long periods. This was highlighted by a recent study showing that 86 per cent of head teachers felt that homelessness had severe adverse effects on the education of children (Power *et al.*, 1995). The recommendation of the Plowden Report that a gradual but long-term government policy of positive discrimination in favour of schools in deprived areas was necessary if such educational inequalities were to decline is as true today as it was then:

> As a matter of national policy, 'positive discrimination' should favour schools in neighbourhoods where children are most severely handicapped by home conditions. The programme should be phased to make schools in the most deprived areas as good as the best in the country. For this, it may be necessary that their greater claim on the resources should be maintained. (Central Advisory Council for Education, 1967, p. 66)

Despite the general improvement in educational standards and the expansion of university education, socio-economic differences remain very strong. The children of the lower socio-economic groups have a much lower chance of reaching university education than do the children of the higher socioeconomic groups. Positions in the highest socio-economic groups that enjoy the highest salaries are overwhelmingly filled by those with university education; similarly, only a very small minority of those in manual and generally low-paid jobs have had university education, as Table 5.9 shows. British society is obviously not a caste society, but neither is it a very open society. Social mobility does take place, but it is rather limited both in volume and range. Family background, educational achievement and occupational status are strongly correlated, and, on present evidence, this is likely to continue in the future.

Table 5.9   Higher educational qualification (degree or equivalent) held by gender and socio-economic group among 25–69-year-olds, Great Britain (percentage), 1995 and 1996

Socio-economic group	Men	Women	Total
Professional	65	68	66
Employers and managers	24	22	24
Intermediate, non-manual	30	24	26
Junior, non-manual	12	4	5
Skilled manual	2	4	2
Semi-skilled manual	1	1	1
Unskilled manual	1	0	0
Total	**16**	**11**	**14**

Source: Office for National Statistics, 1998a, Table 7.4, p. 95.

Health Effects

The relationship between social class and poverty and health is extensively documented. Despite the general improvement in health standards, socio-economic inequalities have remained and have even increased in the past twenty years. Table 5.10 provides the evidence concerning the standardized mortality rates for men. It is clear that, during the twenty-year period covered by the table, the mortality rates for men in classes I and II declined more than the rates for class V or IV and that, as a result, the gap between them widened.

The same picture emerges for perinatal and infant mortality rates. Although they declined substantially over the years for all social classes, they remain stubbornly related to social class, as Table 5.11 shows. Further evidence also shows that both types of mortality rate are higher for babies born outside than inside marriage. Perinatal mortality rates for babies born outside marriage were 10.0 compared with 8.2 for those inside marriage for all classes; the corresponding rates for infant mortality were 5.9 and 7.4 respectively – largely a reflection of the prevailing socio-economic conditions of these two groups.

Table 5.10   Standardized mortality rate (SMR) by social class, men aged 20–64, England and Wales

Social Class		1970–72	1991–93
I	Professional	500	280
II	Management and technical	526	300
IIIN	Skilled (non-manual)	637	426
IIIM	Skilled (manual)	683	493
IV	Partly skilled	721	492
V	Unskilled	897	806
ALL classes		**624**	**419**

SMR is the number of deaths from all causes per 100 000 men in the age group.
Source: Hattersley, 1997, Table 8.5 p. 105.

Table 5.11   Social class differentials in perinatal and infant mortality rates, England and Wales, 1993–95

Class	Perinatal mortality*	Infant mortality†
I	7.0	4.5
II.	7.3	4.8
IIIN	8.4	5.5
IIIM	8.5	5.9
IV	9.9	6.6
V	11.5	7.7
All Classes	**8.7**	**5.9**

* Perinatal mortality refers to the number of stillbirths and deaths for babies under 7 days per 1000 live births.
† Infant mortality refers to the number of deaths of babies under 1 year per 1000 live births.
Source: Hattersley, 1997, Tables 7.2 and 7.3, pp. 85 and 86.

It is, therefore, no surprise that life expectancy at birth varies by social class for both men and women, and that class differentials have widened in recent years despite the improvement that has taken place for all classes. Table 5.12 shows this, as well as the greater life expectancy rates of women over men.

Unemployment, too, is linked to mortality rates. The unemployed run a higher risk of death than those at work. This is partly because of the social class composition of the unemployed, but part of the difference is caused by the stresses that unemployment itself involves. For both men and women, 'unemployment has an independent causal effect on mortality' estimated at 25 per cent of the total mortality rate (Bethume, 1997, p. 167).

Table 5.12   Life expectancy at birth by social class for men and women, England and Wales

Class	Men		Women	
	1977–81	*1987–91*	*1977–81*	*1987–91*
I and II	72.8	74.9	78.2	80.2
IIIN	70.8	73.5	78.1	79.4
IIIM	70.0	72.4	76.1	77.6
IV and V	68.3	69.7	75.7	76.8
ALL classes	70.0	72.3	76.3	77.9

Source: Hattersley, 1997, Tables 6.1 and 6.5, pp. 76 and 78.

People on assistance benefits are more likely to suffer from illness than are all other groups. One study found that 65 per cent of the parents and 70 per cent of the children on assistance benefit reported illness and disability figures that were considerably higher than those reported by working-class people, let alone by professionals (Cohen *et al.*, 1992). As Toynbee puts it: 'The worse-off have not just got relatively less money, their relative chances of surviving have also worsened' (Toynbee, 1997, p. 5).

There is now an established body of research opinion that what affects health in affluent societies is not so much the absolute but the relative income of individuals. It is for this reason that differences of income *between* affluent countries do not affect their mortality rates a great deal. It is differences *within* countries that affect mortality rates. Thus, there is 'a very clear tendency for the developed countries with the highest life expectancy to be those where income differences are lowest' (Wilkinson, 1994, p. 28).

Effects on Crime

As we shall show in the next chapter, poverty and inequality are central elements in male crime in Britain today. This is particularly the case for those living in large geographical concentrations of poor families in either housing estates or inner city areas, where they compound the disadvantage.

Social Isolation

Low incomes inevitably mean that people have less or no money to spend on those social activities which other people take for granted. It means a depressing lack of individual choice to buy the things that are needed, let alone wanted, to take part in the social and recreational activities of the community. Feelings of isolation and exclusion develop and become part of a life in poverty. Such feelings can often feed into states of mental ill health as the dividing line between constant anxiety and depression may be only very thin.

Lack of Power

Poverty also means a lack of power to control, change or even influence events around one. Poverty in this sense is a form of 'disempowerment' and has distinct implications for the efforts of the poor to escape from their poverty (Friedman, 1996). Poverty as a form of disempowerment helps to explain the failure of governments and other bodies to consult the poor themselves about relevant policies. None of the government or other committees that have so far examined issues of inequality and poverty in the UK have included poor people in their membership. Yet, on practical grounds, as Beresford and Croft point out, 'It is only with their involvement that poverty discussion is likely accurately to identify, reflect and advance their needs, concerns and interests' (Beresford and Croft, 1995, p. 91).

The Costs to Sustainability

Poverty and inequality affect not only the individuals or the families who are poor, but society as a whole: they have social, economic and political costs in addition to the individual costs. They alienate whole sections of the population, with all that this implies for work, productivity and national prosperity. They alienate people from work and reduce their productivity. They reduce purchasing power in society and hold back consumption and hence employment. They precipitate illness in society and raise the costs to the NHS. They are one of the contributory factors to the rise of crime that affects everyone, including the very affluent, however much they spend on expensive surveillance and protective devices around their homes. The creation of no-go estates is an abomination not only for those who live in them, but also for everyone in the country because the violence and the fear generated gradually spread to other parts of the country. Social cohesion in society suffers, and, as a result, the quality of life for all suffers. In brief, high rates of poverty and inequality are inimical to a sustainable society.

What Are the Broad Implications for Society?

- Inadequate diets
- Debt
- Homelessness
- Educational failure
- Poorer health
- More crime
- Isolation
- Powerlessness

What Proposals for Action Have Been Made by Conventional Sources?

We divide the various policy proposals on social division into the conventional and the radical, although the two inevitably overlap. Conventional are those proposals which see gradual piecemeal changes to the current system as the best way forward, while radical proposals are those which involve comprehensive and major departures from existing policies.

Neither conventionalism nor radicalism is confined to any one political ideology. Conventional and radical policy proposals on poverty alleviation come from all wings of the party political spectrum. Where they differ is on the definition of poverty. The Right sees it either in pure subsistence terms or with a few social needs added to it, while the Left considers poverty in social participation terms – the resources needed to take part in the way of life customary in society.

It is inequality that really divides the Right from the Left. The New Right and Traditional Conservatives would agree on the inevitability and beneficial nature of inequality, although the Traditional Conservatives would be concerned about the social and political effects of excessive inequality. The Left see inequality as harmful in both economic and social terms, and hence unacceptable, although they will accept moderate levels.

Conventional proposals on poverty tend to identify the main poverty groups and to make proposals for each one of them individually. Unemployment is seen as one of the major causes of poverty, and no set of social policies stands any chance of success in eradicating poverty unless unemployment is tackled first. There is now implicit bi-partisan agreement that, in the drive towards the reduction of unemployment, poverty among the unemployed is an unfortunate but necessary penalty that has to be paid. This is an inherent part of active labour market policies as practised in the UK.

Active rather than passive labour market policies are a bi-partisan approach today. As mentioned in Chapter 2, active labour market policies involve more government intervention in helping the unemployed back to work. On the benefit side, however, these same policies imply a marked degree of coercion: payment of benefits to the unemployed must be accompanied by increasingly strict eligibility conditions; state surveillance must be stepped up to discourage unemployment benefit fraud; the level of benefits for the families of the unemployed should be kept below those paid to other groups of beneficiaries; and benefit to the young unemployed should be stopped.

Low pay at work is another major cause of poverty, particularly for families with children and only one wage earner. Three main approaches to reducing poverty among this group have surfaced over the years among the major political parties in the UK: a minimum wage, child benefits and wage supplementation.

Debates over the pros and cons of a minimum wage have a long history in the UK. Its advantages and disadvantages were crisply discussed in a government report in 1969 and have been repeated by many others since then (Department of Employment and Productivity, 1969). The claimed advantages of a minimum wage are that it reduces earnings inequality; reduces poverty among single people and families with both parents at work; gives due recognition to the contribution that workers in low-paid jobs make to the national economy; reduces risks of poverty traps; and places the responsibility for improving low pay onto the right shoulders – those of the employers. On the other hand, it is argued that a national minimum wage is a blunt and ineffective instrument for reducing poverty among large families or even small families with only one wage earner; if set and maintained at a modest level, it may lead to some loss of jobs; if set at a high level, it may lead to significant numbers of jobs disappearing; by raising labour costs, it may discourage multinational companies from investing in the country and thus increase unemployment; and, if it is used as an excuse by other groups of workers for wage demands to maintain differentials, it will lead to rises in wage costs and inflation.

Supporters of the national minimum wage as a policy for reducing family poverty acknowledge that it will only succeed if it is accompanied by a system of generous child benefits that will be taxable in order to minimize costs. Without such child benefits, a minimum wage cannot tackle poverty among families with two or more children unless both parents are at work. Neither political party, however, intends to improve child benefits to the point that they meet the cost of maintaining children as they both operate on the principle that the cost of bringing up children should be borne by the parents with only some help from the state. They differ, however, on the role of the state, the present Labour government intending to improve the level of child benefits.

It is predominantly the Right which has supported schemes of wage supplementation as a method of reducing poverty among wage earners. Its claimed advantages are that, since it is paid only to those in assessed need, it is effective in reducing poverty and its cost to the Exchequer is low. Its disadvantages are that, being means tested, it carries the usual risks of stigmatization, low take-up rates and poverty traps. It runs the risk of being a subsidy for unscrupulous employers and of depressing wages by unloading wage costs on to the state.

Conventional proposals on poverty reduction among lone parents cut across party political lines. There is general consensus that assistance, rather than insurance, benefits are the most appropriate benefit for lone parents; that the absent parent, usually the father, should be compelled to pay maintenance; and that as many lone parents as possible should be encouraged and pressurized, but not compelled, to obtain paid employment. What is lacking in the policies of both parties is, first, a credible commitment to provide affordable child care facilities in order to enable lone parents to go out to work, and second, an acceptance that earnings disregards have to be increased to reduce the stranglehold of the obvious poverty traps that result from the low wages of many women employees. The recent policy announcement by the Labour government that it intends to provide enough child care places for the under-fives is a welcome departure, although only time will tell whether this will be implemented to the full.

Despite the improved financial position of elderly people over the years, they are still one of the main groups in poverty for sheer demographic reasons. There is agreement between the parties that the flat rate insurance pension should remain as the basic income for the retired. It is also acknowledged that, by itself, it is not sufficient to meet even basic needs, and hence there is a need for a second pension. It is over the nature of the second pension that party policies differ. The Conservative Party view is that all future pensioners should rely on either occupational or private pensions as their second line of defence against poverty. The Labour Party accepts the role of occupational and private pension provision but feels that the state earnings-related pension has a place, too. Neither party has come up with any anti-poverty pension policy proposals for those such as married women, the long-term unemployed, the severely disabled and those with chequered employment careers which render them unable to participate fully in either the basic flat rate or any of the additional earnings-related pension schemes.

The policies of the two parties on benefits for disabled people remain rooted in tradition, with the result that the cause of disability still influences the kind and generosity of benefit provided. Those disabled by war receive better benefits than those disabled at work, who are in turn more favourably treated than those disabled in ordinary life. Benefits for carers have been improved, but neither party has taken the bold step of fully recognizing the importance of caring as a job and drawing up proposals for treating carers as any other group of workers.

Neither political party has given any serious thought to the possibility of reassessing and costing basic needs in the 1990s in order to decide the appropriate level of assistance benefit. Instead, both parties are content to use the Beveridge scales of the 1940s, upgraded at first in an *ad hoc* way from time to time, then according to wages and from 1980 onwards according to prices. There can be no doubt that these scales are too low for the needs of the 1990s and beyond – a fact acknowledged by several publications by the Labour Party in the past, although not by the current Labour government.

The general conclusion from this brief review is that neither party is proposing policies that can be seriously said to have poverty reduction as their direct aim. Both parties insist that the creation of more jobs is a first priority and that this will lead to the reduction of poverty. This is, of course, true as far as it goes. But no one can seriously claim that full employment is around the corner or that the absence of unemployment means that poverty and excessive inequality are taken care of. As a political issue, poverty has been marginalized to a side issue worthy of token attention only, while inequality has ceased altogether to be a serious issue in party politics.

What Proposals for Action Have Been Made by Conventional Sources?

- Active labour market policies
- Minimum wage
- Child Benefit
- Wage supplementation
- Maintenance for lone parents
- Occupational and private pensions or state earnings related pensions

---

What Proposals for Action Have Been Made by Radicals?

This section outlines and assesses the main radical proposals for the replacement of the current social security system, which is based on the twin principles of insurance and assistance. The criteria to be used for the assessment of the various schemes are their contribution to the abolition of poverty, their impact on the redistribution of income, their encouragement of employment, being non-discriminatory in terms of gender or ethnicity, their promotion of social cohesion, and their administrative simplicity and cost. Other attempts to compare social security reform models have used similar, although not identical, criteria (George and Howards, 1991; Harker, 1996).

Although all four proposals discussed here break with tradition, some are more radical than others. They are, therefore, presented in order of proximity to existing social security arrangements – Benefits as of Right (BAOR), Stakeholder Welfare (SW), Negative Income Tax (NIT) and Basic Income Guarantee (BIG).

It is generally agreed that the Beveridge principles that underpin the current social security system have been overtaken by economic, demographic and social changes. In a society with high rates of unemployment, insecure employment and part-time employment on a large scale, the insurance principle loses its validity as a method of social protection. Changes in the family, the growth of divorce, separation and lone parenthood, and the increased employment of married women necessitates a social security system that treats men and women equally. The growth of lone parenthood also seriously questions the notion of insurable and uninsurable risk as defined by Beveridge. Irrespective of whether one can or should apportion blame in family break-up, current social security provision for lone mothers caring for millions of children is well past its sell by date. The growth in the number of frail elderly people has increased the burden on women as carers and calls for official recognition of caring as a form of paid employment, with all the implications for social security provision that this would involve. There is an obvious mismatch between the principles of the Beveridge model and the social, familial and economic conditions prevailing at the end of the twentieth century.

Benefits as of Right Scheme (BAOR)

These and other changes in society over the past fifty years lie behind the proposal for a Benefits as of Right scheme (BAOR) that pays benefits to all those suffering certain contingencies acknowledged by the state. People may still continue paying insurance contributions, but the benefits they receive will not be decided by their insurance contributions record. The contingencies for which 'insurance' benefits will be paid will be similar to those we have today but with the addition of lone parenthood. In all these contingencies, benefits will be paid as of right rather than because of contribution records or means tests.

A BAOR scheme is more likely than the current system to reduce poverty because it will reduce both the role of the insurance principle and the scope of means-tested benefits, thus increasing take-up rates. The redistributive nature of BAOR will not be dissimilar from today's system as insurance contributions will continue to be the main source of funding. In all probability, it will create fewer poverty trap situations, but it may need closer policing to guard against fraud. Its effects on work incentives and labour supply may not be all that different from those of today's system. Without doubt, a BAOR scheme will not discriminate against women or ethnic groups for the reasons already given – recognition of caring as a form of employment and the abandonment of the insurance principle. Any scheme that reduces the scope of means testing of the type practised in the UK today is bound to improve social cohesion in society. A BAOR scheme will be administratively simpler and cheaper. It will do away with the current bizarre practice whereby an individual is refused an insurance benefit only to be offered an assistance benefit after an administratively expensive means test. It will reduce people's sense of stigmatization as they are spared the process of means testing. BAOR will inevitably be more expensive than the current system but not as much more as first appears for it will reduce, although not completely do away with completely, the cost of means-tested assistance benefits.

Stakeholder Welfare (SW)

In recent years, writers of the Left have been searching for ways of providing social services that are in tune with the situations and aspirations of consumer-minded people today but which also maintain such traditional welfare values as social caring and social cohesion. In social security, Field's ideas of SW belong to this category. The underlying principle of his proposals is that 'Self-interest, not altruism, is mankind's (sic) main driving force' (Field, 1996a, p. 19). Reform proposals must take this basic truth into account, otherwise, he argues, they stand no chance of success in today's world. Altruism in small quantities and within recognizable boundaries is necessary in order to achieve comprehensive provision, but it must not dominate reform proposals.

Using retirement pensions as an example, Field argues that, since the current flat rate retirement pension will gradually lose its value because it is upgraded only according to the rise in prices rather than earnings, there is the need for a second tier pension. In contrast to the Conservative reliance on private pensions and the Left's support for state earnings-related pensions, he argues for mutual aid pensions. Everyone should be compelled to pay contributions to mutual aid societies for a pension that they will own themselves although will not be able to sell. Contributions for those who, for good specified reasons – unemployment or caring roles – cannot pay should be met by the state. Similar proposals are made for unemployment and social care.

The advantages of this approach, Field argues, are that it is in line with the public mood. The proposals give control of the schemes to the members, and accrued profits go not to the shareholders but to members. What he does not say is what happens if mutual aid societies' financial fortunes turn sour and they fail to secure a reasonable return on members' investments or go bust.

In terms of the criteria used in this section, stakeholder welfare will probably be no more effective in abolishing poverty than are today's schemes; it will be less redistributive, it is likely to be more supportive of work incentives, it will be just as complex administratively, it will have neutral effects on social cohesion, and it will be less costly to the state, although not to many individuals. The major question mark around this approach from a Left position is how to pay for the premiums of millions of people who are unemployed, who care for others, who are disabled and have never worked, or who simply have low wages. Playing on people's self-interest first and then appealing to their altruism may not prove convincing enough to win continued political support for subsidizing the weak in society. Field's argument, that stakeholder welfare will keep the middle classes on board the welfare state, thus avoiding the growth of a residual welfare state for the poor, while the middle classes go private, is of significance. As already mentioned, however, all this depends on the unlikely willingness of the middle and stable working class to pay the premiums of a very large number of currently disadvantaged people.

If the BAOR and the SW retain some links with existing social security provisions, the next two proposals depart from them completely. In ideological terms, NIT has been identified predominantly with the Right, while BIG is mainly the ideal of the Left.

Negative Income Tax Scheme (NIT)

The NIT proposes that all existing insurance, assistance and other benefits should be replaced with one benefit scheme solely dependent on the individual's or couple's income. In the same way that an individual or family pay income tax when their income exceeds a certain level, they should be entitled to a benefit when their income drops below that level. Proposals for a NIT scheme were first made by Friedman in the USA as a means of reducing both poverty and social security costs. He summarised the advantages of his scheme as follows:

> It is directed specifically at the problem of poverty. It gives help in the form most useful to the individual, namely, cash. It is general and could be substituted for the host of special measures now in effect. It makes explicit the cost borne by society. It operates outside the market. (Friedman, 1962, p. 192)

Since then, however, it has been supported by many in the Centre and on the Left of the political spectrum, who have perceived it in more generous terms. The result is that its effects on the criteria used here vary depending on the level of benefit envisaged, the amount of benefit withdrawn when income exceeds the stipulated amount, the frequency of NIT renewal, the inclusion or exclusion of rent in the family income and so on.

Despite these differences, a NIT scheme can abolish poverty, it is vertically redistributive and it can be non-discriminatory. It is, on the other hand, probable that it will undermine work incentives by creating poverty traps on a large scale, and it is likely to undermine social cohesion because of its stigmatizing nature since it will be paid to the poor only after an income test, albeit one impersonally administered. Assuming that the level of NIT is the same as the current assistance benefit, the cost to the state will be lower than the current combination of insurance and assistance benefits. Indeed, some of its supporters rightly claim that the state can afford to provide a more generous level of benefit than the current assistance benefit. Administratively, it appears simpler than the current system of insurance and assistance benefit although in practice it may prove just as complex if it is to respond quickly to the changing needs of individuals. A final question mark about NIT is the tendency of programmes designed solely for the poor to degenerate in generosity over the years, particularly during hard economic times. They lack the strong political constituency that is so important for the protection of state welfare schemes.

Basic Income Guarantee Scheme (BIG)

Proposals for a BIG go back to the immediate postwar years, and they have appeared under different names ever since. The BIG is the most radical and most inclusive of all schemes as it proposes the payment of a flat-rate amount to all citizens irrespective of income, employment status, age or family membership. The amount should be the same, and it should be sufficient for basic needs. Some variants of BIG, envisage lower benefit amounts for children and higher ones for disabled persons to cater for their specific needs. In its ideal version, it will replace all existing insurance, assistance and other non-contributory schemes. Since it will be funded out of general taxation, there will be no need for insurance contributions (Ashby, 1984).

The BIG scores very highly on five out of the seven criteria used here – the abolition of poverty, the vertical redistribution of income, non-discrimination, social cohesion and administrative simplicity. Its effects on work incentives and labour supply are uncertain and contested. It is argued, on one hand, that the payment of benefits sufficient for basic needs to all will discourage many from work and will create an army of idle people dependent on the state. Behind this argument lie the beliefs that people are selfish, work is boring and people work only for money. On the other hand, there are those who believe that BIG will improve work incentives as most people will be more willing to work in order to raise their standard of living. The flat rate amount will be for basic needs only and will not cover most social needs, which consume most of the income of average and above-average income earners. In a consumer society, a BIG will act as a spur to the low-income groups to improve their standard of living through the labour market.

It is cost, however, that is the Achilles heel of the BIG as it is generally accepted that it will be costly and will necessitate high marginal tax rates for those at work. It is for this reason that several of its advocates have come forth with suggestions for partial, less costly, versions of the BIG (Parker, 1991). The problem is that the more one dilutes a BIG, the more it loses its radical nature and appeal.

It has also been argued that its ethos is alien to contemporary British society. Its central idea involves no reciprocity – people receive benefits without giving back anything visible in return. The recent report by the Council of Churches for Britain and Ireland had this in mind when it commented that, apart from the high taxation implications of BIGs, 'we have to ask whether a separation between income and work for some people along these lines is actually what we would like to see achieved' (Council of Churches for Britain and Ireland, 1997, p. 77) It is also for this reason that some of its supporters have made it conditional on a national scheme of community service.

What Proposals for Action Have Been Made by Radicals?

- Benefits as of right
- Stakeholder welfare
- Negative income tax
- Basic income guarantee

Conclusions

First, there is substantial agreement on what has happened to the distribution of wealth and income during the past twenty years. Despite the very substantial economic growth, Britain is a more unequal society now in terms of income and wealth than it was before 1980. Poverty is also more widespread today than then, when defined in relative terms. This shows that there is no natural economic law dictating that the fruits of economic growth automatically 'trickle down' to everyone in a more or less similar way. If there is any natural law, it is that, in a *laissez-faire* economy, the fruits of economic growth tend to 'trickle up' to benefit most those who already have most.

Second, despite this substantial agreement on what has happened to income and wealth, there is no such agreement on what, if anything, should be done. Many on the right will claim that income and wealth inequalities are natural and beneficial to society – they act as a spur to higher work effort, which benefits all in society. It is not the responsibility of governments to interfere in the way in which the market operates in distributional issues. They will also claim that if poverty were defined in subsistence rather than relative terms, it would not be as widespread as suggested by the government data used to construct the tables presented in this chapter. The quotation from Powell at the beginning of the chapter provides the conceptual framework for this line of argument. Powell's thesis was that citizens have no social rights that the state should be expected to meet.

Many of those in the middle, and all those on the left of the political spectrum will take a different view: people have certain social rights that the government has a responsibility to meet. At the basic level, the state has a responsibility to reduce extreme inequalities and to abolish poverty in both relative and subsistence terms. It will, however, disagree on how exactly to translate this belief into a set of specific government policies.

Third, there is agreement that policies to reduce inequality and to abolish poverty need to be wide ranging. What is needed is a comprehensive approach that incorporates economic, fiscal and social policies in a sustained drive to reverse the trends of the past twenty years. Relying on social security benefits alone to reverse these trends will be both unwise and ineffective. The first line of attack on social division is through employment and education, while the second line is through fiscal and social security measures. Neither line of attack is in itself sufficient – they are both necessary.

Full employment of the various kinds envisaged in Chapter 2 is seen as the cornerstone of all attempts to create a more egalitarian society. Without full employment, attempts to reduce inequality and abolish poverty are almost destined to fail. Large-scale unemployment reduces the wealth of the country, creates a large dependent population, generates a disabling pessimism about social possibilities, accentuates social division and alienation, and fosters the insecurity that militates against redistributional policies.

Affordable child care facilities are essential to full employment. There is abundant evidence that many women, particularly lone mothers, find it difficult to go out to work because of the lack of affordable child care facilities or play facilities for after school hours. Some go beyond child care facilities for the under-fives to argue that the role of schools should be re-examined to find ways in which they can adapt 'to the needs of parents as well as children' (Piachaud, 1993, p. 10) and support parenting and families. Remaining open after formal school hours and during holidays would serve the needs of both working parents and children. The plans announced by the current Labour government, if fully implemented, will go a long way towards achieving this goal.

Low pay at work is not the result simply of the educational, ethnic, gender, motivational or other characteristics of individuals. Imagine a highly educated society without women or ethnic minority groups, for example: there would still be low-paid jobs as they are a necessary ingredient of capitalist enterprise.

Individuals have somehow to be found to fill the low-paid positions. It is, therefore, necessary to introduce social policy measures if low pay is to be moderated. The Labour government's decision to introduce a minimum wage is seen by many as a step in the right direction despite the disagreements on its level and the possibility that it might result in some unemployment, particularly at times of recession. Others, however, believe that, with some improvements, the existing scheme of state supplementation of low wages for family wage earners is a better way of dealing with poverty.

Fiscal policies can play a central role in moderating the pattern of income and wealth inequalities. During the past two decades, they have been intentionally used to encourage gross inequalities. Although this is generally acknowledged, there is no desire by either of the two major political parties to increase direct taxation; if anything, their intention is to lower it further. The Labour government, however, has shown that it intends to close many of the loopholes in both private and corporate taxation. This is particularly the case with wealth taxation, where avoidance is generally agreed to be unacceptably high (Ryan, 1994).

Housing policy is considered by many to be central to the reduction of poverty. It is generally agreed that the emphasis on private ownership is in tune with the public mood and has done much to improve housing standards, yet the neglect of the voluntary and public sector in housing has been a major factor in the rise in homelessness. It is difficult to see how homelessness can be reduced unless there is an improvement in the fortunes of voluntary and public housing, particularly for the young.

Social security is the second, but equally important, line of attack on poverty. There is, however, no agreement on the kinds of social security measure that can do this. Neither of the major political parties supports any of the four radical schemes outlined in the previous section. Instead, they both emphasize the importance of the private and occupational sectors and put forward *ad hoc* reforms of the state sector that they hope will reduce poverty. It is too early yet to identify the course that the Labour Party in government will follow, but the signs are that, in the short term, it will continue with policies that target benefits to those most in need rather than increase benefits for all in line with the rise in earnings, as it was arguing when in opposition. In a sense, this follows naturally from its desire to reduce taxes and strictly control the volume of public expenditure.

The heated debates of the past concerning the relative significance of the state and the private sector in improving living standards for all and abolishing poverty no longer excite much passion. Instead, it is generally acknowledged that they are both important and necessary. Rather, the political debates of today – and of the near future – are going to surround the best ways to integrate the two. Pragmatism rather than ideology will decide the outcome of this. However, it is acknowledged that, although poverty can best be reduced through the operation of both the market and the policies of the state, the responsibility for ensuring that it is achieved lies with the state.

Challenges

- The extent and depth of poverty in the UK today is higher than that of most other EU member countries with a comparable standard of living. Successive Conservative governments either ignored or accepted high levels of poverty or argued that the figures exaggerated the problem. The Labour government has been openly critical of such high levels of poverty, but it has decided that the best way to launch a direct attack on poverty is not so much to increase direct public expenditure on poverty but to improve education and training facilities. This is a very long-term strategy, but there is no guarantee that it will succeed in reducing, let alone eradicating, poverty. If this analysis is correct, poverty will remain a significant problem for many years to come.
- The challenge of excessive inequalities appears even more intractable. To begin with, there is no political agreement on whether the rates should be reduced. Even those who are opposed to such rates do not agree on either the types and levels of inequality that are acceptable or the measures that are necessary to deal with the problem. In such circumstances, it is very unlikely that much will be done to reduce current levels of income and wealth inequality, particularly in view of the globalization pressures referred to in Chapter 2.
- The notion of equality of opportunity receives widespread political support. Every child, it is argued, should be given the opportunity to achieve his or her full potential as both the individual and society as a whole will benefit as a result. All the evidence, however, shows that family background, educational achievement, occupational status, housing and health are strongly correlated. It seems that equality of opportunity is an impossible ideal in a very unequal society. What kind of policies are, therefore, needed to reduce this correlation and hence to create a more open society in Britain?

Further Reading

Journals

Poverty, a quarterly journal published by the Child Poverty Action Group in London and contains short articles on various aspects of poverty in Britain.
Benefits, another quarterly journal, dealing with social security issues mainly in the UK.

Books

Alcock, P. (1993) *Understanding Poverty*, London, Macmillan. A very readable discussion of the various defeinitions of poverty, its dynamics, its extent and its consequences.

Goodman, A., Johnson, P. and Webb, S. (1997) *Inequality in the UK*, Oxford, Oxford University Press. Concerned primarily with trends in the distribution of income in the UK and the reasons behind recent trends. It is also strong on the discussions surrounding the problems of defining and measuring income.

Oppenheim, C. and Harker, L. (1996) *Poverty: The Facts* London, Child Poverty Action Group. This is a concise and well-documented book on poverty based largely on government data. It is revised and updated every two years or so.

6
Law and Order

In democratic countries all over the world. there is a sense of crisis about public security. (Bayley, 1994, p. 11)

Crime presents a major threat to society. (Home Office, 1997a, p. 3)

Introducing the Pattern of Crime

High and increasing crime rates are an indication of society's failure to secure adherence to common norms and patterns of behaviour – something which is obviously central to a society's sustainability. A democratic society that cannot secure majority adherence to the basic values, norms and patterns of behaviour required for its common life is failing in a task essential to its survival and its future. Descent into a Hobbesian state of nature threatens.

What has become increasingly plain in recent years is that (1) order can no longer be assumed, (2) order is absolutely central to individual and social well being – if citizens cannot walk the streets at night without fear, the quality of individual and social life is sadly diminished – and (3) concern about law and order feeds a fearful and defensive attitude that compounds the problem and contributes to a destructive pessimism about society and its future.

There are two main sources of information about the extent of crime in England and Wales – the Home Office's Annual Criminal Statistics of offences recorded by the police and (since 1982) the British Crime Survey's (BCS) bi-annual study of people's experience of crime. The Criminal Statistics 1996 show 5 million notifiable – that is, more serious – offences recorded by the police in 1995. As this book was being completed, the latest Criminal Statistics showed a fall to 4.5 million offences in 1997. The BCS estimated there to be 19.1 million crimes in 1995, but the latest figures corroborate the official picture of a fall in crime – the first recorded by the BCS since it began in 1982 (*Guardian*, 14 October 1998). Most crime goes unreported and unrecorded, hence the discrepancy between the official figures and people's reported experience of crime. The BCS estimates suggest that almost three times as much domestic burglary is committed as is recorded by the police, four times as many thefts from vehicles, four times as many woundings, seven times as many offences of vandalism and eight times as many robberies and thefts from the person (Cook, 1997, p. 55).

In addition to 'crime' – and to some people a matter of greater concern – is what *Misspent Youth* called 'juvenile nuisance' (Audit Commission, 1996a, para. 17), a general fooling around in groups. A quarter of adults told the British Crime Survey that this was a problem. Some 20 per cent of calls to the police are about young people creating a nuisance. Such behaviour is not criminal but contributes to a sense of disorder and a feeling that the streets are not as safe as they once were.

Most – around 92 per cent – of crime is offences against property. Thefts of, or from, vehicles, other thefts and burglary each account for roughly a quarter of all offences. Many of these offences, of course, involve property worth relatively trivial sums. Criminal damage accounts for between 10 and 15 per cent and violence for 5–6 per cent of all recorded crime.

In all types of crime, young men are the key offenders: 80 per cent of known offenders are male, more than 40 per cent being under twenty-one years of age. Figure 6.1 shows the gender balance of offenders. More than half of young men and a third of young women admit to having committed a crime (Home Office, 1997b, p. 5). In 1995, nearly 9 per cent of eighteen-year-old males were cautioned for, or found guilty of, an indictable offence (Office for National Statistics, 1997, p. 160).

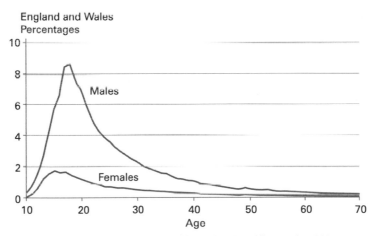

People found guilty or cautioned for indictable offences in 1996; excludes those whose age was not known.

Figure 6.1   Offenders as a percentage of the population by gender and age, 1996

Source: Office for National Statistics, 1998b.

Although a high proportion of young people commit offences, a small proportion are responsible for a large proportion of crime. Thirty-two per cent of males born in 1953 had been convicted of a standard list offence (a relatively serious offence) by the time they reached the age of forty. Seven per cent of the male population, however, had been responsible for nearly 60 per cent of all court appearances for this group (Home Office, 1997c, p. 20).

The other key factor about crime is its uneven distribution. The BCS figures about the statistical risk of suffering a crime are reassuring but, unfortunately, are highly misleading. Crime is not distributed evenly. A small number of victims and a small proportion of areas – generally the poorest – suffer a disproportionate percentage of crime (Trickett *et al.*, 1995, p. 343). Over half of all the property crimes recorded in the BCS are likely to be found in only one fifth of the communities in England and Wales (Hope, 1998, p. 52). According to the 1992 BCS, 4 per cent of victims suffered over 40 per cent of crime. People living in areas with the highest crime rates are more than ten times as likely to be the victims of personal crime and five times as likely to suffer property crime as are those living in more law-abiding areas (Audit Commission, 1996a, para. 10–11).

Young people themselves experience a great deal of crime. In the 1992 BCS, a sample of 12–15-year-olds was drawn for separate study. Over 6–8 months, a third of the sample said they had been assaulted at least once, a fifth had had something stolen, and a fifth had been harassed by other young people of their own age, as well as a fifth by older young people. Four out of ten of the sample said that they felt 'very unsafe' or 'fairly unsafe' when out alone at night (Maung, 1995, pp. vi, x). Fear of crime is now so extensive as to be a social problem in its own right (Hale, 1996, p. 82).

What of the general population's feelings about crime? In the 1994 BCS, 10 per cent of men and 20 per cent of women said that they were worried about being insulted or pestered by young people in public places (Home Office, 1997a, p. 5) In the 1996 BCS, 20 per cent of the adults questioned said that they were very worried about being burgled, mugged or having their car stolen or broken into. If we add those who said they were 'fairly worried', the figures treble for burglary and more than double for muggings and thefts of, or from, cars (Home Office Statistical Bulletin, 1996, Table 7.2). The 12th British Social Attitudes survey asked respondents how safe they felt walking in their own area after dark. More than 50 per cent of women respondents said they felt unsafe, as did 16 per cent of the men (Dowds and Ahrendt, 1995, p. 21). Fear tends to increase with age. It is also strongly associated with poverty (Pantazis and Gordon, 1997).

How does Britain compare with other countries? Nearly all countries in Western Europe experienced sharp increases in recorded crime over the period 1987–96. The increase in England and Wales was 29 per cent – second only to Italy, with 30 per cent (Home Office, 1997c, p. 20). Evidence from the International Crime Victimisation Survey published in 1997 shows that rates of violent crime, burglary and car theft in England and Wales in 1995 were all higher than in any other European country or in the USA. People in England and Wales were also more frightened of being out alone after dark than people in any other of the eleven countries studied (*Independent*, 3 July 1997).

What Has Been Happening?

Six trends stand out as the key ones.

An Increase in Crime

> The crime wave represents one of the more dramatic social trends of the past thirty years. (Utting *et al.*, 1993, p. 8)

In the early 1950s, there were fewer than half a million notifiable offences recorded by the police in England and Wales. In 1964, the figure reached 1 million, in 1975 2 million, and in 1982 3 million. The figure peaked in 1992 at 5.6 million and fell back to 5 million in 1996 and then to 4.5 million in 1997 – the fifth consecutive annual fall (Morris, 1989, p. 90; *Guardian*, 14 October 1998; Office for National Statistics, 1998b, p. 157). In short, there has been a tenfold overall increase in recorded crime in forty years, from 1100 recorded offences per 100 000 population in 1950 to 7700 in 1986 and 9400 in 1996 (Home Office, 1997c, pp. 16 and 34). Figure 6.2 shows the trends in notifiable offences over the ten years 1986–96.

For many crimes, rates of increase accelerated in the 1980s. Between 1981 and 1991, for example, the rate of domestic burglary per household in England and Wales rose by 66 per cent according to the BCS and by 63 per cent according to police records. The rates of increase for vehicle theft were 65 per cent according to the BCS and 70 per cent according to the police (Farrington, 1996, p. 2). There has also been a massive increase in the scale of corporate crime, illustrated by the string of trials for frauds on a massive scale. Within this pattern of overall increase, there are particularly worrying trends – one of which is the increase in violent crime, from 178 000 crimes of violence in 1986 to 345 000 in 1996 (Home Office, 1997c, p. 44) – an almost doubling of the figure. Crimes of violence against the person increased from 126 000 to 239 000. Between 1995 and 1996, while the amount of burglary and vehicle crime fell, violent crime rose by 11 per cent (Home Office, 1997c, p. 16). There may well have been increased reporting, but Levi's conclusion is that 'there seems little doubt that there was a substantial increase in violent crime during the 1980s' (Levi, 1994, p. 319).

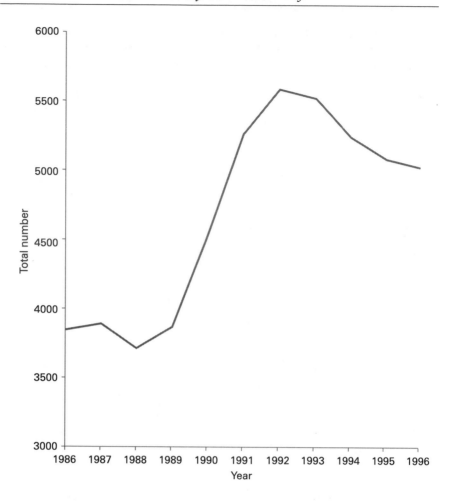

Figure 6.2   Total notifiable offences recorded by the police
for England and Wales, 1986–96

Source: Home Office, 1997c, p. 45.

Violence accounts for a very small proportion of all recorded crime, but to most people, it is the most worrying type of crime. Figure 6.3 shows overall trends in officially recorded violent offences between 1986 and 1996. The BCS gives a breakdown of the trends between 1981 and 1995. Interestingly – and, perhaps to most people, surprisingly – the smallest increase has been in stranger violence – some 12 per cent. Mugging has increased by 54 per cent. The biggest increases have been in acquaintance violence (123 per cent) and domestic violence, which accounts for one quarter of the violence recorded by the BCS (Home Office Statistical Bulletin, 1996, p. 28). Part of the increase in domestic violence may, of course, be a result of increased willingness to report such incidents, but the BCS is likely to be a better indication of the extent of the problem than are the police figures. Most domestic violence is against women. In 1995, 1.3 per cent of women reported incidents of domestic violence – double the proportion of men. Young women were at the greatest risk. Thirty-eight per cent of offenders were said to have been under the influence of alcohol or drugs at the time of the assault. In nearly one third of incidents, the victims needed medical attention (Home Office Statistical Bulletin, 1996, p. 31).

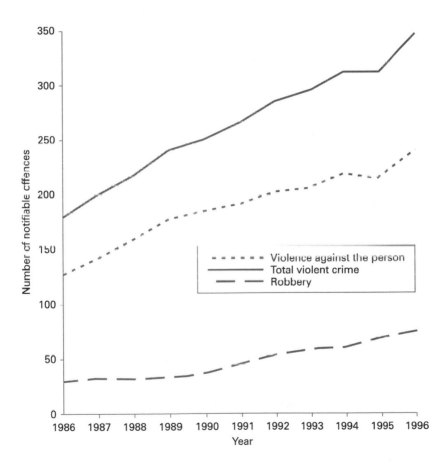

Figure 6.3   Violent offences recorded by the police, 1986–96

Source: Home Office, 1997c, p. 45.

Another striking trend has been the increase in the number of drug offences. Between 1976 and 1995, there was a more than sevenfold increase in the number of people found guilty of drug-related offences, to 94000 in 1996 (Office for National Statistics, 1998, p. 159). Figure 6.4 illustrates the striking increase in drug-related offences. The BCS shows that one in two young people have tried an illegal drug at some time, although only 15 per cent had taken such drugs in the past month. The ONS estimates that the illegal drugs industry in Britain is worth nearly £10 billion per year. Britons may be spending more on illegal drugs than they spend on wine, spirits or DIY (*Guardian*, 19 July 1998).

There are two issues here – the use of illegal drugs and prosecution for such use, and the relationship between drug use and wider patterns of criminal

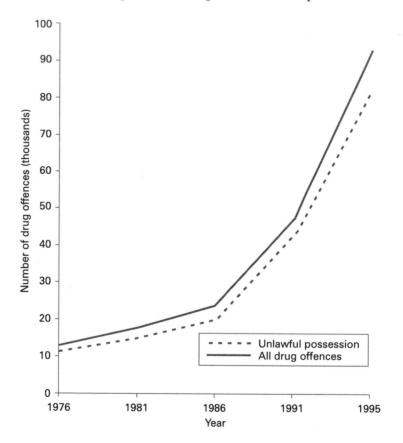

Figure 6.4   Drug offences – persons found guilty,
cautioned or dealt with by compounding

Source: Office for National Statistics, 1998b, Table 9.7.

behaviour. In November 1997, the Home Secretary told the House of Commons that 'perhaps 60–70% of the youngsters who come before the courts have some sort of drug habit' (Parliamentary Debates, 1997). A few months later, he told the House that drugs 'are at the root of much crime and disorder' (Parliamentary Debates, 1998). The precise significance of drugs as a factor in crime is difficult to establish – for example what proportion of thefts are carried out to support a drug habit or the role of drugs in violence – but the evidence suggests a significant connection (see, for example, Home Office Statistical Bulletin, 1996, p. 6; Hough, 1996).

Riots and Disorder

The 1960s and 70s were decades of unprecedented popular protest. In the 1980s, as Downes and Morgan put it, 'street protest turned sour' (Downes and Morgan, 1994, p. 204). The Economist Election Briefing verdict on the years 1979–87 was that 'there has been more public disorder than at any time this century' (*The Economist*, 1997, p. 22).

Riots broke out in the summer of 1981 in a range of inner city areas in the UK – most notably perhaps in Brixton (Scarman, 1982). In these riots, levels of injury unknown for nearly fifty years in English disorder were inflicted on both police and participants by boot, brick, fist, truncheon and petrol bomb (Reiner, 1992, p. 87). In 1977, police riot shields were used for the first time, and the early 1980s riots saw the first use of CS gas in riot control in mainland Britain.

In 1985, there were further riots. In their detailed analysis of thirteen serious riots and disorders in 1991–92, Power and Tunstall reckon that at least twenty-eight areas experienced serious outbreaks of violence and civil disorder between 1991 and 1995 and that over a hundred other areas, not in the list of officially recorded riots and disturbances, also experienced violence, fires, clashes between local youths and the police and so on (Power and Tunstall, 1997, p. i).

The riots and disturbances represent criminal behaviour, but they are more than simply part of the increase in crime that we discussed earlier: they represent a much broader and more significant rejection of, and challenge to, authority. They suggest alienation, stakelessness and a rejection of basic social norms and patterns. They threatened social order in what they actually did and in the attitudes and behaviour they represented.

The Politicization of Law and Order

It was not until 1959 that law and order issues were mentioned in a party manifesto, and the issue only gradually became politicized in the 1960s. What

Downes and Morgan make very clear is how, in the 1970s, the Conservatives hijacked the issue with far more Conservative than Labour election addresses mentioning law and order. They were triumphantly successful. In the 1979 election campaign, their policies on law and order gave the Conservatives their biggest lead over Labour (Downes and Morgan, 1994).

Other factors also contributed to politicization. In 1978, the Police Federation launched a campaign on law and order designed to influence the outcome of the 1979 election. Their proposals were strikingly similar to those put forward by the Conservative Party (Reiner, 1992, p. 92). A few years later, the 1981 riots and the 1984–85 miners' strike gave policing a new and sharper political dimension. Those who saw the riots and the miners' strike as the product of Thatcherite policies saw the police as being involved in a political conflict. Conservative supporters, on the other hand, saw the police, as Morris puts it, as 'the heroic defenders of a civilised society' (Morris, 1989, p. 156). In the late 1980s, the police drew back from their overtly pro-Tory stand but, as Reiner put it, 'the years of partnership had tarnished, possible irretrievably, the sacred aura hitherto enjoyed by the British police of being, like the Queen, above party politics' (Reiner, 1992, p. 96).

Both parties sought in the 1980s and 90s to make political capital from rising crime rates. Labour blamed them on the more divided society produced by Conservative policies. Conservatives blamed the unemployability and permissiveness generated by thirty years of the welfare state.

A Decline in Confidence in the Police and in the Criminal Justice System Generally

There is a mass of telling evidence of declining public confidence in the police from the supposed golden days of the 1940s and 50s. For example, research for the 1962 Royal Commission on the Police showed that 83 per cent of the people interviewed had 'great respect' for the police. A MORI poll in 1993 showed that this 83 per cent had dropped to 43 per cent (Bennett, 1994, p. 225). The research on the riots and disorder of the 1980s and 90s again and again pinpoints declining confidence in the police as an element in those events. Writing of the 1980s, Newburn speaks of 'the precipitous decline in public faith in the police' (Newburn, 1995, p. 79). Reiner describes the late 1980s as witnessing 'a haemorrhage of public confidence in the police' (Reiner, 1992, p. 262). There were highly publicized and very serious cases of police corruption and serious malpractice, and deeply disturbing evidence of racism and sexism – and a crime clear-up rate of 45 per cent in the 1960s was down to 26 per cent by the mid 1990s.

There was an almost parallel decline in faith in the traditional approach to criminal justice, culminating in the despairing cry in the late 1970s that 'Nothing Works'. The 1960s were the golden age of the rehabilitation ideal;

in the 1970s, it was substantially rejected. Positivist-type approaches to establishing the 'causes' of crime, which, it was assumed, would point the way to cures and solutions, were abandoned The result was that the 1980s saw bewildering oscillations in policy, epitomized by the denunciation of the ineffectiveness of imprisonment by one Home Secretary and then the adoption of the line that 'Prison Works' by another.

The significance of declining faith in the police and the criminal justice system was essentially fourfold. First, it compounded the problem. Effective policing depends on good relations with the public – for information and support, for example. Without it, police effectiveness inevitably declines. Second, it produced and exacerbated a sense of despair and hopelessness, particularly among the most at-risk groups and communities, which further compounded the problem. Third, it led people to seek their own private solution – alarms, security devices, bigger dogs. Finally, it fed the politicization of the problem of law and order, which further reduced the chances of constructive policies.

Criminology Loses its Optimism

The criminology of the 1960s and early 1970s had two central concerns: (1) to tease out the supposed 'causes of crimes' so that they could be analysed, understood and then eliminated, and (2) to analyse the effectiveness of the various methods of dealing with offenders and to improve and promote 'effective' treatments.

Both these concerns were vigorously and effectively challenged in the late 1970s and 80s. What the BCS and other victim studies showed was just how widespread, and therefore how normal, crime was. Given its normality, the assumption that offenders were somehow different and that the causes of their offending could be established took a nasty blow. Research shifted in response to this realization from a focus on causes to one on the situations in which crime took place and the possibilities for what came to be known as situational crime prevention. This new interest was also fuelled by the 'Nothing Works' judgement about treatment approaches. A Home Office publication in 1984 expressed the conclusion that 'the scope for reducing crime through changes to the Criminal Justice system itself is very limited' (Heal, 1992, p. 258). Through the 1950s and 60s, criminological research was regarded sympathetically by Labour and Conservative governments alike. As crime became politicized in the 1970s, so political concerns increasingly defined and determined agendas and approaches. To survive, criminological research had to be useful, and it had to find a way out of the academic cul-de-sac up which it had paddled in the 1960s and early 1970s.

What is plain is that there was a crisis in academic criminology in the 1980s – a sense of its limited contribution in the past and present in the face of rising crime rates and more incidents of civil disorders. It contributed to the pessimism that led to the reassertion of instinctive policies – 'Prison Works' – which flew in the face of research and experience.

The Weakening of a Dominant Morality

It is obviously exceedingly difficult to measure this kind of trend, but there is certainly a strong sense in Britain in the 1980s and 90s of a weakening of traditional morality and a declining respect for authority of all kinds. Comparing the 1940s with the 1980s, Terence Morris sees the 1940s as characterized not only by a greater degree of consensus about the canons of social propriety, but also by the fact that the dominant morality was both more effectively and more widely asserted. Transgressions, of whatever kind, brought greater stigma and disgrace (Morris, 1989, p. 26). In the 1980s, there is a declining sense that anything is absolutely right and wrong. Morality is relative, therefore less clear cut and thus less compelling.

In a sense, late industrial society in the 1970s and 80s was living on a legacy of moral capital inherited from a more structured, deferential, religious past. By the 1980s, that legacy was almost exhausted. The vigorously proclaimed virtues of individualism and choice were the final nails in the coffin of the old authority for good and ill. The situation is illustrated by the number of calls to the police about young people being a nuisance and individuals' unwillingness or inability to assert any kind of authority or influence over them. It is epitomized, too, by the growth of 'sleaze' in the 1990s and revelations about the behaviour of, for example, police and MPs. It is epitomized in increasing numbers of children excluded from school because of the school system's inability to assert its authority over them. It is epitomized by the finding, reported by Cook, that only one employee in twelve considered stealing from work to be a crime (Cook, 1997, p. 60).

What Has Been Happening?

- Riots and disorder
- Politicization of law and order
- Decline of confidence in the criminal justice system
- Criminology loses its optimism
- An increase in crime
- Weakening of a dominant morality

Why Have Things Been Changing as they Have?

There is a huge literature seeking to explain the changes sketched above. The aim of this section is not to review that literature but to indicate the broad lines of the analysis under four headings – weakening of informal and formal order-maintaining mechanisms, increased opportunity for crime, increased poverty and social division, and a crisis of youth and masculinity.

Weakening of Informal and Formal Order-maintaining Institutions

There is little dispute that the central mechanisms for maintaining social order are the family, community, work and religion. All these have been weakened or changed by crucial elements in the modernization process – industrialization and de-industrialization, urbanization and secularization. The process of change has been taking place for two centuries, but many residual elements of a pre-modern system survived into the postwar years. The accelerating economic and social changes of the past three decades have quickened their decline.

Felson, writing about the USA, points up the significance of changes in the family as a force for social order. Comparing young people in the 1940s and the 1970s, he sees a very clear trend for adolescents to be increasingly independent of parental settings. They have much greater access to cars. Families take fewer meals together. More mothers are in the formal labour market. There are fewer adult relatives sharing the same household (Felson, 1994, pp. 104–5). The family is a very different kind of unit, exercising much less informal and formal supervision over young people. Society encourages teenagers to independence, but independence is a two-edged sword.

The market economy has led directly to a stress on individualism and competition. Braithwaite sees the crucial element in the maintenance of social order as what he calls 'reintegrative shaming' – the expression of community disapproval followed by gestures of re-acceptance into the community. He sees individualism as dismantling the sanctioning capacities of communities by weakening those intermediate groups which come between the individual and the state (Braithwaite, 1989).

Attributing what has gone wrong to the forces of modernization is one interpretation. Prime Minister Margaret Thatcher favoured a quite different one. Taking responsibility away from people had, she argued, quite simply made them irresponsible (Thatcher, 1993, p. 626). She also argued that both formal and informal order-maintaining mechanisms had been sadly weakened by the dominant philosophy of seeking to understand offenders rather than to assert their responsibility and punish them, which was both an ineffective way of dealing with them and gravely weakened the respect for law in the community.

Increased Opportunity for Crime

A more affluent society offers more opportunity for crime. There is more tempting movable property – radios, TVs, videos, computers, cars. Ninety-two per cent of crime is property crime. Property crime is likely to grow with the availability of stealable property. In the 1950s, for example, crimes involving motor vehicles were relatively rare – cars were much less numerous, and the car had not become an icon of contemporary society. The increased number of cars on the road – up by 38 per cent, for example, in the 1980s alone – and the dominant position of the car in contemporary culture go a long way to explain increased car crime, now a quarter of all crime.

Other social changes have also increased opportunity. Smaller households mean that there is less likely to be someone at home at any given time to guard property. The increase in the number of women in paid employment has had the same effect. The supermarket offers much readier opportunities for crime than the shop where goods are protected by a counter and an individual shopkeeper.

Increased Relative Deprivation and Social Division

Much of the increase in crime since 1945 took place at a time of full employment when the fruits of rising national prosperity were widely shared. It is when we focus on the 1980s – the years of most rapidly increasing crime – from 3 million to well over 5 million serious offences – that explanations in terms of relative deprivation, division and exclusion became most relevant. These were years when affluence was increasing, the poor were getting relatively poorer and there was consistently high youth unemployment.

Crucial to order is a stake in society and an attachment to the future. Unemployment and social exclusion undermine such order-maintaining commitments. Dahrendorf speaks of 'those who are being defined out of the edifice of citizenship' (Dahrendorf, 1985, p. 98). A society and a system that excludes you is not going to attract your commitment or endorsement. It loses legitimacy. The prevalence of high rates of youth unemployment is a probable explanation for the fact that young people do not seem to be growing out of crime as they did in the past. Unemployment, as Mrs Thatcher never tired of saying, is no excuse for crime and rioting. But it may be a contributory factor.

Power and Tunstall, in their analysis of thirteen riots and disorders in 1991–92, show how the areas where the disorder actually took place had strikingly higher rates of unemployment than did the local authority areas in which they were set. The social conditions in the areas, in Power and Tunstall's view, 'generate aggression, law breaking and destructiveness' (Power and Tunstall, 1997, p. 1). Scarman's earlier analysis was similar (Scarman,

1982, para. 2.38). For Downes and Morgan, 'the real cause' of the riots is 'the economic marginalization and political exclusion of disadvantaged youths, whether black, white or both' (Downes and Morgan, 1994, p. 201). James argues powerfully that increasing inequality is the vital element in the increasing violence of the 1980s (James, 1995, Chapters 4 and 5).

Another important link between deprivation and crime is one stressed by Utting and his colleagues. They argue that economic and environmental deprivation are powerful stress factors that conspire to make it more difficult to be an effective parent. There are simply not the resources – financial, physical or emotional – to socialise the next generation satisfactorily (Utting *et al.*, 1993, p. 19) – hence our stress on the need for an attack on family poverty in Chapter 3. Levi links the trebling of reported domestic violence between 1981 and 1996 with 'the general social and economic insecurity of the 1980s and 1990s' and the tensions in relationships which that can generate (Levi, 1994, p. 337).

Increasing inequality and social division, as well as high rates of long-term unemployment, are clearly less than the whole story, but they contribute to a weakening of the legitimacy of authority, to a weakening or non-development of informal or formal mechanisms of social control and to a dangerous lack of a stake in society.

A Crisis of Youth and Masculinity

Men account for 80 per cent of people cautioned by the police and nearly 90 per cent of those found guilty of indictable offences. Men are responsible for over 90 per cent of crimes against the person and 97 per cent of burglaries. 'The most significant fact about crime', say Newburn and Stanko, 'is that it is almost always committed by men' (Newburn and Stanko, 1994, p. i). The fact that men, more particularly young men, are the chief offenders is central to understanding both crime and masculinity.

The issue is one of role. Young men have always been the main law breakers – traditionally in their last year at school. Entry to employment solved the problem for all but a tiny minority, but now there is no such easy transition. Young people are, in Campbell's words, 'adrift from all institutions', without jobs, training, income or voice (Campbell, 1993, p. 96). During the winter of 1995–96, 281 000 16–19-year-olds were unemployed. The unemployment rate among young males is the highest of any age group – just under 20 per cent in 1995–96 (Cook, 1997, p. 147). The old ways in which boys learned to be men have disappeared, but no officially accepted new routes have been established. Coote suggests that 'it is the unequal struggle to be masculine in modern times that gets so many boys into trouble' (Coote, 1994, p. 4).

Why Have Things Been Changing as they Have?

- The weakening of informal and formal order-maintaining institutions
- An increased opportunity for crime
- Increased relative deprivation and social division
- A crisis of youth and masculinity

What has the Government Response Been to these Changes?

The government response is analysed under five headings – what *The Economist Election Briefing* called 'a flurry of law and order policy making' (*The Economist*, 1997, p. 22), the expansion and reform of the police, the move to crime prevention, the search for scapegoats and the call for the remoralization of society.

A Flurry of Law and Order Policy Making

Between 1851 and 1979, there were only five Criminal Justice Acts – great landmark pieces of penal legislation marking major changes of philosophy, policy and practice. Between 1979 and 1997, there were no fewer than nine Criminal Justice Acts, and the Labour Government elected in May 1997 quickly introduced the major Crime and Disorder Bill. The pendulum of policy swung back and forth in a quite bewildering fashion. The Criminal Justice Act 1991, for example, sought to consolidate and further develop punishment in the community and introduced four forms of community order for adults. It reflected Home Secretary Douglas Hurd's view that prison was an expensive way of making bad people worse. In 1993, in contrast, Home Secretary Michael Howard asserted the view that 'Prison Works', and the 1993 Criminal Justice Act, led to a 50 per cent increase in the prison population in four years. That Act, and the Criminal Justice and Public Order Act 1994, introduced a wide range of new or extended custodial sentences for young offenders between the ages of ten and seventeen.

The 1980s also marked a clear retreat from welfarist principles in juvenile justice, although, at the same time, the period marked a decline in the use of custody for juveniles. The number of juveniles in prison, for example, halved between 1984 and 1989, reflecting the view of the White Paper *Punishment, Custody and the Community* that 'Even a short period of custody is quite likely to confirm them as criminals particularly as they acquire new criminal skills from the more sophisticated offenders' (Home Office, 1988, para. 2.15). A series of Circulars in 1978, 1985 and 1990 encouraged the courts in the use of cautioning for young offenders.

One interesting innovation was the introduction of parental responsibility for fines or compensation orders for juveniles. The 1991 Act gave the courts power to 'bind over' parents to enforce their obligations to provide proper care and control over their (male) children. These developments pre-figure the commitment by both the main political parties in their 1997 manifestos to enforce responsibilities on parents via Parental Control Orders (Conservatives) and Parental Responsibility Orders (Labour).

The years 1979–97 are clearly not years of consistent policies or of the simple pursuit of old-fashioned forms of custodial punishment. The story is much more complex than that. The striking fact is how the absence of any kind of coherent penal philosophy, and sharply rising crime figures, led to policies that simply reflected the idiosyncratic views of particular Home Secretaries. These policies were desperate attempts to deal with pressing problems when no one really knew what was best.

Expansion and Reform of the Police

The initial instinctive response of the Conservative governments to the increasing problem of law and order was to pour extra resources into the police. Expenditure increased by 65 per cent in real terms in the first eight years of Conservative rule (Hale, 1992, p. 179). Over the sixteen years of Conservative rule, the number of police officers rose by 16000, and an additional 18000 civilians were recruited to the police service (Conservative Central Office, 1997, p. 36).

Conservative enthusiasm for the police, which was matched in the early years by police enthusiasm for the government, was soon challenged. There were critical accounts of poor police–community relations as a factor in the 1981 riots. There was the fact that extra resources did not seem to lead to either less crime or improved clear-up rates. There was pressure from the Treasury to subject the police to the same kind of keen financial discipline that was being imposed on the rest of the public sector. The result was a series of reforms attempting to secure police financial and community accountability.

By the end of the 1980s, many more perceptive senior police officers were seeking to distance themselves from the government. Once the Audit Commission began to get its teeth into traditional assumptions about the effectiveness of the police and into the way the police were actually used – only 5 per cent of a force's total strength was found to be actually patrolling the streets at any one time (Audit Commission, 1996b, p. 5) – the government had to adopt a more critical and reflective stand. More police and more expenditure on policing were clearly not the answer to the problem.

The Move to Crime Prevention

The adoption of crime prevention as a major element in government policy was a response to rising crime rates, a decline of faith in the 'treatment model', loss of faith in increased expenditure on the police, and faltering belief in general social reform as the answer to increasing crime. In the late 1970s, the Home Office Research Unit made a fundamental shift in focus from the individual offender to the situation in which the crime took place. Situational prevention 'became the main form of government prevention during the 1980s' (Davidson, quoted in Gilling, 1997, p. 60).

In 1983, a Standing Committee on Crime Prevention was formed, chaired by a Home Office Minister. In the same year, a Crime Prevention Unit was set up in the Home Office, and there was a major drive to develop Neighbourhood Watch Schemes. In 1986, a Ministerial Group on Crime Prevention was set up, composed of ministers and civil servants from twelve government departments to coordinate government action in order to reduce crime. Heal sees this as a development of major importance – marking the recognition that crime reduction was a responsibility of all central government departments (Heal, 1992, p. 257). Various projects followed – the Five Towns demonstration projects in 1986–87, the Safer Cities Programme and the launch of Crime Concern in 1988. By 1987, the Manpower Service Commission's Community Programme had 8000 places committed to crime prevention work. 1991 saw the first National Crime Prevention Week (Hale, 1992, p. 181).

There was, predictably, more talk than action. Cynical critics saw the whole initiative as no more than an attempt to shift the blame for rising crime rates and police failures from 'the government' to 'the community'. Pease's verdict was that the real failure was the absence of any effort to generalize the major successes that were achieved – for example, reductions in domestic burglary recorded in the crime prevention project on the Kirkholt estate in Rochdale (Pease, 1992). There was a failure, too, to switch resources in line with the new rhetoric of priorities. 'The mismatch between the alleged primacy of crime prevention as a police purpose', says Pease, 'and its resourcing has been grotesque' (Pease, 1994, p. 683). Bright calculates that less than half of 1 per cent of the criminal justice budget is spent on prevention (quoted in the *Guardian*, 2 June 1997).

What the move to crime prevention did was to mark, in theory at least, a major change of approach to the problem of law and order – a recognition, in Mrs Thatcher's words, that 'Combating crime is everyone's business' (quoted in Brake and Hale, 1992, p. 10).

The Search for Scapegoats

If the government was to avoid being blamed for rising rates of crime and disorder, it had to put the blame elsewhere – hence the search for scapegoats. Five figured prominently in discourse about crime in the 1980s – the family, schools, social workers, the penal system and the welfare state generally.

The family was blamed for permissive methods of child rearing and inadequate discipline. Parents were failing to teach children the distinction between right and wrong. Lone parent families, in particular, were singled out for failing to socialize the next generation to accepted norms (see, for example, Dennis and Erdos, 1993; Thatcher, 1993, p. 629).

Schools were criticized for failing to instil a sense of discipline and self-discipline – partly because of failures in the training of teachers, partly because of mistaken ideas about child development and the nature of education, partly because of the way in which large comprehensive schools increased problems of maintaining discipline (see, for example, Boyson 1975, 1995).

Social workers were criticized for putting too much emphasis on understanding, for explaining antisocial behaviour in terms of circumstances, for stressing people's right to help from society and for putting too little emphasis on their obligations. Their ways of dealing with juvenile delinquents were criticized for their preoccupation with understanding, treatment and training rather than condemning and punishing.

Finally, the welfare state was indicted for taking responsibility away from people – responsibility for working, responsibility for their failures, responsibility for their children, responsibility for providing for their own and their families' needs, responsibility for their behaviour. By taking responsibility away from people, they were made irresponsible, and one of the chickens that was coming home to roost was the increase in antisocial and criminal behaviour (Thatcher, 1993, p. 8).

The Remoralization of Society

The fifth element in the government's response was a call for the remoralization of society, variously a restoration of Victorian values (Thatcher) and 'back to basics' (Major). Society was to be remoralized by stressing individual responsibility, rewards for hard work and punishment for failure. Explanations for crime and disorder and unmarried motherhood in terms of poverty and unemployment were not to be countenanced.

People were to take more responsibility for their lives, their failings, their future and society. As John Patten put it when at the Home Office, 'At the very centre of our ideas on how to control crime should be the energy and initiative of the active citizen' (quoted in Hale, 1992, p. 180). People must look to themselves rather than to government. Looking to government was the route to individual and social demoralization; the answer to crime, as to a range of other social ills, was remoralization.

The Government Response
▦ A flurry of law and order policy making
▦ Expansion and reform of the police
▦ A move to crime prevention
▦ A search for scapegoats
▦ The remoralization of society

What are the Broad Implications for Society?

There are five implications that stand out as key: the costs of crime; the impact of high and rising crime rates on social and community life; the impact on the national mood; the broad public and social policy implications; and the way in which current crime rates constitute an additional element in social deprivation.

Costs

Computing the costs of crime is an art rather than a science. In 1995, the Labour Party published estimates for the cost of crime in England and Wales in 1993–94. They reckoned the overall cost to be over £20 billion. The two biggest elements were the cost of the Criminal Justice System, reckoned to be £9.5 billion and the cost to business of £7.5 billion. The cost of private security was reckoned at £2 billion, the loss from car crime at £775 million and that of residential burglary at £495 million (*Guardian*, 21 February 1995). The overall estimate is close to Utting's. He puts the total figure at £18 billion in 1988 – roughly the same then as the cost of the NHS (Utting *et al.*, 1993, p. 67). In 1990, the Confederation of British Industries (CBI) reckoned that workplace crime was costing about £5 billion per year (Cook, 1997, p. 60). The latest estimate from the Association of British Insurers is that crime costs Britain £35 billion per year – £31 per week per household, which is only £9 less than the cost of the NHS (*Guardian*, 15 September 1998).

The 1996 BCS sought to work out the cost of burglaries to individuals. Only 56 per cent of burglaries were covered by insurance. Half of those who claimed had had their claim met in full by the time they were interviewed, and a third had had the claim met in part. The average net loss incurred, taking into account insurance repayments and any property recovered, was £370. This rose to £620 for burglary with loss (Home Office Statistical Bulletin, 1996, p. 42). In 1995, 779 000 burglaries with loss were recorded by the BCS. Those without insurance, who often tend to have the highest rates of victimization, suffer all the loss themselves.

In 1995 the BCS recorded 423 000 thefts of cars, 2.5 million thefts from cars and 1.3 million attempted thefts. The proportion of stolen cars recovered has dropped from 83 per cent in 1987 to 64 per cent in 1995. For the individuals concerned, the average net loss was calculated to be £470 when cars were recovered and £2190 when they were not recovered. For thefts from cars, the average net loss was £270 (Home Office Statistical Bulletin, 1996, pp. 43–7).

Rising crime rates also push up the cost of property and car insurance. The Labour Party study showed bills for household and car insurance rising by more than 20 per cent between 1988 and 1992 – to £556 for the average family – largely as a result of a sharp rise in claims. Households with no insurance suffer almost twice as much fear of crime as households with insurance, despite having similar crime rates (Pantazis and Gordon, 1997, p. 131).

There are also emotional costs of crime for the victims – anger, fear and shock of varying degrees were the common responses to all kinds of crime from violence to theft, significant numbers being very emotionally affected, particularly by stranger violence and by burglars who got into the house. Half of all burglary victims report emotional problems, and a quarter are still experiencing problems six months later (Audit Commission, 1996a, para. 10).

Community Life

The impact of crime on community life is considerable, worry about crime being a significant issue. Twenty-two per cent of men and women are 'very worried' about burglary and 62 per cent 'very or fairly worried'. Nineteen per cent are very worried about mugging, 47 per cent being 'very or fairly worried', while 32 per cent of women are very worried about rape. Eighteen per cent of men and women are very worried about the theft of their car (Home Office Statistical Bulletin, 1996, p. 51). In general, women are more worried than men about crime. Of women aged 16–59, around 12 per cent said that they felt, or would feel, very unsafe walking in their own area alone after dark. For women over 60, the percentage rose to 31 per cent (Home Office Statistical Bulletin, 1996, p. 53), although the evidence shows very clearly that elderly people are at less risk from crime than the young. As we saw earlier, 40 per cent of young people aged 12–15 interviewed in the 1992 BCS said that they felt 'fairly unsafe' or 'very unsafe' when out alone at night (Maung, 1995, p. x). Fear about crime is not, of course, spread uniformly through the population. Being able to afford the technology to 'target harden' your home is likely to reduce fear. Access to a car, or the ability to afford taxi fares, reduces the fear and the risks of going out at night.

High crime rates have costs for individuals. They also have a damaging impact on social and community life. Predatory crime, argues Wilson, causes the kind of fear that drives people apart from one another and thus impedes, or even prevents, the formation of meaningful human communities. Such acts 'are destructive of the very possibility of society' (Wilson, 1983, pp. 4, 252).

The National Mood

A third important implication for society is the sense of social crisis and pessimism that high crime rates induce. It seems to indicate, and to threaten, the collapse of moral order and civic society, raising questions about the future of society. The BCS's most significant, and perhaps most worrying, finding concerns the extent and therefore the normality of crime.

The failure of increases in police number and expenditure to stem the increases in crime feeds a pessimistic fatalism. So does the seeming ineffectiveness of the rest of the Criminal Justice System. So does the failure of criminology to offer answers. Crime is so pervasive, and its impact so widespread, that it raises questions about the whole enterprise of society. The only logical responses exacerbate the problem – not going out, installing home security devices, using cars and taxis to avoid public transport and the street. The social dimension of life narrows, and with it any hopes or visions for society and its future.

The Need to Plan for Social Order

A fourth implication for society is the need consciously to plan for social order. We have discovered our inability effectively to combat disorder via the Criminal Justice System. The alternative strategy, which circumstances and our failures are pressing upon us, is the need to seek to plan for order. Most societies have, historically, taken order for granted. They have assumed order rather than disorder to be the natural state. However, the evidence challenges that comforting view. As a society, we can now begin to appreciate order in the sense of low crime rates, the absence of disorder, respect for authority and shared norms and values as the happy, rather than the inevitable, result of particular patterns of economic, social and cultural development.

What we have to do is to explore more carefully the nature and basis of social order and law-abiding behaviour and seek to develop services to promote them. Modern society has to see disorder as a new giant to be set

alongside Beveridge's traditional five giants barring the route to social reconstruction. We have to set out carefully and coolly to promote order as a critical and central task – just as the promotion of health, rather than simply
treating disease, has become a key objective (at least in theory) of the NHS.

An Element in Social Deprivation

The final implication is that much crime must be seen as an additional pain
of deprivation because those who suffer the heaviest burdens are the poor –
those living on the poorest and most run-down housing estates or in the inner
city. Using a very general characterization of 'inner city', the British Crime
Survey shows that inner city households are twice as likely to be the victim of
a burglary as other households (Office for National Statistics, 1997, p. 157).

Sharpening the analysis, *Misspent Youth* quotes research showing that
people living in areas with the highest crime rates are more than ten times as
likely to be victims of personal crime and five times more likely to suffer property crime as those living in more law-abiding areas (Audit Commission,
1996a, para. 11). Such high crime areas are characterized by general
economic and social deprivation.

The 1988 BCS showed that, generally, council house tenants face over twice
the risk of burglary faced by owner occupiers. However, council tenants in areas
of majority council housing, with the highest levels of poverty, have a risk of
burglary five times that faced by tenants in areas where council tenure is not the
majority tenure and where incomes are higher (Foster and Hope, 1993, p. 5).

The risks of crime are not evenly spread through society: they are greater
for those who already suffer a raft of deprivations. High risks of crime victimization are an additional element in other deprivations. They need to be seen
as part of the broader coexistence of adversities with which the worst off have
to contend.

What Proposals for Action Have Been Made by Conventional Sources?

The 1997 election manifestos published by the Conservative and Labour
Parties were strikingly similar in what they had to say about law and order,
and are striking, too, in the way in which they epitomize the conventional
approach. They take the existing Criminal Justice System as a given, their
essential concern being with fine-tuning current responses – the Conservatives because, after eighteen years in office, it is difficult to launch completely
new initiatives and retain any vestiges of credibility, and Labour because they
had to cover themselves against the electorally wounding charge of being
'soft on crime'.

The Conservatives pledged themselves to provide an extra 5000 police in the three years 1997–99 and to set up a National Crime Squad. The police will be encouraged to pursue a policy of zero tolerance in relation to petty crime. Labour make no commitment to provide additional police officers but promise steps to get more officers back on the beat. The Liberal Democrats promise the resources to provide an extra 3000 officers on the beat within a year. Labour is also committed to a zero tolerance approach to petty criminality.

There is no sign in the manifestos of any attempt to think radically about the role, function, ideologies and organization of the police. Community policing, police–public relations, the nature of the police task, the evidence of the minimal impact of the police on crime levels, and/or of additional resources on clear-up rates, fail to get a mention. What both parties are offering is more of much the same rather than a response to two decades of research, review and debate – and rising crime rates.

There is the same, rather tired fine-tuning approach to the other side of the Criminal Justice System. Both parties commit themselves to speeding up the time taken to get young offenders to court and deal with them. Both parties aim to enforce parental responsibility for young offenders. The Conservatives promise Child Crime Teams. Labour offer Youth Offender Teams. The Conservatives promise – and, of course, we have seen it all come and go before – tough new regimes at young offender institutions. Labour promise stricter punishment for serious repeat offenders and guideline sentencing. The Conservative manifesto promises mandatory minimum sentences for certain offenders and life sentences for anyone committing a second serious sexual or violent crime, and they reiterate the belief that 'Prison Works', promising an additional 8500 prison places by the year 2000. Labour pledges an audit of the resources available, proper ministerial responsibility and constructive regimes that require prisoners to face up to their offending behaviour.

The two parties' manifesto proposals epitomize the conventional approach of tinkering and fine-tuning – expanding provision here, mildly reforming organization and administration there, modifying the law at the edges, toughening an established approach, genuflecting in the direction of current concerns.

The two manifestos offer a brief insight into Conventional approaches. Two recent White Papers – one, *Preventing Children Offending* (Home Office, 1997a), produced by the Conservatives in March 1997, and the other, *No More Excuses* (Home Office, 1997b), produced by Labour later in the same year help us to amplify this characterization. Five further characteristics emerge.

First, both documents are essentially reactive. Action is to be triggered by an offence or by a strong sense of a child or a young person being at risk (Home Office, 1997a, p. 3, 1997b, p. 14). There is much stress in both documents on prevention, but it is prevention focused on at-risk young people rather than genuine prevention in the sense of action designed to prevent children and young people ever becoming at risk of offending.

Second, the focus in both White Papers is strongly on parents and families. The Conservatives propose Parental Control Orders, requiring parents to exercise proper care and control over their children. Labour proposes a new Parenting Order 'designed to help and support parents to control the behaviour of their children' (Home Office, 1997b, p. 14). This focus is significant for various reasons. The implicit message is that it is parents who have failed and that it is they who are to blame. Requiring parents to exercise proper care and control suggests that the problem is simply one of wilfully neglecting a duty. Labour talk of 'help and support' is to mean counselling and guidance sessions. There is no sense of the way in which economic and social conditions can make it extremely difficult for parents actually to do what they know they should do. When the White Paper goes on to talk about support for families, the first proposal is for assistance to one-parent families so they can get off benefits and get back to work – a rather limited view of support for families. Blaming the parents seems a clear strand in Labour's thinking, implicitly if not explicitly. Obviously, some parents do wilfully neglect their duty as parents. Many more find it difficult to be the good parents they would like to be because of circumstances.

A third element in the two sets of proposals is the faith in better coordination – so often the last refuge of the despairing. Child Care Teams (Conservative) and Youth Offending Teams (Labour) will aim at a better coordinated strategy from relevant local agencies.

Fourth, there is much stress by Labour on 'responsibility'. 'The government is determined', says the White Paper, 'to reinforce the responsibility of young offenders – and their parents – for their delinquent behaviour' (Home Office, 1997b, p. 12), and there is emphasis on ending the so-called 'excuse culture'. That is one very important side of the coin. The other side, which gets no mention, is ensuring that the economic, social and family conditions that are required to enable parents to be responsible are in place. Nothing is said about this.

Fifth, Labour's pre-election commitment to be tough on crime is very clear – there are curfews, wider powers to lock up under thirteen-year-old offenders and stress on reparation. What is missing, however, is any parallel emphasis on the reintegration of offenders to prevent punishment and shame simply producing stigma, alienation and deviance amplification.

Labour's White Paper is a mix of conventional and more radical elements, but the conventional elements are very strong, brought out very clearly in what is stated as 'the Government's top priority' – halving the time taken for persistent young offenders to move from arrest to sentence (Home Office, 1997b, p. 2). This is certainly important but, given all we know about the problems of young people and the pattern, nature and extent of crime, displays a very narrow approach to the law and order issue.

What Proposals for Action Have Been Made by Radicals?

Those who adopt a radical stance in the face of the problem of law and order start from five beliefs and assumptions. Their first assumption is the most central fact about the Criminal Justice System – its very limited impact on crime. So few crimes are solved, so few of those committing offences end up in court, Cook argues, that 'to assume that anything we do to offenders (by way of punishment), will have any impact on crime rates is simply a nonsense' (Cook, 1997, p. 146).

The second assumption is that the police have only a marginal impact on crime. Bayley's conclusion is that really big increases or cuts might make a difference, but 'the increases and decreases that are likely to occur in the number of the police as a result of normal political and budgetary pressures will not make any difference in the incidence of crime' (Bayley, 1994, p. 5). The cry of 'more police on the beat' is an immensely popular one. Research shows, however, just how ineffective in terms of crime control such beat policing is – although it may be good for public confidence.

The third point is that law and order policy should focus on maintaining and promoting social order rather than responding to breaches of the law. Radicals would endorse Felson's judgement and try to go on to work out its implications – 'Any society that has to rely on these slow and uncertain public agencies [that is, the Criminal Justice System] as the main source of prevention has already lost the battle against crime' (Felson, 1994, p. xi).

The fourth assumption is that government in modern industrial society has to adopt an active policy of promoting and maintaining order. Order can no longer be taken for granted and simply assumed. It has to be seen as a central focus of social policy, although, because our knowledge of how to do it is limited, what will be required, at least initially, is experiment and evaluation – and there will certainly be failures.

Finally, there is the rather different weight that radicals give to certain types of criminal behaviour compared with conventional assessments. Radicals stress the major significance of domestic violence to an understanding of violent crime and to an effective response to violence given that a quarter of all violent crime revealed by the BCS is domestic (Home Office Statistical Bulletin, 1996, p. 28). Radicals argue that the salience of domestic violence has for too long been underestimated. Similarly, they express more concern about the extent of racially motivated crime and its seeming underrecording by the police – in the early 1990s, the police recorded under 8000 offences involving a racial element, whereas the BCS estimated 130 000 racially motivated crimes (Cook, 1997, p. 58). Radicals also emphasize how black people are much more likely to be stopped and searched by the police than white people and the very different ways in which they are dealt with by the

Criminal Justice System. Overall, radicals are much more concerned about gender and race issues as aspects of the law and order problem.

Radical proposals can usefully be explored under eight headings.

A Broad Approach to the Problem of Law and Order

Radicals stress the need for an approach that focuses on society rather than on the specific problem of law and order because they see crime and disorder as indications of an ill-ordered, ill-functioning society.

No one argues that a successful anti-poverty strategy or full employment would eliminate crime, but tackling economic, social and work deprivation is, for radicals, a necessary, even if insufficient, element in any serious law and order policy. As Downes argues, 'Policies to tackle unemployment and under-employment and to reintegrate youths into schools and family life are... essential if crime rates are to be slowed in their rate of increase, let alone reduced' (Downes, 1995, p. 142). Simply reacting to offending behaviour with new criminal justice policies is, for radicals, to ignore the central importance of economic and social factors in the genesis of criminal behaviour and to ignore the possible dysfunctional effects of criminalizing certain kinds of behaviour.

The most obvious example is approaches to dealing with drug abuse. Conventional approaches emphasize the necessity for the firm use of law to 'crack down' on substance abuse. Radicals urge a more careful examination of the broader implications of a hard-line policy, arguing that such a stance may well be counterproductive, blurring the distinction between different kinds of illegal substance, creating a drug subculture and forging a link between illegal drug use and organized crime (Downes, 1997, p. 11). What radicals urge is a careful, measured examination of the issues rather than a knee-jerk reaction.

A Social Development Strategy as a Necessary Response to Crime

Radicals urge such a strategy because of their belief that the community and civic culture are the key forces for maintaining social order. Pantazis and Gordon's conclusion is that 'high levels of victimisation seem to be associated more with a lack of social cohesion in a community rather than with high levels of poverty' (Pantazis and Gordon, 1997, p. 133). The thesis is that the key force in maintaining people in law-abiding ways is bonding with groups or institutions that disapprove of law-disregarding behaviour. It is fear of 'community' disapproval and the potential and actual impact of family and community disapproval that are the key elements in low crime rates. Society, therefore, has to work to re-establish the essential characteristics of such communities.

What is required for such communities? There is support for Dahrendorf, who argues that 'The answer to the problem of law and order can be put in one word, institution building' (Dahrendorf, 1985, p. 121). He saw 'a conscious effort to build and rebuild institutions' as the only way to avoid the normlessness and lawlessness that destroys law and order, and therefore society. Dahrendorf see the crucial need as being the need for institutions that 'define in' young people by reaching out to them and involving them in society (Dahrendorf, 1985, p. 137). Alderson (writing while still a Chief Constable) argues along very similar lines. Order in society, he says, 'depends upon a whole system of cultural and institutional networks. When such networks are strong and effective, the role of the police in maintaining order is marginal' (Alderson, 1984, p. 19).

'It is not the "Thin Blue Line"', say Matthews and Young, 'but the social bricks and mortar of civil society which are the major bulwark against crime' (Matthews and Young, 1992, p. 45). It is the recognition of this truth that leads radicals to press for strategies to re-establish a sense of community responsibility for law and order, and the confidence and power to seek to assert and enforce common standards of behaviour in local communities. No one pretends that it will be easy or straightforward. There is no noddy's guide recipe on how to do it, but we know enough to get started and that we have to learn as we experiment.

The Need to Confront the Most Obvious Central Fact about Crime and Disorder – that they Are Problems Dominated by Young Men

'Crime Statistics', says Campbell, 'tell a story about masculinity and crime prevention must, therefore, contemplate the reform of masculinity' (Campbell, 1993, p. 211). The radical view is that society clearly does not provide legitimate avenues and opportunities through which young men can find satisfaction. Partly, of course, it is a problem of the shortage of unskilled work, which has in the past given young men identity, status and income. It is partly the failure of society to recognize the need for the provision of leisure activities to capture their interest, commitment and energy. Partly it is also a matter of socialization.

Society has created an image of youth and masculinity that is at odds with what is legally available to young men. The result is alienation, a rejection of social norms, disorder and crime on a significant scale. Society has to work to give young people a role and to create a new model of masculinity that does not require law-disregarding behaviour for its authentication.

Dealing with the Concentration of Crime

As we saw earlier, the concentration of crime in terms of the multiple victimization of individuals and the high rates of property victimization in particular areas in one of the most striking 'facts' about crime. This unequal distribution, radicals argue, should be seen as the starting point for policy – for policing, for crime prevention policies of opportunity reduction, for broader social development policies and for broader anti-crime economic and social policies. Hope analyses the concentration effects that afflict high-crime communities in Britain and emphasizes how research evidence supports 'the strategic importance of targeting crime prevention efforts on high crime communities and applying comprehensive community initiatives to tackle the interlocking problems of social dislocation, of which crime plays an important part' (Hope, 1998, p. 128).

The Socialization of the Next Generation is a Societal Responsibility

Radicals accept that the family has a central role to play in the prevention and correction of delinquency. Where they differ from much conventional opinion is on their insistence that families have both the right and the need to claim the help of government in socializing the next generation. Their argument is that, in a more morally pluralist society, less certain of the nature of right and wrong and with less regard for authority, it has become more difficult for families adequately to perform the function of bringing up children. It has become even more difficult for that large fraction of families struggling to bring up children in poverty.

Radicals urge the general value of a policy of support for all families. They see such support as 'central' to any delinquency prevention strategy (Utting *et al.*, 1993, p. 68). They believe that being an effective parent requires more than instinct, that parents need training and preparation for parenthood, both before they embark on parenting and at different stages on the parental journey. That, they insist, requires public investment on a considerable scale, although with the prospect of an excellent return.

Sherman *et al.*, on the basis of research and experiment in the USA, urges intensive home visiting during pregnancy and infancy focused on families that face, or seem likely to face, problems in the future in bringing up their children as being highly effective in preventing crime (Sherman *et al.*, 1997). Farrington and Utting are both strong supporters of pre-school and nursery education. Farrington's research suggests that nursery education is the single most effective crime prevention policy (*Guardian*, 22 February 1993). It gives children a 'head start' and reduces the educational failure that is so clearly linked with early delinquency. Research very clearly suggests that schools can inhibit delinquency in their pupils by integrating them in a law-abiding value system and giving them a sense of worth and of achievement, but they need extra resources to tackle the task effectively (Graham, 1988). Research suggests very strongly that prevention programmes for children should focus on risk factors affecting all aspects of a child's life rather than just on those which seem more directly connected with delinquency (Graham, 1998, p. 3).

Radicals accept the reality and implications of a society in which increasing numbers of women with young children are in paid employment. The implications are threefold – pre-school care, after school care and holiday care. A society that purports to be concerned about delinquency has to take action in a situation in which around one in five primary school children returns home every day to an empty house (Utting *et al.*, 1993, p. 31).

They accept that rearing and socializing the next generation is properly a shared enterprise. In a complex world, many parents lack the capacity to succeed. Society cannot simply allow failure to happen. It must join forces with parents, offer them support and provide a network of those services that research shows would be conducive to success in socializing the nation's children and young people. There is no mystery about what is needed. The lines of policy are very clear (see, for example, Cavadino, 1997, p. 11).

The Adoption of a Radical Model of Crime Prevention

Early discussion of crime prevention was very much in terms of situational prevention. Since then, discussion has moved on to embrace a broader social model. Radicals see crime prevention as embracing a variety of social policies and as a key element in central and local government responsibility. *No More Excuses* promised that the Crime and Disorder Bill would establish prevention as a statutory aim of the youth justice system (Home Office, 1997b, p. 1). That is radical and encouraging – as long as preventive policies are not seen as solely the responsibility of the youth justice system and as long as its strategies are genuinely proactive, preventive and not simply reactive in the face of emergent problems of delinquency. Crime prevention has to be a concern of all public policies.

At the local level, a radical policy for crime prevention will give the police a central role – for example, they have much of the information about patterns of crime on which a crime prevention strategy will need to draw. But the police must operate as part of a team; their role cannot be the dominant one. A radical crime prevention strategy will give the lead role to the local authority because no other body has the ability to take the necessary broad view of the issues involved or the resources to tackle them. If crime prevention involves the renovation of run-down housing estates, the use of housing management to avoid the concentration of particular population groups on particular estates or in particular parts of particular estates, the provision of training and work opportunities for young people, the use of schools as sites for crime prevention initiatives, then only the local authority can lead and facilitate such action. Hence radical support for the local authority's central role.

A New Approach to Dealing with Juveniles – 'Reintegrative Shaming'

Braithwaite is the great advocate of the policy of 'reintegrative shaming', as he styles it (Braithwaite, 1989). In essence, it is a form of community response to crime through which members of the offender's community – local or interest based – actively participate in shaming offenders and then work hard to reintegrate them into the community of law-abiding citizens (Braithwaite, 1989, p. 8). Braithwaite tries to distinguish shaming from stigmatization. The former has positive possibilities because of its parallel emphasis on reintegrating offenders. Stigmatization has negative results because it excludes offenders from the community of law-abiding citizens and gives them a new identity – that of a criminal.

Shaming expresses the strong disapproval to the offender of those who are significant in his life: family, friends and work colleagues. It also acts as a deterrent to further criminal behaviour because is shows the immediate social consequence and costs of criminal activity – and none of us likes to incur the disapproval of those close to us. What shaming does – or tries to do – is to condemn an act while striving to preserve the identity of the offender as essentially good (Braithwaite, 1989, pp. 75, 71 and 101). It builds on what we know – that nearly all offenders are anxious about what family will think about their offences and worry about that more than about formal punishment.

Can shaming work in urban, industrial societies? Braithwaite argues vigorously that it can (Braithwaite, 1993, p. 15), through mechanisms such as Community Conferences or Family Group Conferences. He sees two elements in such conferences as helping the process of reintegrative shaming. First, giving the victim of the offence and his or her supporters a role builds shaming into the process. Equally, the presence of the offender and his or her supporters builds reintegration into the process. Braithwaite argues that the Family Group Conference as a way of dealing with young offenders can be a method of reintegrative shaming.

There have been various experiments in recent years in Britain and elsewhere that try, usually implicitly, to use some of these ideas. The results have been encouraging, but society is still too bound by a commitment to punishment rather than to the ultimate purpose of punishment – the prevention of re-offending and the promotion of social order.

A New Approach to Policing

Both too much and too little is expected of the police. They are expected, somehow, to arrest criminals, to deter potential criminals and to reduce the total volume of crime in the community. At the same time, they are not seen as key players in the broader task of crime prevention, for example as working constructively with industry to 'design out' the criminal potential from new or existing products and reduce their stealabilty. Radicals want to see a change in the expectations of the police. If law enforcement is not the primary answer to crime, the police role is not as central to the maintenance of social order. Radicals want to see the role of the police put in context – as an important element, but certainly not the most important one, in the maintenance of order in society. They would assert the importance of the police working 'to strengthen society's ability to police itself' (Leadbeater, 1996, p. 25). Radicals believe that local democratic accountability of the police is central to this aim.

Radicals insist in this area, as in others, that policy and practice should be guided by research. *Reducing Offending* has an illuminating list of current orthodoxies about policing and the research evidence on whether or not the particular strategies actually reduce crime (Jordan, 1998, pp. 64–5). What the research evidence shows is that instinct is not enough. Policy and practice must be shaped by evidence.

What Proposals for Action Have Been Made by Radicals?

- A broad approach to the problem of law and order
- A social development strategy as a necessary response
- The need to confront the fact that crime is a problem of young men
- The need to deal with the concentration of crime
- That the socialization of the next generation is a societal responsibility
- The need to adopt a radical model of crime prevention
- The need for a new approach to dealing with juveniles
- The need for a new approach to policing

Conclusions

Comparing and contrasting conventional and radical approaches illuminates the key debates and dilemmas in how to produce a safe and sustainable society. This section draws out the differences of approach to clarify the choices that need to be made and the policies that need to be developed.

There is a sharp difference over the fundamental nature of the approach that needs to be taken. The conventional approach starts from the offence and the offender, its preoccupation being with the Criminal Justice System – even if broadly defined. In contrast, radical proposals are much broader. Their focus is on the nature of the society that produces crime and disorder and what can be done to change it.

Conventional approaches start from two basic beliefs – that problems of law and order are marginal rather than systemic. That is to say that they can be dealt with by particular, carefully crafted services and systems pointed at offenders rather than requiring major changes in society, and that the current Criminal Justice System is, *broadly speaking*, on the right lines. It certainly needs development and fine-tuning, but in essentials its approach is sound and there are no real alternatives.

Radicals, on the other hand, start from the belief that the law and order problem is systemic, produced by the very nature of our society and its institutions and their failings. The primary, although not sole, focus must, therefore, be on broader social changes to make society less criminogenic rather than simply on efforts to deter or change the criminal or make the Criminal Justice System more efficient or more effective. The problem for radicals is to do with society and not simply with the Criminal Justice System. They do not ignore the need for reform in the Criminal Justice System, but they see such reform as offering no more than a small contribution to solving the problem.

Conventional responses to the problem of law and order are essentially reactive, reactive to a problem – the crime, a person – the offender, and an act – the offence. Radicals favour a much more proactive approach. Their major concern is to promote order and law-abiding behaviour rather than with how to respond more effectively to disorder.

It is this concern actively to promote order and law-abiding behaviour that leads radicals to much broader policy proposals. They see the socialization of the next generation as central to order and thus of central concern to society. This means more financial and general support for families, the development of better day care and universal pre-school education, the promotion of social education, a commitment to full employment and so on. Radicals urge a special proactive focus on areas of acute disadvantage because of their criminogenic nature.

Radicals are concerned to develop proactive strategies both to promote order and to attack those social conditions known to be strongly associated with disorder. Of course, there must be a direct and immediate response to disorder, but radicals believe that policy cannot be limited to such a reactive role. If it is, it is doomed to fail because it is getting nowhere near the roots of the problem.

Conventional responses focus strongly on parents in trouble – parents with children who have committed offences and parents with children regarded as at risk of offending. There is concern to make parents face up to their responsibilities and to provide various kinds of training in parenting and emotional support.

Radicals, on the other hand, in line with their broader more proactive approach, want the focus to be on *all* parents – on the conditions that parents need to be effective parents in today's world – which leads directly to concerns about poverty, housing, day care, pre-school education and so on. This mirrors the difference between residual and institutional approaches – minimalist help for failures, or more generous broadly conceived help for all.

Conventional and radical proposals are different partly, at least, because they have rather different audiences. Conventional proposals are produced by those in power, close to power or hopeful of securing power. Hence, proposals have to have popular political appeal. More police on the beat is a very popular idea. All the main British political parties succumbed in their 1997 manifestos to this siren song. All the evidence, however, points to the very dubious value of such an initiative. Equally popular is the new approach of 'zero tolerance' towards any kind of law-disregarding/ law-breaking behaviour.

Radicals by virtue of their position outside power can afford to be more rational and less political, more sensitive to research evidence and less swayed by the demands of the moment or populist sentiment. They can, for example, question the longer-term effectiveness and implications of zero tolerance.

The two different groups use the same words – for example prevention – in very different ways with very different meanings. Conventional proposals tend to give prevention a narrower more limited meaning. Essentially, it is prevention in the sense of preventing things getting worse – preventing young people continuing a delinquent career or preventing 'at-risk' children and young people sliding on down the slippery slope. Radicals, in contrast, take a much broader and bolder view of what constitutes prevention, as could be deduced from the characteristics of their approach discussed above. They urge what they see as genuine preventive strategies – strategies that are designed to promote order and law-abiding behaviour generally in society, to inculcate accepted norms at school, to support all parents.

Both groups are concerned about prevention, but the conventional and radical approaches actually define the term in ways which have very different implications for policy.

Conventional proposals are essentially incremental. They start from the existing Criminal Justice System as the baseline for discussion. They propose incremental changes – new responsibilities here, new statutory duties there, better coordination between relevant departments, a change of nomenclature to indicate new emphases and so on. There is nothing wrong with incrementalism. Experience needs to be drawn on. In a rapidly changing world that has seen dramatic increases in crime in recent decades, incrementalism is, however, dubiously adequate as a primary response.

Radicals try to respond to what they define as a new situation and get to the root of the problem rather than focus on existing systems. An obvious example of radicalism is the focus on young men and masculinity. The predominance of young men in the ranks of law breakers must have a message for those concerned about law and order. Radicals seek to explore what that message might be – and to devise responses, not simply to accept it as a fact without broader implication as do conventional approaches.

Conventional and radical proposals both stress the importance of responsibility – of making offenders take responsibility for their offence and for what it has meant to the victims, and of making parents take responsibility for their children and their children's offences. Radicals, however, see responsibility as dependent on the social context not as something which exists in a social vacuum. They would stress that being responsible depends on having access to certain goods and services, and if society wants people to be properly responsible, it has to ensure that appropriate supporting services are in place. People have to be enabled to be responsible. Radicals would also go on to stress that emphasizing the responsibility of offenders is of limited value unless accompanied by measures to ensure the reintegration of offenders.

Challenges

In any law and order policy there has to be a balance between long- and short-term goals and policies, between policies to deal with offenders and breaches of the law, and policies to promote a more orderly society. The key challenges for the future are about the balance between these strategies and how actually to achieve them:

- Although recorded offences have fallen in the past five years, crime is still a massive and daunting social problem in terms of cost to individuals and society, and the way in which it diminishes the quality of life of the whole community. It seems clear that, in Britain, the focus of policy has been too much on the offender and the offence and too little on reinforcing and strengthening the natural order-maintaining mechanisms in society. The focus has been on crime rather than on order. More attention needs to be given to order as a complement to policies that focus on offenders and disorder. A crucial issue is the balance and the links between them.
- The next and possibly the most important challenge is what needs to be done to promote a more orderly society. What are the key potential order-promoting and maintaining mechanisms and forces in society, and how can they be developed and strengthened without trespassing on important individual freedoms?
- The third great challenge is how to deal with offenders in order to turn them into law-abiding citizens. The ineffectiveness of current methods of

dealing with offenders is all too obvious. We have to work harder to try out radical new ideas and new approaches. There is a growing bank of information and ideas that has to be built on, tested and evaluated. We have to discover what works best with whom and when.

It is plain that the size and scale of the task of maintaining order in society has been underestimated. Crime is hugely expensive. Order is central to individual and societal well being, and needs as much attention as other major areas of social policy. What society has developed so far are reactive ambulance-type services rather than proactive institutional-type approaches. Order is clearly no longer natural and cheap. That has to be accepted. Order-maintaining institutions that were once self-sustaining are no longer so. Law and order requires a new approach to ensure a sustainable society.

Further Reading

Journals

There are many specialist journals, and general sociology and social policy journals also carry relevant articles. The two most useful specialist journals are probably *The Howard Journal* and *The British Journal of Criminology*.

Books

Audit Commission (1996) *Misspent Youth*, London, Audit Commission. Possesses all the usual virtues of the Audit Commission's work – sharp, critical, very up to date and splendidly presented.

Cook, D. (1997) *Poverty, Crime and Punishment*, London, Child Poverty Action Group. A very accessible introduction to major aspects of the issues considered in this chapter.

Farrington, D.I. (1991) *Understanding and Preventing Youth Crime*, York, Joseph Rowntree Foundation. An excellent distillation of a huge body of research.

Maguire, M., Morgan, R. and Reiner, R. (eds) (1994) *The Oxford Handbook of Criminology*, Oxford, Oxford University Press. Contains everything most students would want to know about criminology.

7

A Sustainable Society

A map of the world that does not include utopia is not even worth glancing at, for it leaves out the one country at which humanity is always landing. Progress is the realisation of utopias. (Wilde, 1891/1954, p. 340)

This book had three main aims: first, to provide a critical account of the issues and problems in the five areas that were considered central to a sustainable society; second, to compare and contrast the policies advocated by conventional and radical approaches to the solution of these problems; and third, to put forward a programme of policies, borrowing from both the conventional and the radical approaches, in order to secure a sustainable society in Britain.

Current policies do not live up to the demands created by the massive changes – economic, social, political and demographic – that have transformed British society during the postwar era. Many of these changes have been positive and have resulted in progress in various areas of life: people live healthier and longer lives; standards of living have risen; gender relations are on a more equal footing; discrimination on the grounds of race has been made illegal; there is a greater public awareness of environmental problems; and so on. Other changes have made individual and public life more difficult: crime rates have risen; full employment has come and gone; certain aspects of environmental pollution have worsened; social cohesion has suffered; and so on. Still other changes have had effects that are open to more than one interpretation: marriage instability; the spread of part-time and insecure employment; the increase in inequality; the greater emphasis on individualism. British society today is inevitably 'better' in some ways and 'worse' in others than the postwar society. If it is to retain what is positive and to reform what is negative, changes are needed in the dominant values, the behaviour of individual citizens and the policies of governments.

This chapter attempts the daunting task of outlining these changes cognisant of the fact that what is attempted is not a detailed account of the changes that are needed but rather a sketch of the nature of these changes. Affluent societies possess the wealth and are equipped with the political and administrative institutions that are needed for the pursuit of specific policy agendas. A web of interrelated factors – structural and cultural – influences the nature of the policies pursued or not pursued by governments. Important among these is the nature of the dominant value system of society. Without changes to the dominant values of contemporary Britain, the likelihood that governments will pursue the policies needed to tackle the negative changes in British society outlined in previous chapters is diminished. This is not to deny the significance of structural factors at both the national and the international level but to stress the relevance of cultural factors that are often ignored.

The Problem of Sustainability

Sustainability requires four essential elements: environmentally friendly economic growth; an opportunity for all to contribute to their own, as well as to the general, welfare through their work effort; a just distribution of the fruits of economic growth so that poverty and excessive economic inequalities are abolished; and the inculcation of a shared value system that stresses the values of respect for others and a commitment to collective action to promote the common good without suffocating creative individualism.

If these are accepted as a summary of the core characteristics of a sustainable society, sustainability in Britain is clearly under threat. Lip service is paid to the need to pay more attention to the protection of the environment, but concern stops well short of what is required to protect our common future. The present, rather than the future, continues to dominate our thinking. Government has abandoned any commitment to full employment and refuses to face the revolution in attitudes and practices that is essential to secure work for all.

Poverty and gross inequality remain striking characteristics of British society. There is no longer any commitment to the redistribution of income or wealth even in the Labour Party. Getting people off welfare and into work is an important element in any anti-poverty strategy, but it has to be accompanied by two equally important parallel emphases – managing the economy in order to create jobs for people to move into and setting benefit levels that provide an adequate level of living.

Values are perhaps the key element in sustainability. The key value is commitment to the common good and an acceptance of the importance of the collective as against the assumed rights of the individual. Britain remains too individualistic a society for its assured sustainability.

The Value Mix for a Sustainable Society

Social values are rarely held as absolutes by either individuals or societies. Support for this or that value tends to be both partial and conditional. Endorsement of, say, equality is never so absolute as to be diametrically opposed to the support of inequality. Similarly, support of any one value may vary from one aspect of life to another and may also depend on the prevailing societal circumstances. Altruism, as a value, may be more influential within the family circle than in relationships with strangers, and it may also be more widely and strongly held during times of war than in peace time.

Government policies are rarely based on unadulterated absolute values. More often than not, they reflect specific value mixes in which seemingly contradictory values coexist, although to different degrees. This is not to underestimate the importance of specific values to policy making but to point out that the value shifts that are necessary for the pursuit of different policies are not as impossible as may first appear. With this in mind, value shifts are necessary in at least six areas for the pursuit of a sustainable society.

First, the long standing ideological debate over the relative importance of rights versus duties seems sterile today. It needs to give way to a more pragmatic approach that recognizes the importance of both and concentrates on the relative balance between them. For two or three decades after the end of the Second World War, the emphasis was on guaranteeing people their economic and social rights. The Thatcher years changed the emphasis from rights to duties – from entitlements to responsibilities. If the emphasis on rights weakened individual responsibility, the stress on duties has undermined social cohesion because it has been used as an argument to restrict the public support that people need to fulfil their responsibilities.

The experience of the past fifty years suggests that a new public philosophy is needed that acknowledges the symbiotic relationship between rights and duties. People, as citizens, need to accept that the satisfaction of their rights presupposes the fulfilment of their duties and vice versa. What little evidence there is on this issue suggests that this is not always so. Etzioni quotes a study showing that young Americans expect to be tried before a jury of their peers – their right – but are at the same time reluctant to serve on a jury – their duty (Etzioni, 1995, p. 3). Several surveys in this country show that many respondents in public opinion studies feel strongly about the provision of high-quality social services but show far less enthusiasm for paying the taxes that are required to finance the services. Excessive emphasis on rights can exacerbate conflicts in society; similarly, too much stress on duties can ignore people's needs for the resources to fulfil them. Self-respect is built, in part, on the belief that one has rights. To gain and preserve self-respect, and to gain the respect of others, one must perform the duties expected of a citizen. What is at issue is the appropriate balance between rights and duties in different situations and between different groups in society. It is a principle that is difficult to translate into practical policy measures, but it is fundamental to further social and economic progress.

Second, the heated political debate surrounding the relative advantages of public or private provision has also run its course as it is now generally acknowledged that neither is intrinsically superior to the other. Both have their strengths and weaknesses, and they merge into each other rather than being two diametrically opposed forms of enterprise or service provision.

There is now ample evidence from British experience that nationalized industries, public utilities and social services run the risk of being excessively bureaucratic, overdominated by professional interests, inefficient and insensitive to the wishes of their users. There is no iron law that makes public services inherently prone to these weaknesses, but the risk is a possibility and steps have to be taken to guard against it. Conversely, there is firm evidence that private provision, particularly when unregulated by government, can become overdominated by the pursuit of profit, by short termism, responsive to wants rather than to needs, restricting supply in order to maintain prices and profits, and ignoring any notion of the common good. They can, as Pierson puts it, be 'corrosive of those forms of sociability and communality upon which a truly socialist society can be built' (Pierson, 1995, p. 124) – and the same is true of a truly sustainable society.

The emerging consensus sees different forms and degrees of private and public provision as necessary in contemporary society and sees the state not only as provider, but also as regulator, planner and financier. The Thatcherite view that governments are overbearing and inefficient while markets are unobtrusive, dynamic and efficient has done considerable damage to the economic, political and social fabric of British society. Markets may be better than the state in profit making, but they are grossly inadequate in providing essential public services for all. Governments require markets if they are to run the economy on a day-to-day basis but markets need governments to provide the necessary framework of law, a stable currency, a guarantee of social and political stability and the necessary infrastructure. The view that individual choices can only be satisfied through the market is a caricature of a far more complex situation. For many situations, this may be true, but equally, for many people in many other situations, 'individual choices depend on collective provision, support and regulation' (Blackstone *et al.*, 1992, p. 3).

Third, a better-educated, more mature and more articulate electorate has a lot to offer to decision making at the local level of service provision as well as in the workplace. Public participation is a troublesome concept to operationalize but, if well implemented, is of great value to effective service provision and to society in more general ways. Democracy must mean more than just casting a vote every five years. As Tawney pointed out many years ago, 'Democracy is unstable as a political system as long as it remains a political system and nothing more, instead of being, as it should be, not only a form of government, but a type of society' (quoted in Castle, 1994, p. 180). More recently, the same case was made by Taylor: 'The case for making individuals count, by providing more information, education and the means of participation is wholly irrefutable' (Taylor, 1992, p. 104).

If public participation is to be made a reality, a change is needed in the traditional dominant ideology that the professional or the expert always knows best and that public or user participation runs counter to efficiency. There are situations in which public participation can slow the decision-making process down but without leading to better decisions. But, overall, there are more situations in which the opposite can be the case – public participation preventing the wrong decisions being taken, enhancing the quality of services or improving productivity to the benefit of all in society.

The notion of participation is related to the notion of procedural rights. People have a right to be treated in certain ways that are considered fair and that are laid down in enforceable regulations. This notion has found partial expression in such recent developments as the idea of social charters, which, despite their many problems, are a way of empowering the individual and making the organization and the professional more accountable. It is an approach that is different from some strands of the New Right philosophy which claim that only private provision can provide freedom and fairness to the public, as well as from some strands of the Fabian tradition that have implicitly maintained that the professional knows best. Administrative procedures are not neutral technical issues. The way in which they are pursued can either empower or disempower people. Procedural rights are not only good in themselves, but also ensure that the citizen is treated fairly and can have a positive influence on the quality of service outcomes (Galligan, 1992).

Fourth, a greater public acceptance of the primary importance of the collective good is vital for a sustainable society. 'Our society', says Etzioni, 'is suffering from a severe case of deficient me-ness' (Etzioni, 1995, p. 25). Too many people on too many occasions put their own interests above those of the rest of society. This is not to suggest that individuals must always sacrifice their own welfare for the good of the community but instead that they need to accept the fact that there are situations in which this is necessary and right, and that the number of such situations may well increase in the future. The recent influence of New Right philosophy that extols aggressive individualism has obscured the fact that a long tradition in political thought has argued that this type of individualism is a threat to social order and stability (see, for example, Lukes, 1973, pp. 195–9).

A better balance between aggressive individualism and communitarianism can be facilitated by governments policies. Most people accept that behaviour damaging to the environment ought to be avoided, but unless there is an adequate public transport system, most people will continue to use their cars in environmentally unfriendly ways. There is evidence, however, showing that the public is beginning to accept the importance of the common good. Every year, the UK Henley Centre asks people whether they think that society does best when people look after their own interests or when society acts collectively. The proportions of people supporting each option did not change much from the mid 1980s until the mid 1990s, but the 1996 figures tell a very different story. Those believing in collective action now number 70 per cent, and the individualists have shrunk to 30 per cent (*Guardian*, 1 February 1997). As Wright puts it, 'We have become less of a community and want to become more of a community' (Wright, 1997, p. 103).

Perhaps the best evidence for the public's support of a communitarian spirit is the general acceptance of an adequate and fair personal taxation system. Many of the government's policies stand or fall on the availability of financial resources. Even the reduction of unemployment is as much a political as an economic problem. As the report of the Council of Churches for Britain and Ireland aptly put it, 'We see paying taxes as a contribution to the common good, which people should make without resentment' (Council of Churches for Britain and Ireland, 1997, p. 9).

Fifth, the claim that maximum levels of inequality in rewards are essential to efficiency, hard work and economic growth is, as Chapter 5 argued, not supported by empirical evidence. For a sustainable society, a more egalitarian ethic is needed that accepts moderate degrees of inequality and, at the same time, fosters policies that are designed to ensure an adequate minimum income for all. Such an ethic will both encourage incentives as well as reduce the heavy social costs to individuals, families and communities engendered by the current ethic of absolute inequality of rewards. As Hattersley has argued, such a distributional principle is both possible and beneficial to society:

> A fairer distribution of the nation's resources would reduce not crush differences. That is no more difficult to achieve – and no more in conflict with the natural order of things – than to organize society and distributive resources in a way which promotes inequality. (Hattersley, 1987, p. 41)

Sixth, the definition of welfare in economic terms alone is inadequate for capturing the quality of life in today's world. Social stability, an absence of crime and disorder, and a clean environment are essential parts of the quality of life and should be included in the calculation of welfare at the individual and national levels. The non-material aspects of life become more important as material needs are met. Moreover, it makes no sense to consider environmental degradation or crime as increasing our welfare simply because they provide work and thus increase the national GDP. Acceptance of this new approach to measuring welfare can encourage people to support public policies that appear initially to be either contrary to, or irrelevant to, their immediate economic welfare. What is needed is a composite – rather than unitary – measurement of welfare. Income, environment, health, crime and so on are important indicators of welfare, and there is no good reason why they should be subsumed under one indicator. As Jacobs has argued:

> It is much better that the changes in the different indicators are out in the open, where they can be seen. We can all then make our own judgements on whether any given change from one year to another represents progress or not; and economic policy can be decided accordingly. (Jacobs, 1991, p. 241)

Policy Proposals for a Sustainable Society

The policy proposals outlined below for a sustainable society are informed by the value principles sketched out above. Inevitably, reform proposals are ideological – they reflect the authors' understanding of the problems, their perception of the causes of these problems and their vision of a good society. All visions of a good society, whether expressed in technical or non-technical language, are ideological – they depend on the values and beliefs of their protagonists irrespective of whether this is openly stated or simply implied.

A Modern, Full-employment Society

One of the main conclusions of Chapter 2 was that the traditional pattern of full-time full employment is no longer viable, but full employment with reduced hours of work, with sabbaticals, with work sharing and with a wider definition of work to include caring can be achieved. The following principles, combining features from both the conventional and the radical approach, are offered as guidelines for the achievement of a modern full-employment society.

First, neither a totally free market nor a centrally planned economy has any future. As Hain puts it, 'if the command economics of state socialism is obsolete, so too is free market capitalism' (Hain, 1995, p. 119). The experience of the Soviet Union and of Thatcherite policies in the UK provides the clearest evidence that what is needed is a mixed economy, with the government playing a significant role in strategic long-term planning and in the regulation of the economy, but with little in the way of public ownership, the private sector remaining responsible for most day-to-day activity and also being involved in long-term planning. It is a partnership between state and private industry, each with separate roles albeit merging into each other.

Second, while it is true that no one single economic policy by itself can deliver a modern full-employment society, it is also true that relying on traditional employment policies will be as futile in the future as it has been in the recent past in achieving full employment. Somehow governments, employers and trade unions need to agree on employment policies that reduce the hours of work in order to create more jobs; policies that create more jobs in the state and voluntary sector for social and community care as well as for environmental purposes; job sharing schemes; regional and local policies that reduce the mismatch between jobs and labour availability; and more emphasis on education and training for all throughout people's working lives.

Third, there is an urgent need to pay as much attention to the quality of the work environment as to creating more jobs. This makes sense not only from the workers' point of view and that of their families, but also from that of the employers as a good working environment can reduce absenteeism and sickness absence and can be conducive to good motivation and higher productivity. Work insecurity and unsocial hours will always exist, but they can be mitigated through explicit agreements between management and workers on their mutual rights and responsibilities.

Fourth, the achievement of a modern full-employment society requires changes not only in policies and practices, but also in attitudes among all sections of the community, particularly among employers and trade unions, that a less inegalitarian and more socially cohesive society improves the welfare, broadly defined, of all its members. While statutory wages policies are unenforceable, a freely entered into broadly based policy to promote less adversarial industrial relations stands a better chance of success. This implies some form of worker involvement in the decisions affecting their employment as well as an expectation by employers that wage demands will not exceed the firm's ability to pay, bearing in mind the need both to invest for the future and to pay dividends to its shareholders.

Fifth, a modern policy of full employment stands a better chance of success if it is adopted by all EU member countries than by only some of them. It will make social dumping, capital flight and company tax evasion more difficult in the modern globalized world of work. By pooling their powers, governments are in a better position to withstand the pressures from multinational enterprises, which are increasingly demanding deregulated economies, tax concessions and low labour costs.

Finally, any radical programme for a full-employment society can only be implemented gradually and unevenly. This has always been accepted, even by the most radical of reformers. Reflecting on his own radical proposals, Handy commented that 'we shall probably, in the end, muddle towards a compromise blend' of the various ways of creating and sharing jobs (Handy, 1984, p. 185).

The choice facing industrial societies today is between two types of work sharing: the largely unmanaged, unplanned operation of the labour market leading to part-time work, contract work, insecure work, early retirement and unemployment; or the methods outlined above. A return to traditional full-time full employment is no longer an option. Neither is the *status quo*, which generates an inequitable and unsustainable situation. It is important that British society moves forward into a new world of work.

Sustainable Families

It is now widely accepted that, in Prime Minister Tony Blair's words, 'Families are the core of our society but they are under pressure' (Department for Education and Employment, 1998, p. 2). The six proposals outlined below grow out of this realization.

First, a new relationship between state and families has to be forged. The state needs families, and families need the state. The state needs to adopt a positive, proactive stance shaped by a concern and commitment to support families in the performance of their key roles – socializing the next generation, caring for the dependent, providing for the emotional needs of members. A minimalist approach concerned only for families deemed to be 'at risk' is no longer adequate. The focus of policy has to be on all families – and it has to be broad – with what families need to function effectively. This new commitment by the state to a bold, broad sphere of family-focused activity is the crucial basis for more specific policies.

Second, this commitment to a vigorous, proactive families' policy has to be institutionalized by government. There have to be institutions and mechanisms to make sure that aspirations get translated into policies, that policies get implemented and that the impact of all government policies on families gets evaluated and registered. There is no easy guaranteed way of achieving this. Tacking responsibility for family policies on to other ministerial responsibilities is a sure recipe for neglect – ministers will always give first attention to their departmental responsibilities. Creating a separate ministry is also unlikely to work. Experience makes it very plain that ministers without departments count for little at Westminster or in Whitehall.

A vigorously independent Commission for Families, with membership drawn from all types of family and household, appears to be the best way forward. Obviously such a suggestion is not unproblematic. The key issue is how to ensure that such a body remains independent and critical – a terrier rather than a poodle – and is not colonized and corrupted by the appointment of docile yes-persons or government trusties. That cannot be guarded against completely, but membership could be specified in ways which would do something to guarantee a radical, critical independence. It would obviously need courage for a government to appoint a Commission whose job it is to call government to account, but that is what is required. Such a Commission would receive Family Impact Statements on their policies from other government departments and would make Family Impact Analyses. It would produce annual reports and would have the right to report to Parliament on any issue affecting families that it regarded as important. A possible alternative to such a Commission for Families would be a Standing Select Committee of the House of Commons supported by a strong secretariat.

Third, the focus of government policy for families must be on families in all their contemporary diversity, so its primary focus must be on family functions rather than on supporting particular family structures – with what good families do and should do rather than with the assumed structure and shape of good families. Given such a focus on functions, the key concern has to be on parenting, children and broader caring responsibilities. Policies have to be developed and directed towards helping parents to be good parents and helping children to get as good a start in life as possible, preventing the disadvantages and deprivations that currently arise from particular family structures.

Where the concern is families with children, the primary focus must be on parenting, on enabling parents to be good parents, which has very clear and specific policy implications in terms of work, income, day care and the general support and services provided through the proposed families, children and young person's service.

Fourth, policies to help parents to reconcile the competing, and often conflicting, demands of work and family life are central to a policy for families. There must be policies that allow parents with young children a genuine choice between full-time work and access to appropriate day care, and part-time work with an adequate income. As the Labour government's *Meeting the Child Care Challenge* put it, 'Families must be given genuine choices: to look after their children full time, or to combine work, education or training with parenting in a balanced way' (Department of Education and Employment, 1998, para. ES2).

Policies to make such a reconciliation possible require four elements – appropriate and affordable day care available to all those who need it; a legally guaranteed right for all parents to limit their hours of work or to work part time if they so wish when their children are young, and then subsequently to return to full time employment; rights to a given number of days of parental leave for child care purposes; and a guarantee of an income adequate for the bringing up of children.

Fairness at Work promises an extension of maternity leave to eighteen weeks and implements the EU Parental Leave Directive, which provides three months unpaid leave for both men and women to be taken in a child's early years with protection from loss of job. It also provides for time off for urgent family reasons (Department of Trade and Industry, 1998, pp. 32–3).

Fifth, family and child poverty have to be tackled and abolished. One third of children are being brought up in poverty in Britain simply because governments have lacked the courage and initiative to face the problem and its implications. Solving the problem is not difficult – and it is only seen as expensive because it is so much easier to calculate the costs of action than the costs of inaction. The official view is that the new Working Families Tax Credit 'will substantially raise the incomes of working families' (Department of Education and Employment, 1998, para. ES1).

The policies needed to abolish family and child poverty need to be rooted in policies to restore full employment (as defined in Chapter 2), the provision of day care services that allow women with young children to engage in paid work, a guaranteed minimum wage and a system of child benefit that makes a realistic contribution to the costs of children.

Sixth, there must be policies directed at the particular needs and disadvantages of lone parent families. Policies directed at helping lone parents to get back to work – given impetus by the Labour government's 'New Deal' for lone parents – are necessary and desirable, but far from sufficient. Policies must be based on the principle of choice – that lone parents have the right and responsibility to decide what feels best for them and their children in terms of full-time work, part-time work or full-time child care at different stages. What is needed are (1) policies that ensure them an adequate income whatever the balance of paid work and caring they adopt, and (2) policies that enable them to take up paid employment if that is what seems best to them. Few lone parents want to depend long term on state benefits. Many, however, see staying at home to care for their young children as the right course of action when children are very young – as would majority opinion in the UK.

What is needed are policies guaranteeing a sufficient income to avoid the gross deprivations such families currently suffer and policies encouraging and supporting a move from benefits to paid employment as children grow older. What are quite inappropriate are policies that pressurize lone parents to return to work, or policies that accept benefit dependence and provide none of the services such parents need if they are to enter or re-enter paid work. What is needed are sensitive and balanced policies.

A Sustainable Environment

There is now general agreement that the quality of the environment is so central to the welfare of people everywhere that every effort needs to be made to preserve and improve it. Disagreements, however, run deep on how serious the threat to the environment is from current ways of living. This very fundamentally affects the kinds of proposal made to protect the environment. The proposals made in this section are based on the belief that the threat to the environment from current industrial lifestyles is serious enough to warrant wide-ranging and radical policies at the individual, local, national and international levels. It is an approach similar to that of the Brundtland report.

First, economic growth is essential to human welfare. It should, however, be pursued in environmentally friendly ways, and its fruits should be more equally distributed than at present. This means redistributive measures both within and between nations so that subsistence poverty can be abolished. Balanced social and economic development rather than simply economic growth should be the guiding principle for achieving a sustainable environment.

Second, while the debate around the 'limits to growth' issue remains unresolved, it is a matter of prudence that non-renewable resources should be used with care, that greater use should be made of renewable resources and that a reduction in environmentally damaging waste disposal should be vigorously pursued. The technology now exists for far greater reliance on energy from the sun, wind and water. This type of energy is less polluting than fossil or nuclear energy, it is, or will be, no more expensive and it is renewable. There are ample examples of how the problems of waste disposal could be reduced and disposal carried out in ways that do not harm the environment providing governments, local authorities and the public accept it as a worthwhile policy.

Third, even motoring organizations acknowledge that the car is the worst environmental polluter today. While pollution from many other sources has declined, pollution from cars has risen despite the fact that new cars are less polluting than old ones. There are more cars on the road and greater use is made of them today than before, with the result that total pollution has risen. There is the technology to produce cars with minimum emissions, but the price would supposedly be prohibitive for the manufacture of such cars. No doubt the search for such a car will continue, but there is an equally urgent need to improve public transport and encourage the public to walk short-distance journies. As the Royal Commission put it, 'For national sustainability goals to be met, transport in the UK must be radically modified'(Royal Commission on Environmental Pollution, 1997, p. 105).

Governments are beginning to accept that the traditional transport policy of constantly undertaking more road building to accommodate the car is unsustainable and a new policy is needed that involves greater use of public transport and less use of the car. So far, governments in Britain have found it impossible to implement policies that incorporate this approach, partly because of cost implications and partly because of opposition from vested interests.

Fourth, despite some progress in some areas in recent years, industry needs to improve its overall performance *vis-à-vis* the environment. Although this will not be easy, it is not a futile endeavour either, as the deep ecologists have argued over the years. It is possible to combine profitability with environmental concerns, particularly if governments legislate in order to create a level playing field among firms both in the same country and between countries. In agriculture, consumer demand for organically produced food is quite strong in the light of recent human disasters following intensive farming. It is clearly not possible, and perhaps not necessary, totally to replace intensive with organic farming because of price costs and the demand for food. Even a modest reduction in the scope and excesses of intensive farming will be a welcome step in the right direction.

Fifth, it is generally accepted that low-income people and their neighbour-hoods suffer the most from environmental pollution. Discussion about the environment in terms of the atmosphere, the forests, the oceans and biodiversity rings hollow to those who are homeless, overcrowded or live in run-down districts. 'To bring a decent home within the reach of every family' (Department of the Environment, 1997a, p. 19) is, therefore, a top priority if large sections of the community are to be convinced about the realities of the dangers to the less immediate aspects of the environment. In addition, there is now enough knowledge and technology to build greener housing that is weather tight, more energy efficient and less polluting than at present.

Sixth, progress towards a sustainable environment depends on changes in the public's values and attitudes, a process that is bound to be slow, erratic and full of disappointments. There is considerable evidence that people can gradually adapt their values both through fear and hope – the realization that the changed situation requires new approaches without unduly threatening their livelihood and preferably with conferring some benefits. Changes in public values and practices towards the environment have already begun, although they all belong to the Light Green type of environmentalism – the acceptance of recycling, of solar energy, of animal and bird protection, of organic farm production and so on. It is changes in the more fundamental values that will prove more difficult to achieve – acceptance of the necessity for some reductions in consumerism in affluent countries, abolition of poverty at the national and global levels and so on.

Seventh, the government's role is crucial in the progress towards a sustainable environment. All political parties in the UK accept that environmentally friendly policies are necessary, although they differ on the interpretation of what this actually means. Governments so far have preferred the use of regulations and financial incentives as instruments of environmental policies as these involve little public expenditure. Such policies, however, are not by themselves sufficient to protect and improve the environment apart from the fact that they can also have the disadvantage of making the poor poorer, as in the case of raising taxes on energy in order to reduce consumption. Public expenditure for environmental purposes is therefore necessary, particularly if environmental targets are to be set and enforced. Without such targets, progress towards a sustainable environment becomes both haphazard and fanciful. As Jacobs puts it when concluding his discussion on this issue:

> Unless government expenditure is allowed to cushion the effects of environmental change, a policy of sustainability is likely to find itself defeated before it is even attempted. (Jacobs, 1991, p. 163)

Unless we pursue the goal of a sustainable environment, we cannot achieve the broader goal of a sustainable society.

The Abolition of Poverty

Whether poverty is defined in subsistence or social participation terms, whether it is viewed in strictly monetary or broader terms, government data show that it increased during the 1980s and 90s. Some of the reasons for this growth were beyond government control, but others were of governments' own making. Poverty in affluent societies is both morally unacceptable and economically destructive to individuals, communities and the whole society. Chapter 5 outlined both the conventional and the radical approaches to poverty eradication. The proposals made here draw from both traditions as they overlap and both have something useful to say.

First, it has to be acknowledged that the free market by itself never solves the problem of poverty. Markets create wealth and raise general standards of living, but they always leave behind several sections of the population in poverty. Only state action can ensure that those left behind by rising affluence can be lifted out of poverty. Without state action, poverty and affluence can coexist, sometimes in open conflict, sometimes in muted indifference but never in open harmony.

Second, the various population groups in poverty include people at work, people out of work and the retired. Poverty afflicts people of all age groups, marital statuses and ethnic backgrounds as well as men and women. For these reasons, policies to abolish poverty need to be wide ranging: they include education, employment, training, pay, housing, fiscal and social security policies.

Third, full employment of the kind outlined above is the cornerstone of all attempts to abolish poverty and reduce excessive inequalities. Large-scale unemployment, on the one hand, reduces the wealth of the country and the government's ability to finance services, while on the other increasing the demand for services in addition to its alienating effects on individuals and communities. In brief, full employment is a necessary, although not a sufficient, prerequisite for the abolition of poverty.

Fourth, affordable child care facilities are essential to full employment and to the abolition of poverty in contemporary labour markets where a rising proportion of both parents is at work. The role of schools should also be re-examined to find ways in which they can adapt 'to the needs of parents as well as children' (Piachaud, 1993, p. 10). The UK lags behind most other EC member countries in the provision of pre-school care facilities, and this needs to be rectified through the provision of allowances to parents, vouchers or the direct state provision of nursery facilities. Taking steps to help both parents to engage in paid employment can be a major way to help them and their children to avoid poverty.

Fifth, enabling more parents to work has to be accompanied by pay policies ensuring that the problem of low pay is resolved. Low pay at work is not the result simply of the educational, ethnic, gender or motivational characteristics of individuals. As Chapter 2 pointed out, it is also the result of structural factors relating to the nature of the labour market where low-paid jobs are seen as essential to profitability irrespective of the personal characteristics of workers. It is, therefore, necessary to introduce a minimum wage and adequate child benefits to abolish both low pay and family poverty. As the Low Pay Commission put it, 'Poverty wages cannot encourage people to move from benefits to work. Such wage levels encourage feelings of detachment and alienation' (Low Pay Commission, 1998, p. 160). For this to succeed, trade unions will have to abandon their traditional policy of fighting to preserve wage differentials, which is partly responsible for the fact that the gap between the low paid and other workers remained pretty constant for about a century up to the 1970s, after which it widened further (Gosling *et al.*, 1994, p. 3).

Sixth, public housing policy has been neglected in recent years because of the excessive emphasis on private home ownership. Private ownership of housing has an important role to play in the achievement of the sustainable society but so, too, does public housing. The years of discrimination against public and cooperative housing must be ended, and public authorities should be allowed to use their resources to expand both these types of housing. A vigorous initiative is needed to avoid homelessness and to end the proliferation of housing estates where civilized living has become endangered by alienation, decay, unemployment and crime. Recent government initiatives suggest that the Labour government is beginning to accept the necessity of action in this area in its New Deal for Communities.

Seventh, tax policies in the 1980s played a significant part in the growth of poverty and the widening of inequalities. Direct personal taxation rates have been drastically reduced, and an increasing proportion of government revenues has been raised through indirect taxation, which weighs more heavily on low incomes. The pendulum has swung far too much in the inegalitarian direction and needs to be corrected by a modest rise in personal taxation, for example to a higher rate of 50 per cent, to enable the government to raise adequate funds for the public services without endangering work incentives. Also, loopholes for corporate taxes and wealth taxes should be closed as they are at present unacceptably wide (Ryan, 1994). It is true that the forces of globalization militate against such a policy, and, although governments cannot ignore them completely, they need not be totally subservient to them either.

Eighth, social security is the second, and equally important, line of attack on poverty. So far, it has had a measure of success in alleviating poverty, but it has also failed in several important ways. Chapter 5 outlined the various radical social security approaches that have been put forward in an attempt to deal with poverty. They all have their strengths and weaknesses, and the choice between them depends, in the final analysis, on the kind of society that is envisaged. A sustainable society implies that the abolition of poverty should be pursued in ways that encourage self-respect, that minimize stigmatization and that maximize social cohesion in society. This means that large-scale means testing, whether the incremental, random ways pursued by governments in the UK since 1979, or the wholesale approach of the Negative Income Tax scheme, is unacceptable. The BIG scheme abolishes poverty in a socially acceptable and cohesive way, but its costs are too high and its ethos is rather alien to contemporary British society. Its central idea involves no explicit reciprocity, and the report of the Council of Churches for Britain and Ireland correctly observed that 'we have to ask whether a separation between income and work for some people along these lines is actually what we would like to see achieved' (Council of Churches for Britain and Ireland, 1997, p. 77). It is also for this same reason that some of its supporters have made it conditional on a national scheme of community service. Thus, the proposals made here approximate to the BAOR approach, although the two differ in three important respects.

In the first place, the social security proposals put forward here envisage a broad definition of work. This means that caring for children or adults at home constitutes work and should be treated as such for wage and social security purposes. In the second place, part-time work and self-employment should be covered by social security in a comprehensive way rather than patchily and inadequately as at present. In the third place, although the scheme should be financed out of social security contributions as at present, the contribution record should not be taken into account in deciding benefit eligibility. What matters is whether the person falls into any of the categories recognized by the state as meriting social security support.

Benefits should be earnings related, amounting to half pay for those on average incomes; more than half pay for those on lower incomes; and less than half for those with higher incomes. There will inevitably still be a need for means-tested benefits, but their role will be limited. Equally importantly, the level of means-tested benefits should be based on a new calculation of poverty that takes account of the living and consumption standards of the 1990s as the current assistance benefit levels reflect the way of life of the 1940s and do not abolish poverty (Bradshaw, 1993a).

Ninth, beyond the generous, universal benefit scheme for all as defined above, it is the responsibility of individuals to make more substantial arrangements for themselves, either through the work place or privately. These provisions, however, should be neither necessary nor compulsory for those who either cannot or do not want to embark on such schemes and who prefer to rely on an already satisfactory state scheme.

Although the proposals put forward here for the reduction of poverty involve both the state and the market, it has to be acknowledged that the two play rather different roles. The market's dominant role is to increase productivity, economic growth and profitability; it is the state's role to ensure that the fruits of economic growth trickle down to all in order to abolish poverty and reduce social division.

Sustainable Law and Order

There is no need to argue the case for seeing crime as a significant social problem that threatens society's sustainability. One serious recorded offence for every ten members of society – men, women and children – is a sufficient ground for concern, as is the contrast between crime rates now and crime rates a mere ten years ago. Crime obviously threatens the sustainability of society. What then is to be done?

First, the focus of law and order must be society and the promotion and maintenance of order rather than offenders and law-breaking behaviour. Our society is very clearly criminogenic: aspects of its nature and culture generate crime – or at least fail to inhibit it as they did in the past. The focus of law and order policy must, therefore, be on society and the promotion of orderly, law-regarding behaviour rather than on law-breaking behaviour. That priority leads to a broader conceptualization of law and order policy. It must be concerned with the effective socialization of the next generation and thus with families, pre-school education, the nature of the educational experience offered to children, the transition to work, employment opportunities and what it means to be young and male and black in late twentieth-century society.

Second, following logically from an order-promoting strategy must be a vigorous emphasis on crime prevention broadly conceived. Speaking on the forthcoming Crime and Disorder Bill, the Home Secretary said that the Bill 'will make it clear for the first time that the principal aim of the youth justice system is to prevent offending by young people' (Parliamentary Debates 301 c. 77). Situational crime prevention clearly has a place in any anti-crime strategy, but genuine crime prevention has to move on to develop a broader social model embracing a range of policies and activities. The local authority has to take a lead role, defining crime prevention as a key thread in all its policies – in education, in housing policies and housing management, in training and employment creation, in youth provision and in work with families.

This means coordinated work across and between different local authority departments. It also requires a partnership between the local authority and key elements in the criminal justice system. The Youth Offender Teams set up under the Crime and Disorder Act reflect this new concern for coordination, but they seem likely to remain essentially reactive and *post hoc* rather than genuinely preventive in their orientation. Obviously, too, the police have a key role to play in a preventive approach because of their local knowledge, expertise, resources and standing as the most visible manifestation of society's concern for order.

Genuine prevention involves situational prevention and the adoption of a broader social model of prevention, which will occupy the policy and practice space between situational prevention and the social order-promoting strategies sketched in the first point above.

Third, intervention has to be focused – because of what we know about patterns of crime and the nature of offenders. We know that certain areas – usually the poorest urban areas – show extraordinarily heavy concentrations of crime. We know, too, that young men dominate the criminal statistics. Policy needs to respond to these known facts. Of course, we need general policies directed to the promotion of order, but we also need policies and strategies that target the 'hot spots', tackle the chronic social problems and service deficiencies that so often afflict such areas, and aim to rebuild the fabric of civil society.

There may be a case, in the short term, in such areas for policies of 'zero tolerance' or for imposing curfews on young people, but such approaches only tackle the outward manifestations of disorder rather than its roots – even though this may give a harassed local community a much-needed breathing space from endemic disorder. What is really required is a broader, holistic strategy for community development and the economic and social integration and reintegration of young men.

Fourth, the youth justice system clearly need reform and rationalization – if not revolution! *Misspent Youth* presented a chilling indictment of an expensive, inefficient and ineffective system (Audit Commission, 1996a, Chapter 1). The Crime and Disorder Act created the Youth Justice Board to chase reform through the system and bang a few heads together. The sorts of delay and mismanagement exposed by the Audit Commission are, clearly, totally unacceptable, but the problems are actually more fundamental than the charges that the Commission levelled.

The basic problem is simply that we do not know what can be done to turn law-breaking offenders into law-abiding citizens. We lack the answer to this basic and central question. Improving the speed and throughput of the courts and so on is all very well, but it is really peripheral as long as the ways in which we eventually dispose of offenders are so ineffective.

What is needed is radical and creative thinking on new methods of dealing with today's offenders and the production of a synthesis of radical experiments on the lines of the Home Office's *Reducing Offending*, with an analysis of what seems to work, with whom and when. Then, we need further experiment so that we build up a bank of expertise on the potential and actual success of different radical methods. For example, there is interesting evidence of the promising nature of schemes that confront offenders with their victims, for example the Thames Valley Police's pilot scheme in restorative justice (*Guardian Weekly*, 26 October 1997). There are hints of government's acceptance of this line of thinking in the expressed determination 'to reinforce responsibility of young offenders and their parents for their delinquent behaviour' and the idea of reparation orders (Home Office, 1997b, p. 12, 14). There is also the very interesting and promising work on 're-integrative shaming'. As a society, we have essentially continued to recycle old established methods of dealing with offenders when the methods have long proved to be of little value, apart from keeping offenders off the streets. The need now is to think more radically and creatively using different sociological and psychological assumptions.

Fifth, there must be radical changes in police practice – in the sexism and racism that still disfigure police practice and reputation – but also more generally in concepts of policing and the use of police resources. The police need to be firmly integrated into the local authority's crime prevention strategies, their work needs to be sharply focused in the light of analysis of crime activity patterns, and they need to reconceptualize their primary role as the maintenance of order rather than the apprehension of villains.

The police service is very expensive – and on all the available evidence – not effective. The police have to find a new role – in crime prevention, both situational and more generally, as a key resource in the planning and development of local authority order-promoting strategies and in the community development strategies that are needed in areas where crime is concentrated.

Crime threatens the sustainability of society in a variety of ways, as we saw in Chapter 6. It is a dominating concern for many of the poorest and most vulnerable people in society.

The Prospects for a Sustainable Society

Government planning is usually both pragmatic and incremental. Its vision of the future departs little from the present, while the reform process is *ad hoc* and incremental. Only in very exceptional circumstances is the vision radical and the reform process all embracing. Such a period was, perhaps, the immediate postwar era of the Labour government; the Thatcher years were radical in vision but mostly incremental in process. A radical vision and an all-embracing reform process presuppose a high degree of social consensus in a democracy. This rarely happens, and, when it does, it is usually in response to a real or perceived national crisis – be that economic, political, social or military. Radical ideas for alternative solutions to existing problems may come to be accepted at such times. It is, therefore, the responsibility of academics to advance solutions to society's ills that may seem impossible in normal times but which may become quite acceptable – and necessary – at times of national crisis.

It is a matter of opinion whether the vision of the policies required for a sustainable society outlined in this chapter is too radical or Utopian. Clearly, the view of the authors is that this is not the case – it is radical but not Utopian. Judgement depends on one's diagnosis of the seriousness and significance of the current problem of sustainability and on one's social values. Many of the proposals put forward here are being discussed by official bodies and can be found in the manifestos of social democratic political parties. The implementation possibilities naturally vary from one proposal to another, and they are far greater if viewed from a long-term perspective. It is worth remembering that much public provision – compulsory and free education, a NHS, retirement pensions and so on – which is taken for granted by the public today was considered impossible, extravagant or even foolish a hundred years ago; what is radical varies considerably from one generation to the next.

The implementation of any serious reform agenda is always constrained by a variety of factors. It could thus be argued that radical, let alone Utopian, agendas serve no useful policy purpose. On the other hand, however, it could be counterargued that over estimating the difficulties can lead to arid, pragmatic agendas that do not really tackle the serious challenges facing society.

Although all reforms meet with obstacles, this is obviously far more the case with radical rather than pragmatic reforms. The proposals for a sustainable society sketched out here are likely to meet a range of obstacles, although most of them do not appear insurmountable.

First, some of society's current dominant values run counter to the proposals advocated here. The dominant value of the economic merits of and necessity for inequality militates against some of the proposals on work, the environment and the abolition of poverty. The dominant value of aggressive individualism runs counter to the proposals on the family and law and order, yet these dominant values have always been challenged by counter values as well as by empirical evidence. As argued earlier in this chapter, a sustainable society has to recapture a sense of the salience of the common good, of individual and social responsibility and of participatory politics and management. At present, the balance between the two competing values is in favour of aggressive individualism and needs to be tilted more towards communitarianism if society is to hold together as a common enterprise.

Second, various interest groups will feel threatened by some of the reform proposals. The path to a sustainable environment may involve additional restrictions on motorists, the abolition of poverty and the reduction of inequality may well face opposition from the more affluent groups and so on. This is, of course, nothing new as most reforms have been resisted by entrenched interests. A sustainable society, however, involves many measures that are also to the benefit of a wide range of groups in society. In other words, there are no strong sectional interests in society that are totally threatened and that have nothing to gain from the reforms outlined in this book. Indeed, all groups in society stand to benefit from some of the reforms – a cleaner environment, law and order and even the abolition of subsistence poverty.

Third, there is the issue of resources, of whether society can afford the measures proposed in the book. Looking back at the history of welfare in this country, the two most expansive reform periods were the early 1900s and the immediate post-Second World War period – and these were not dominated by any lengthy discussions on cost and affordability. The country believed that the reforms were necessary and was willing to raise the necessary funds. It is a paradox that the issue of affordability is so dominant today when the country is so much more affluent. Rich countries possess the resources to implement the policies that they will politically. This is why countries with very similar levels of economic affluence can spend very different proportions of their GDP on welfare – compare the USA with Germany, Japan with

Sweden, the UK with France and so on. Affordability in affluent countries is far more a political than an economic issue.

Fourth, some of the reforms proposed in the book raise the issue of whether we possess enough knowledge to deal with the problems involved. How to reduce crime, how to improve child rearing and how to make the environment safer are such examples. This is a legitimate concern and applies to all reform proposals rather than just to those of this book. It is one of the arguments in favour of gradual reform, of experimentation and of monitoring. Doing nothing because of possible uncertainties about the effectiveness of reforms is no way forward. It is a recipe not only for stagnation but for further deterioration in the relevant problems. We accept that many of our proposals require testing and careful evaluation.

Fifth, limited administrative capacity is a further constraint on reform. Although the New Right view on the inevitable incompetence of government is not substantiated by evidence, there are situations in which the reach of governments can exceed their grasp. It is for this reason that partnerships between the various social actors – governments, communities, voluntary societies, users' groups and private business – can often be useful. Governments in pluralist societies need to marshal the administrative capacities of as many social actors as possible.

Sixth, electoral considerations always feature highly in the implementation of any reform programme. All governments want to be re-elected, and they are likely to shy away from implementing proposals that directly contravene the wishes of significant sections of the electorate. They may never adopt them in the first place, or, if they do, they will legislate at the beginning rather than the end of their term of office; they will implement them in a gradual way and a watered-down version. This applies to many reforms, including some of those proposed in this book.

Seventh, opposition to reform does not always reflect self-interest or group interests. Sometimes, opposition to reforms stems from the feeling that they are contrary to, or not in line with, traditional values or customs. It is a reluctance, or perhaps a conscious refusal, to accept that, because the world has changed, governments need to take that into account in their policies. Opposition to, for example, a generous treatment of lone parent families is sometimes the result of a strongly held belief in the importance of the two-parent family and hence the fear that such treatment may undermine cherished family values. The evidence may be dubious, but it does not deter opposition. Social scientific evidence on such complex issues as family cohesion is never robust enough to overcome hostility to measures that are perceived to be contrary to long established values. Governments and others, however, have a clear responsibility to lead.

Conclusions

There is clearly a problem – even if not a crisis – of sustainability in contemporary Britain. A wide range of problems damage society and threaten its future order and well being. There is no shortage of economically affordable and politically and administratively practicable policy proposals for tackling the problems. What is lacking, however, is confidence that the problems can be overcome and the will to confront them and experiment with the policy proposals on offer – be they conventional or radical.

The market experiment that was tried in Britain between 1979 and 1997 was a response to what was perceived to be a failure of state-led economic and social development. The market experiment failed to achieve its basic economic, social or political aims and ended in disarray. Markets may have lost favour – but so, too, have states. For an effective response to the problems we outline in this book, state action is clearly necessary. Equally clearly, it is insufficient for the achievement of sustainability.

An effective state depends on a strong economy, which depends in turn on an effective state–market partnership. It depends, too, on a substantial stock of social capital – norms of reciprocity, a sense of the common good, an ethic of public as well as individual responsibility and a general willingness to pay the taxes required to fund the economic and social services needed to ensure a sustainable society. The state has to facilitate the development of a healthy market economy, a strong civic culture, effective families and the values necessary to sustain social stability and the collective action on which sustainability depends.

The years between 1945 and the mid 1970s were the golden age of the state. Reaction was inevitable in the form of the market-led experiment. What is very clear now is that strong states and strong markets are both necessary and that they both depend on each other – as well as on a strong society. As Putnam puts it: 'Strong society, strong economy; strong society, strong state' (Putnam, 1993, p. 176).

What we have tried to provide in this book is an analysis of the nature of the problem of sustainability and a review of some of the complementary and competing policy options. The uncompromising message that we have tried to convey is that the problems we describe are systemic. They are not amenable to solution by gentle, piecemeal social engineering. What has to be forged is a new social order, a new way of managing the problems of economic and social life for a new century.

Bibliography

Addison, P. (1997) *The Road to 1945*, London, Cape.

Alderson, J. (1984) *Law and Disorder*, London, Hamish Hamilton.

Alexander, S. and Radford, T. (1994) 'Jobs uncertainty hits women hardest', *Guardian*, 6 September.

Amin, K., with Oppenheim, C. (1992) *Poverty in Black and White*, London, Child Poverty Action Group.

Anderson, M. (1994) 'Today's families in historical context'. Paper presented to the seminar on the History of the Family, organized by the Board for Social Responsibility of the Church of England and the Joseph Rowntree Foundation, York, February 1995.

Anderson, V. (1991) *Alternative Economic Indicators*, London, Routledge.

Anderson, V. (1993) *Energy Efficiency Policies*, London, Routledge.

Ashby, P. (1984) *Social Security After Beveridge – What Next?*, London, Bedford Square Press.

Audit Commission (1996a) *Misspent Youth*, London, Audit Commission.

Audit Commission (1996b) *Streetwise*, London, Audit Commission.

Barnett, A. (1998) 'Work hard, pay hard leaves the UK off the pace', *Observer*, 3 May.

Barnett, C. (1986) *The Audit of War*, London, Macmillan.

Barnett, C. (1995) *The Lost Victory*, London, Macmillan.

Basiago, A. (1995) 'Methods of defining "sustainability"', *Sustainable Development*, 3(3): 109–19.

Bassett, P. (1996) 'Decline of full-time work will continue', *The Times*, 29 October.

Bassett, P. (1997) 'Absent workers costing £13bn', *The Times*, 3 March.

Bastian, J. (1994) 'Work sharing: the reappearance of a timely idea', *Political Quarterly*, 65(3): 302–12.

Bayley, D.H. (1994) *Police for the Future*, New York, Oxford University Press.

Beck, B. (1998) 'Women and work', *Economist*, 18 July, pp. 1–17, special section.

Beck, U. (1992) *Risk Society*, London, Sage.

Beckerman, W. (1995) *Growth, the Environment and the Distribution of Income*, Aldershot, Elgar.

Beer, S. (1982) *Britain Against Itself*, London, Faber & Faber.

Bennett, T. (1994) 'Community policing on the ground', in Rosenbaum, D.P. (ed.) *The Challenge of Community Policing*, London, Sage.

Bentham, G. (1994) 'Global environmental change and health', in Phillips, D.R. and Verhasselt, Y. (eds), *Health and Development*, London, Routledge.

Beresford, P. and Croft, S. (1995) 'It's our problem too! Challenging the exclusion of poor people from poverty discourse', *Critical Social Policy*, 15(2/3): 75–95.

Berger, B. (1993). 'The bourgeois family and modern society', in Davies, J. (ed.) *The Family: Is It Just Another Life Style Choice?*, London, Institute of Economic Affairs.

Berthoud, R. and Kempson, E. (1992) *Credit and Debt*, London, Policy Studies Institute.

Bethune, A. (1997) 'Unemployment and mortality', in Drever, F. and Whitehead, M. (eds) *Health Inequalities*, London, Stationery Office.

Bhatti, M. (1996) 'Housing and environmental policy in the UK', *Policy and Politics*, 24(2): 159–70.

Bhatti, M., Brooke, J. and Gibson, M. (eds) (1994) *Housing and the Environment*, Coventry, Chartered Institute of Housing.

Blackstone, T., Cornford, J., Hewitt, P. and Miliband, D. (1992) *Next Left: An Agenda for the 1990s*, London, Institute for Public Policy Research.

Blowers, A. (ed.) (1993) *Planning for a Sustainable Environment*, London, Earthscan.

Blowers, A. (1995) 'Nuclear Waste Disposal', in Gray, T.S. (ed.) *U.K. Environmental Policy in the 1990s*, London, Macmillan.

Boissonnat, J. (1996) 'Combating unemployment, restructuring work: reflections on a French study', *International Labour Review*, **135**(1): 5–15.

Boltho, A. and Glyn, A. (1995) 'Can macroeconomic policies raise employment?', *International Labour Review*, **143**(4–5): 451–71.

Bowcott, O. (1998) 'How to make the rubbish go round' *Guardian*, 10 June.

Bowis, J. (1996) 'Opening address', in *Families and Parenting*, London, Family Policy Studies Centre.

Boyer, R. (1995) 'Wage austerity or/and an educational push: the French dilemma', *Labour*, special issue, pp. S19–S66.

Boyson, R. (1975) *Crisis in Education*, London, Woburn Press.

Boyson, R. (1995) *Speaking my Mind*, London, Peter Owen.

Bradshaw, J. (1993a) *Budget Standards for the United Kingdom*, Aldershot, Avebury/Ashgate.

Bradshaw, J. (1993b) 'Foreword', in Kumar, V., *Poverty and Inequality in the UK: The Effects on Children*, London, National Children's Bureau.

Bradshaw, J. (1997) 'Does Britain need a family policy?', in The Barbara Rodgers Memorial Lectures, Manchester, Department of Social Policy and Social Work, University of Manchester.

Bradshaw, J., Kennedy, S., Kilkey, S. *et al.* (1996) *The Employment of Lone Parents*, London, Family Policy Studies Centre.

Braithwaite, J. (1989) *Crime, Shame and Reintegration*, Cambridge, Cambridge University Press.

Braithwaite, J. (1993) 'Shame and modernity', *British Journal of Criminology*, **33**(1): 1–18.

Brake, M. and Hale, C. (1992) *Public Order and Private Lives*, London, Routledge.

Brayshaw, A.J. (1980) *Public Policy and Family Life*, London, Policy Studies Institute.

Brenner, H. (1980) 'Mortality and the national economy', *Lancet*, 15 September, pp. 568–73.

British Medical Association (1997) *Road transport and health*, London, BMA.

Brittan, S. (1975) 'The economic tensions of British democracy', in Tyrrell, R.E. (ed.) *The Future that Doesn't Work*, New York, Doubleday.

Brown, J. (1992). 'Which way for the family: choices for the 1990s', in Manning, N. and Page, R. (eds) *Social Policy Review 4*, Canterbury, Social Policy Association.

Brown, L.R. (ed.) (1990) *State of the World 1990*, London, Unwin Hyman.

Brown, L.R. (ed.) (1996) *State of the World 1996*, London, Earthscan.

Brown, L.R., Flavin, C. and Postel, S. (1990) 'Picturing a sustainable society', in Brown, L.R. (ed.) *State of the World 1990*, London, Unwin Hyman.

Brown, P. (1997) 'The Planet's hottest problem', *Guardian*, 10 October.

Buck, N. and Scott, J. (1994) 'Household and family change', in Buck, N., Gershuny, J., Rose, D. and Scott, J. (eds) (1994) *Changing Households: the British Households Panel Study 1990–1992*, Colchester, ESRC Research Centre on Micro Social Change.

Bunyard, P. and Morgan-Grenville, F. (eds) (1987) *The Green Alternative*, London, Methuen.

Bush, J. (1997) 'Keeping up UK allure', *Times*, 11 February.

Button, K. (1995) 'UK environmental policy and transport', in Gray, T.S. (ed.) *U.K. Environmental Policy in the 1990s*, London, Macmillan.

Cable, V. (1995) 'The diminished nation state', *Daedalus*, **124**(2): 23–53.

Campbell, B. (1993) *Goliath: Britain's Dangerous Places*, London, Methuen.

Cannan, C. (1992) *Changing Families, Changing Welfare*, Hemel Hempstead, Harvester.

Carter, M. (1995) *Out of Sight... London's Continuing Bed and Breakfast Crisis*, London, CHAR.

Casper, L. and McLanahan, S. (1994) 'The gender poverty gap: what we can learn from other countries', *American Sociological Review*, **59**(4): 594–605.

Castle, B. (1994) *Fighting All the Way*, London, Pan.

Cavadino, P. (1997) *Families and Crime*, London, NACRO.

Central Advisory Council for Education (1967) *Children and their Primary Schools* (Plowden report), London, HMSO.

Central Statistical Office (1996) *Social Trends No. 26*, London, HMSO.

Christie, I. (1994) 'Britain's sustainable development strategy', *Policy Studies*, **15**(3): 4–20.

Church House (1995) *Something to Celebrate*, London, Church House Publishing.

Clark, A.E. and Oswald, A.J. (1994) 'Unhappiness and unemployment', *Economic Journal* **104**: 648–59.

Clark, M., Burall, P. and Roberts, P. (1993) 'A sustainable economy', in Blowers, A. (ed.) *Planning for a Sustainable Environment*, London, Earthscan.

Cockett, M. and Tripp, J. (1994) *The Exeter Family Study: Family Breakdown and its Impact on Children*, Exeter, University of Exeter Press.

Cohen, R., Coxall, J., Craig, G. and Sadiq-Sangster, A. (1992) *Hardship Britain, Being Poor in the 1990s*, London, Child Poverty Action Group.

Commission on Social Justice (1994) *Social Justice*, London, Vintage.

Conservative Party (1994) *The Environment: Principles and Policies*, London, Conservative Central Office.

Conservative Central Office (1997) *You Can Only Be Sure with the Conservatives*, London, Conservative Central Office.

Conservative Research Department (1995) *The Economy: Policies for Enduring Prosperity*, London, Conservative Central Office.

Cook, D. (1997) *Poverty, Crime and Punishment*, London, Child Poverty Action Group.

Cooper, D. (1994) 'Making a meal of it', *Search 21*, Winter, pp. 5–8.

Coote, A. (1994) 'Introduction', in Coote A. (ed.) *Families Children and Crime*, London, Institute of Public Policy Research.

Corry, D. (1996) 'Hard times ahead? A Response to E.J. Mishan', *Political Quarterly*, **76**(2): 158–60.

Corry, D. and Glyn, A. (1994) 'The macroeconomics of equality, stability and growth', in Glyn, A. and Miliband, D. (eds) (1994) *Paying for Equality*, London, Rivers Oram Press.

Council of Churches for Britain and Ireland (1997) *Unemployment and the Future of Work*, London, Council of Churches for Britain and Ireland.

Craig, G. and Dowler, E. (1997) 'Let them eat cake! Hunger and the UK state', in Riches, G. (ed.) *First World Hunger*, London, Macmillan.

Crosland, A. (1971) *A Social Democratic Britain*, London, Fabian Society.

Cullingworth, J.B. and Nadin, V. (1994) *Town and Country Planning in Britain* (11th edn), London, Routledge.

Dahrendorf, R. (1985) *Law and Order*, London, Stevens.

David, M.E. (ed.) (1998) *The Fragmenting Family: Does it Matter?*, London, Institute of Economic Affairs.

Dean, H. (1994) 'Social security: the cost of persistent poverty', in George, V. and Miller, S. (eds) *Social Policy Towards 2000,* London, Routledge.

Dean, H. and Thompson, D. (1996) 'Fetishing the family: the construction of the informal carer', in Jones, H. and Millar, J. (eds) *The Politics of the Family*, Aldershot, Avebury.

Delsen, L. (1997) 'A new concept of full employment', *Economic and Industrial Democracy*, **18**(1): 119–35.

Dennis, N. and Erdos, G. (1993) *Families without Fatherhood*, London, Institute of Economic Affairs Health and Welfare Unit.

Department of Education and Employment (1998) *Working Families Tax Credit*, London, Stationery Office.

Department of Employment (1995) 'Ethnic groups and the labour market', *Employment Gazette*, June.

Department of Employment and Productivity (1969) *A National Minimum Wage*, London, HMSO.

Department of the Environment (1993) *English House Condition Survey 1991*, London, HMSO.

Department of the Environment (1997a) *Transport Statistics, GB*, London, Stationery Office.

Department of the Environment (1997b) *Annual Report 1997*, Cm 3607, London, HMSO.

Department of the Environment (1997c) *Digest of Environmental Statistics No. 19*, London, Stationery Office.

Department of Social Security (1996) *Households Below Average Income 1979–1993/94*, London, Stationery Office.

Department of Social Security (1997) *Households Below Average Income, a Statistical Analysis 1979–1994/95'*, London, Stationery Office.

Department of Social Security (1998) *Households Below Average Income 1979–1996/97*, London, Stationery Office.

Department of Trade and Industry (1998) *Fairness at Work*, Cm 3968, London, Stationery Office.

Derber, C. (1994) '*Communitarian economics: criticisms and suggestions from the Left*' Responsive Community, **4**(4): 29–43.

Deshormes La Valle, F. (ed.) (1987) *Women and Men of Europe*, Brussels, Commission of the European Community.

Ditch, J., Barnes, H., Bradshaw, J. *et al.* (1995) *A Synthesis of National Family Policies 1994*, York, European Observatory on National Family Policies, University of York.

Dobson, A. (1995) *Green Political Thought* (2nd edn), London, Routledge.

Dobson, B., Beardsworth, A., Keil, T. and Walker, R. (1994) *Diet, Choice and Poverty*, London, Family Policy Studies Centre.

Dorling, D. (1997) *Death in Britain: How Local Mortality Rates Have Changed: 1950s to 1990s*, York, Joseph Rowntree Foundation.

Dowds, L. and Ahrendt, D. (1995) 'Fear of crime', in Jowell, R., Curtice, J., Park, A. *et al.* (eds) *British Social Attitudes: The 12th Report*, Aldershot, Dartmouth.

Downes, D. (1995) 'Broken windows of opportunity: crime, inequality and employment', in Jones, H. and Lansley, J. (eds) *Social Policy and the City*, Aldershot, Avebury.

Downes, D. (1997) 'What the next government should do about crime', *Howard Journal*, 36(1): 1–13.

Downes, D. and Morgan, R. (1994) 'Hostages to fortune? The politics of law and order in postwar Britain', in Maguire, M., Morgan, R. and Reiner, R. (eds) *The Oxford Handbook of Criminology*, Oxford, Oxford University Press.

Eadie, M. (1997) 'Radiating energy', *Financial Times*, 18 September.

Economist (1997) *Election Briefing*, London, *Economist*.

Edwards, R. and Duncan, S. (1997) 'Supporting the family: lone mothers, paid work and the underclass debate', *Critical Social Policy*, 17(4): 29–49.

Edwards, R. and Tritter, J. (1993) *The Experience of Homeless Families in the Private Sector Leased Accommodation*, London, London Homeless Forum.

Elkington, J. (1987) *The Green Capitalists*, London, Gollancz.

Equal Opportunities Commission (1993) *Women and Men in Britain*, Manchester, Equal Opportunities Commission.

Esping-Andersen, G. and Korpi, W. (1984) 'Social policy as class politics in post war capitalism: Scandinavia, Austria and Germany', in Goldthorpe, J.H. (ed.) *Order and Conflict in Contemporary Capitalism*, Oxford, Clarendon Press.

Etzioni, A. (1995) *The Spirit of Community*, London, Fontana.

European Commission (1994) *Employment in Europe*, Brussels.

European Commission (1996) *Employment in Europe*, Brussels.

Fagan, C. (1996) 'Gendered time schedules: paid work in Britain', *Social Politics*, 3(1): 72–107.

Fagin, L. and Little, M. (1984) *The Forsaken Families*, Harmondsworth, Penguin.

Farrington, D.P. (1996) *Understanding and Preventing Youth Crime*, York, Joseph Rowntree Foundation.

Felson, M. (1994) *Crime and Everyday Life*, Thousand Oaks, CA, Pine Forge Press.

Ferri, E. and Smith, K. (1996) *Parenting in the 1990s*, London, Family Policy Studies Centre.

Field, F. (1996a) 'A rejoinder', in Deacon, A. (ed.) *Stakeholder Welfare*, London, Institute of Economic Affairs.

Field, F. (1996b) 'Making welfare work: the underlying principles', in Deacon, A. (ed.) *Stakeholder Welfare*, London, Institute of Economic Affairs.

Finch, J. (1989) *Family Obligations and Social Change*, Cambridge, Polity Press.

Finch, J. and Mason, J. (1993) *Negotiating Family Responsibilities*, London, Routledge.

Flavin, C. (1996) 'Facing up to the risks of climate change', in Brown, L. (ed.) *State of the World 1996*, London, Earthscan.

Foster, J. and Hope, T. (1993) *Housing, Community and Crime: The Impact of the Priority Estates Programme*, Home Office Research Study 131, London, HMSO.

Francis, A. (1986) *New Technology at Work*, Oxford, Clarendon Press.

Fraser, D. (1984) *The Evolution of the British Welfare State*, London, Macmillan.

Friedman, J. (1996) 'Rethinking poverty: empowerment and citizen rights', *International Social Science Journal*, No. 148, pp. 161–73.

Friedman, M. (1962) *Capitalism and Freedom*, Chicago, Chicago University Press.

Fukuyama, F. (1995) *Trust: The Social Virtues and the Creation of Prosperity*, London, Hamish Hamilton.

Fukuyama, F. (1997) *The End of Order*, London, Social Market Foundation.

Gallie, D., Marsh, C. and Vogler, C. (1993) *Social Change and the Experience of Unemployment*, Oxford, Oxford University Press.

Galligan, D. (1992) 'Procedural rights in social welfare', in Coote, A. (ed.) *The Welfare of Citizens*, London, Rivers Oram Press.

Gauthier, A.H. (1996) *The State and the Family*, Oxford, Clarendon Press.

General Household Survey (1994) London, HMSO.

George, V. and Howards, I. (1991) *Poverty Amidst Affluence*, Aldershot, Edward Elgar.

George, V. and Miller, S. (eds) (1994) *Social Policy Towards 2000: Squaring the Welfare Circle*, London, Routledge.

George, V. and Taylor-Gooby, P. (eds) (1996) *European Welfare Policy*, London, Macmillan.

Gershuny, J. and Brice, J. (1994) 'Looking backwards: family and work 1900–1992', in Buck, N., Gershuny, J., Rose, D. and Scott, J. (eds) *Changing Households: The British Household Panel Study 1990–1992*, Colchester, ESRC Research Centre on Micro Social Change.

Gibbons, J. (1995) 'Family support in child protection', in Hill, M., Hawthorne Kirk, R. and Pait Hill, D. (eds) *Supporting Families*, Edinburgh, HMSO.

Giles, C. and Johnson, P. (1994) *Taxes Down, Taxes Up: The Effects of a Decade of Tax Changes*, London, Institute of Fiscal Studies.

Gill, C. (1985) *Work, Unemployment and New Technology*, Oxford, Polity Press.

Gilling, D. (1997) *Crime Prevention*, London, UCL Press.

Gittins, D. (1993) *The Family in Question*, London, Macmillan.

Glyn, A. and Miliband, D. (eds) (1994) *Paying for Inequality*, London, Rivers Oram Press.

Goldsmith, E., Allen, R., Allaby, M., Davoll, J. and Lawrence, S. (1972) 'A blueprint for survival', *Ecologist*, January, special issue.

Goldthorpe, J.H. (1978) 'The current inflation: towards a sociological account', in Hirsch, F. and Goldthorpe, J.H. (eds) *The Political Economy of Inflation*, London, Martin Robertson.

Goodman, A. and Webb, S. (1994) *For Richer for Poorer, the Changing Distribution of Income in the United Kingdom, 1961–1991*, London, Institute of Fiscal Studies.

Goodman, A., Johnson, P. and Webb, S. (1997) *Inequality in the UK*, Oxford, Oxford University Press.

Gornick, J.C. and Jacobs, J.A. (1996) 'A cross-national analysis of the wages of part-time workers', *Work, Employment and Society*, **10**(1): 1–27.

Gorz, A. (1989) *Critique of Economic Reason*, London, Verso.

Gosling, A., Machin, S. and Meghir, C. (1994) *What Has Happened to Wages?* London, Institute for Fiscal Studies.

Gossop, C. and Webb, A. (1993) 'Getting around: public and private transport', in Blowers, A. (ed.) *Planning for a Sustainable Environment*, London, Earthscan.

Gough, I. (1996) 'Social welfare and competitiveness', *New Political Economy*, **1**(2): 209–33.

Government Statistical Service (1994) *Employment Gazette Historical Supplement* **102**(10).

Government Statistical Service (1997) *Inland Revenue Statistics*, London, Stationery Office.

Government Statistical Service (1998a) *Living in Britain*, London, Stationery Office.

Government Statistical Service (1998b) *Social Focus on the Unemployed*, London, HMSO.

Graham, J. (1988) *Schools, Disruptive Behaviour and Delinquency*, Home Office Research Study 96, London, HMSO.

Graham, J. (1998) 'What works in preventing ciminality', in Goldblatt, P. and Lewis, C. (eds) *Reducing Offending*, London, Home Office.

Gray, T.S. (ed.) (1995) *U.K. Environmental Policy in the 1990s*, London, Macmillan.

Gunderson, M. and Craig Riddell, W. (1995) 'Jobs, labour standards and promoting competitive advantage', *Labour*, special issue, pp. S125–S148.

Hain, P. (1995) *Ayes to the Left: A Future for Socialism*, London, Lawrence & Wishart.

Hain, P. (1996) 'Swap a small rise for a secure future', *Observer*, 22 December.

Hale, C. (1992) 'Crime and penal policy', in Manning, N. and Page, R. (eds) *Social Policy Review 4*, Canterbury, Social Policy Association.

Hale, C. (1996) 'Fear of crime: a review of the literature', *International Review of Victimology*, 4(2): 79–150.

Handy, C. (1984) *The Future of Work*, Oxford, Blackwell.

Harding, L. Fox (1996) *Family, State and Social Policy*, London, Macmillan.

Harker, L. (1996) *A Secure Future?*, London, Child Poverty Action Group.

Harris, J. (1994) *Private Lives. Public Spirit: Britain 1870–1914*, Harmondsworth, Penguin.

Haskey, J. (1994) 'Stepfamilies and stepchildren in Great Britain', *Population Trends*, 76: 17–28.

Haskey, J. (1995) 'Trends in marriage and cohabitation: the decline of marriage and the changing pattern of living in partnerships', *Population Trends*, 80: 5–15.

Haskey, J. (1998) 'Families: their historical context, and recent trends in the factors influencing their formation and dissolution', in David, M.E. (ed.) *The Fragmenting Family: Does it Matter?*, London, Institute of Economic Affairs.

Hattersley, L. (1997) 'Expectations of life by social class', in Drever, F. and Whitehead, M. (eds) *Health Inequalities*, London, Government Statistical Service.

Hattersley, R. (1987) *Choose Freedom*, Harmondsworth, Penguin.

Hawkins, K. (1979) *Unemployment*, Harmondsworth, Penguin.

Heal, K. (1992) 'Changing perspectives and crime prevention', in Evans, D.J., Fyfe, N.R. and Herbert, D.T. (eds) *Crime, Policing and Place*, London, Routledge.

Heath, A. and Mcmahon, D. (1997) 'Education and occupational attainment: the impact of ethnic origins', in Karn, V. (ed.) *Ethnicity in the 1991 Census*, Office for National Statistics, London, Stationery Office.

Heclo, H. (1980) 'Welfare: progress and stagnation', in Gwyn, W.B. and Rose, R. (eds) *Britain: Progress and Decline*, London, Macmillan.

Hedges, B. (1994) 'Work in a changing climate', in Jowell, R. *et al.* (eds) *British Social Attitudes, 11th Report*, Aldershot, Dartmouth Press.

Hempel, L.C. (1996) *Environmental Governance: The Global Challenge*, Washington, DC, Island Press.

Hennessy, P. (1993) *Never Again*, London, Vintage.

Hewitt, P. (1994) 'Families in flux', *Political Quarterly*, 65(2): 168–79.

Hewitt, P. and Leach, P. (1993) *Social Justice: Children and Families*, London, Institute for Public Policy Research.

Hill, M. (1995). 'Family policies in Western Europe', in Hill, M., Hawthorne Kirk, R. and Pait Hill, D. (eds) *Supporting Families*, Edinburgh, HMSO.

Himmelfarb, G. (1994) *The Demoralisation of Society*, New York, Knopf.

Hirsch, P. (1977) *Social Limits to Growth*, London, Routledge & Kegan Paul.

HMSO (1990) *This Common Inheritance: Britain's Environmental Strategy*, Cm 1200, London, HMSO.

HMSO (1994a) *Sustainable Development: The United Kingdom Strategy*, Cm 2426, London, HMSO.
HMSO (1994b) *Biodiversity: The UK Action Plan*, Cm 2448, London, HMSO.
HMSO (1995) *A Waste Strategy for England and Wales*, London, HMSO.
HMSO (1997a) *No More Excuses – A New Approach to Tackling Youth Crime in England and Wales*, Cm 3809, London, HMSO.
HMSO (1997b) *This Common Inheritance: UK Annual Report 1997*, London, HMSO.
HM Treasury (1979) *The Government's Expenditure Plans 1980–81*, London, HMSO.
Holman, B. (1988) *Putting Families First*, London, Macmillan.
Holtermann, S. (1995) *All our Futures*, Ilford, Barnardos.
Home Office (1997a) *Preventing Children Offending*, Cm 3566, London, Home Office.
Home Office (1997b) *No More Excuses – A New Approach to Tackling Youth Crime in England and Wales*, Cm 3809, London, Home Office.
Home Office (1997c) *Criminal Statistics England and Wales 1996*, Cm 3764, London, HMSO.
Home Office (1988) *Punishment, Custody and the Community*, London, HMSO.
Home Office (1998) *Reducing Offending*, London, Home Office.
Home Office Statistical Bulletin (1996) *The 1996 British Crime Survey*, London, Home Office.
Hope, T. (1998) 'Community crime prevention', in Goldblatt, P. and Lewis, C. (eds) *Reducing Offending*, London, Home Office.
Hough, M. (1996) *Drug Misuse and the Criminal Justice System*, London, Home Office.
Hough, M. and Roberts, J. (1997) *Attitudes to Punishment: 1996 British Crime Survey*, London, Home Office.
House of Lords (1995) Report from the Select Committee on Sustainable Development, Volume I, HL Paper 72, London, HMSO.
House of Lords (1996) Towards Zero Emissions for Road Transport HL Paper 13, London, HMSO.
Huby, M. (1998) *Social Policy and the Environment*, Buckingham, Open University Press.
Hudson, R. and Williams, A.M. (1995) *Divided Britain* (2nd edn), Chichester, Wiley.
Hutton, W. (1995) *The State We're In*, London: Cape.
Hutton, W. (1996) 'The stakeholder society', in Marquand, D. and Seldon, A. (eds) *The Ideas that Shaped Post War Britain*, London, Fontana.
Hutton, W. (1997) *The State To Come*, London, Vintage.
Ineichen, B. (1993) *Homes and Health*, London, E. & F.N. Spon.
International Labour Office (1995) *World Employment 1995*, Geneva, International Labour Office.
Jacobs, M. (1991) *The Green Economy: Environment, Sustainable Development, and the Politics of the Future*, London, Pluto Press.
Jahoda, M. (1979) 'The impact of unemployment in the 1930s and the 1970s', *Bulletin of the British Psychological Society*, **32**: 309–14.
James, O. (1995) *Juvenile Violence in a Winner–Loser Culture*, London, Free Association Books.
Jenkins, R. (1998) 'Britain's beaches are dirtier than ever', *Guardian*, 27 April.
Jones, H. and Millar, J. (1996) 'Introduction', in Jones, H. and Millar, J., *The Politics of the Family*, Aldershot, Avebury.

Jordan, P. (1988) 'Effective policing strategies for reducing crime', in Goldbatt, P. and Lewis, C. (eds) *Reducing Offending*, London, Home Office.

Joseph, K. and Sumption, J. (1979) *Equality*, London, Murray.

Joseph Rowntree Foundation (1995) *Inquiry into Income and Wealth*, Volume I, York, Joseph Rowntree Foundation.

Jossa, B. (1996) 'Working time reduction as a remedy against unemployment' *Economic Notes*, **25**(1): 1–20.

Jowell, R., Brook, L. and Taylor, B. (1994) *British Social Attitudes, 11th Report*, Aldershot, Dartmouth Press.

Kavanagh, D. (1980) 'Political culture in Great Britain: the decline of the civic culture', in Almond, G. and Verba, S. (eds) *The Civic Culture Revisited*, Boston, Little, Brown.

Kiernan, K. (1998) 'Family change: issues and implications', in David, M.E. (ed.) *The Fragmenting Family: Does it Matter?*, London, Institute of Economic Affairs.

Kiernan, K and Wicks, M. (1990) *Family Change and Future Policy*, York, Joseph Rowntree Memorial Trust.

Kiernan, K. and Estaugh, V. (1993) *Cohabitation*, London, Family Policy Studies Centre.

King, A. (1975) 'Overload: problem of governing in the 1970s', *Political Studies*, **XXIII**: 2–13.

Knight, J. (1997) Sparks fly in debate on cause of cancer', *South China Morning Post*, 25 August.

Kumar, V. (1993) *Poverty and Inequality in the UK: The Effects on Children*, London, National Children's Bureau.

Labour Market Trends (1998) **106**(4): S4.

Labour Party (1997) *New Labour Because Britain Deserves Better*, London, Labour Party.

Labour Party (undated) *Families in Focus*, London, Labour Party.

Labour Party Policy Commission on the Environment (1994) *In Trust for Tomorrow*, London, Labour Party.

Lampard, R. (1993) 'An examination of the relationship between marital dissolution and unemployment', in Gallie, D., Marsh, C. and Vogler, C. (1993) *Social Change and the Experience of Unemployment*, Oxford, Oxford University Press.

Land, H. (1994). 'Reversing "the inadvertent nationalization of fatherhood": The British Child Support Act 1991 and its consequences for men, women and children', *International Social Security Review*, 47(3–4): 91–100.

Layard, D. (1986) *How to Beat Unemployment*, Oxford, Oxford University Press.

Leach, P. (1994) *Children First*, Harmondsworth, Penguin.

Leadbeater, C. (1996) *The Self Policing Society*, London, Demos.

Lee, E. (1997) 'Is full employment still desirable and feasible?', *Economic and Industrial Democracy*, **18**(1): pp. 35–54.

Leisink, P. and Coenen, H. (1993) 'Work and citizenship in the New Europe', in Coenen, H. and Leisink, D. *Work and Citizenship in the New Europe*, Cheltenham, Edward Elgar.

Levi, M. (1994) 'Violent Crime', in Maguire, M., Morgan, R. and Reiner, R. (eds) *The Oxford Handbook of Criminology*, Oxford, Oxford University Press.

Lewis, J. (1992) 'Gender and the development of welfare regimes', *European Journal of Social Policy*, **2**(2): 159–74.

Lewis, J. (1998). 'Work, welfare and lone mothers', *Political Quarterly*, **69**(1): 4–13.

Lewis, J. and Piachaud, D. (1987) 'Women and poverty in the twentieth century', in Glendinning, C. and Millar, J. (eds) *Women and Poverty in Britain*, Brighton, Wheatsheaf.

Leys, C. (1989) 'From the paralysis of social democracy to the crisis of the 1970s', in Anderson, J. and Cochrane, A. (eds) *A State of Crisis*, London, Hodder & Stoughton.

Liberal Democrat Party (1994) *Supporting Families*, London, Liberal Democrat Party.

Lister, R. (1996) 'Back to the family: family policies and politics under the Major government', in Jones, H. and Millar, J. (eds) *The Politics of the Family*, Aldershot, Avebury.

Long, B. (1997) 'Environmental regulation: the third generation', *OECD Observer*, Number 206, pp. 14–18.

Low Pay Commission (1998) *The National Minimum Wage, First Report*, London, HMSO.

Low Pay Unit (1996) 'Coming apart at the seams', *New Review of the Low Pay Unit*, Number 42, pp. 8–11.

Lowry, S. (1991) *Housing and Health*, London, *British Medical Journal*.

Lukes, S. (1973) *Emile Durkheim*, Harmondsworth, Penguin.

Luper-Foy, S. (1992) 'Justice and natural resources', *Environmental Values*, 1(1): 55–68.

Macarov, A. (1996) 'The employment of new ends: planning for permanent unemployment' *Annals of the American Academy of Political and Social Science*, **544**: 191–203.

McCormick, J. (1991) *British Politics and the Environment*, London, Earthscan.

McKay, S. and Marsh, A. (1994) *Lone Parents and Work*, Department of Social Security Research Report 25, London, HMSO.

Mackintosh, J. (1976) 'The declining respect for the law', in King, A. (ed.) *Why Is Britain Becoming Harder to Govern?*, London, BBC.

McLaughlin, E. (1994) 'The demise of the institution of the job', *Political Quarterly*, 65(2): 179–91.

Maclean, M. and Eekalaar, J. (1997) *The Parental Obligation*, Oxford, Hart.

Maguire, M., Morgan, R. and Reiner, R. (eds) (1994) *The Oxford Handbook of Criminology*, Oxford, Oxford University Press.

Mannion, A.M. (1992) 'Acidification and eutrophication', in Mannion, A.M. and Bowlby, S.R. (eds) *Environmental Issues in the 1990s*, Chichester, Wiley.

Mannion, A.M. and Bowlby, S.R. (eds) (1992) *Environmental Issues in the 1990s*, Chichester, Wiley.

Mannion, R., Hutton, S. and Sainsbury, R. (1994) *Direct Payments from Income Support*, DSS Research Report Number 33, London, HMSO.

Marsh, D. (1996) 'Reinventing German capitalism', *German Politics*, 5(3): 395–403.

Matthews, R. and Young, J. (1992) 'Reflection on realism', in Young, J. and Matthews, R. (eds) *Rethinking Criminology; the Realist Debate*, London, Sage.

Maung, A. (1995) *Young People, Victimisation and the Police: British Crime Survey Findings on Experiences and Attitudes of 12 to 15 Year Olds*, Home Office Research Study 140, London, HMSO.

Meadows, D.H., Meadows, D.L., Randers, J. and Behrens, W. (1972) *The Limits to Growth*, London, Pan.

Meadows, D.H., Meadows, D.L. and Randers, J. (1992) *Beyond the Limits*, London, Earthscan.

Middlemass, K. (1986) *Power, Competition and the State*, 1, London, Macmillan.

Middlemass, K. (1990) *Power, Competition and the State*, 2, London, Macmillan.

Mishan, E.J. (1996) 'Technological unemployment: why there are hard times ahead', *Political Quarterly*, 76(2): 151–7.

Morgan, D.H.J. (1985) *The Family, Politics and Social Theory*, London, Routledge & Kegan Paul.

Morgan, K. (1985) *Labour in Power 1945–51*, Oxford, Oxford University Press.

Morgan, P. (1998) 'An endangered species', in David, M.E. (ed.) *The Fragmentary Family: Does it Matter?*, London, Institute of Economic Affairs.

Moroney, R. M. (1976), *The Family and the State*, London, Longman.

Morris, L. and Ritchie, J. (1994) *Income Maintenance and Living Standards*, York, Joseph Rowntree Foundation.

Morris, T. (1989) *Crime and Criminal Justice Since 1945*, Oxford, Blackwell.

Moss, P. (1991). 'Day care for young children in the UK', in Melhuish, E.C. and Moss, P. (eds) *Day Care for Young Children: International Perspectives*, London, Routledge.

Mullard, D. (1995/96) 'The politics of unemployment in Europe', *East-West Review of Social Policy*, 1(2): 260–71.

National Association of Citizens Advice Bureaux (1993) *Make or Break? CAB Evidence on Deductions from Benefit*, London, NACAB.

National Children's Home (1991) *Poverty and Nutrition Survey*, London, National Children's Home.

National Children's Home (1992) *Deep in Debt: A Survey of Problems Faced by Low Income Families*, London, National Children's Home.

Naylor, K. (1994) 'Part-time work in Great Britain – an historical analysis', *Employment Gazette*, 102(12): 473–85.

Newburn, T. (1995) *Crime and Criminal Justice Policy*, London, Longman.

Newburn, T. and Stanko, E. (1994) *Just Boys Doing Business*, London, Routledge.

Norris, P. (1997) 'Are we all green? Public opinion on environmentalism in Britain', *Government and Opposition*, 32(3): 330–40.

Novak, M. (1991) *The Spirit of Democratic Capitalism*, London, Institute of Economic Affairs.

Nuttall, N. (1997) 'Satellites reveal extent of Europe's forest loss', *Times*, 9 October.

OECD (1977) *Economic Surveys UK 1977*, Paris, OECD.

OECD (1994a) *Economic Outlook*, Number 55, June, Paris, OECD.

OECD (1994b) *Economic Outlook*, Number 56, December, Paris, OECD.

OECD (1994c) *The Jobs Study*, Paris, OECD.

OECD (1995) *Review Statistics 1965–1994*, Paris, OECD.

OECD (1996) *Social Expenditure Statistics of OECD Member Countries*, Occasional Paper Number 17, Paris, OECD.

OECD (1997) 'Low Wage Jobs: Stepping Stones or Traps?', *OECD Observer*, Number 208, pp. 38–42, OECD.

Office for National Statistics (1997a) *Social Focus on Families*, London, Stationery Office.

Office of National Statistics (1997b) *Social Trends 27*, London, HMSO.

Office for National Statistics (1998a), *Living in Britain: Results from the General Household Survey*, London, Stationery Office.

Office for National Statistics (1998b) *Social Trends, 28*, London, Stationery Office.

Olsen, G.M. (1996) 'Re-modelling Sweden', *Social Problems*, 43(1): 1–21.

Oppenheim, C. and Harker, L. (1996), *Poverty: The Facts*, London, Child Poverty Action Group.

Ormerod, P. (1996) 'Unemployment and the distribution of income', *Economic Affairs*, **16**(2): 21–35.

Owen, D. (1997) 'Labour participation rates, self-employment and unemployment', in Karn, V. (ed.) *Ethnicity in the 1991 Census*, Office of National Statistics, London, Stationery Office.

Packman, J. and Jordan, B. (1991) 'The Children Act: looking forward, looking back', *British Journal of Social Work*, **21**: 315–27.

Pantazis, C. and Gordon, D. (1997) 'Poverty and crime', in Gordon, D. and Pantazis, C., *Breadline Britain in the 1990s*, Aldershot, Ashgate.

Parker, H. (1991) *Basic Income and the Labour Market*, London, Basic Income Research Group.

Parliamentary Debates, 301, c.1095, 27 November 1997.

Parliamentary Debates, 310 c.377, 8 April 1998.

Pascall, G. (1996) *Social Policy: A New Feminist Perspective*, London, Routledge.

Pearce, D. (1993) *Blueprint 3: Measuring Sustainable Development*, London, Earthscan.

Pearce, D. (1995) *Blueprint 4*, London, Earthscan.

Pease, K. (1992) 'Preventing burglary on a British public housing estate', in Clarke, R.V.G. (ed.) *Situational Crime Prevention*, New York, Harrow & Heston.

Pease, K. (1994) 'Crime prevention', in Maguire, M., Morgan, R. and Reiner, R. (eds) *The Oxford Handbook of Criminology*, Oxford, Oxford University Press.

Phalter, A. Gough, I. and Thorborn, G. (eds) (1991) *Can the Welfare State Compete?*, London, Macmillan.

Phillips, D. and Verhasselt, Y. (eds) (1994) *Health and Development*, London, Routledge.

Philo, C. (ed.) (1995) *Off the Map: The Social Geography of Poverty in the UK*, London, Child Poverty Action Group.

Philpott, J. (1994) 'The incidence and cost of unemployment', in Glyn, A. and Miliband, D. (eds) *Paying for Inequality*, London, Rivers Oram Press.

Philpott, J. (ed.) (1997) *Working For Full Employment*, London, Routledge.

Piachaud, D. (1993) *What's Wrong with Fabianism?*, London, Fabian Society.

Pierson, C. (1995) *Socialism after Communism: The New Market Socialism*, London, Polity Press.

Plant, R. (1996) 'Social democracy', in Marquand, D. and Seldon, A. (eds) *The Ideas that Shaped Post War Britain*, London, Fontana.

Platt, S. and Kreitman, N. (1984) 'Trends in parasuicide and unemployment among men in Edinburgh 1962–1982', *British Medical Journal* (289).

Powell, E. (1972) *Still to Decide*, London, Elliott Right Way Books.

Power, A. and Tunstall, R. (1997) *Riots and Violent Disturbances in Thirteen Areas of Britain, 1991–2*, York, Joseph Rowntree Foundation.

Power, S., Whitty, G. and Youdell, D. (1995) *No Place to Learn: Homelessness and Education*, London, Shelter.

Putnam, R.D. (1993) *Making Democracy Work*, Princeton, Princeton University Press.

Ratcliffe, P. (1997) '"Race", ethnicity and housing differentials in Britain', in Karn, V. (ed.) *Ethnicity in the 1991 Census*, Office for National Statistics, London, HMSO.

Reiner, R. (1992) *The Politics of the Police*, Hemel Hempstead, Harvester Wheatsheaf.

Richards, A. and Madden, K. (1996) 'An international comparison of taxes and social security contributions (1984–1994)', *Economic Trends*, Number 517, pp. 16–29.

Rifkin, J. (1995) *The End of Work*, New York, Putnam's Sons.

Rifkin, J. (1996) 'A new social contract', *Annals of the American Academy of Political Science*, **544**: 16–27.

Roch, W.K., Fynnes, B. and Morrissey, T. (1996) 'Working time and employment: a review of international experience', *International Labour Review*, **135**(2): 129–57.

Rodgers, B. and Pryor, J. (1998) *Divorce and Separation*, York, Joseph Rowntree Foundation.

Rose, R. (1979) 'Ungovernability: is there fire behind the smoke?', *Political Studies*, **XXVII**(3): 351–70.

Rosen, S.M. (1996) 'Jobs: new challenges, new responses', *Annals of the American Academy of Political Science*, **544**: 27–43.

Royal Commission on the Distribution of Income and Wealth (1977) *Report No 5*, Cmnd 6999, London, HMSO.

Royal Commission on Environmental Pollution (1997) *Transport and the Environment – Developments since 1994*, 20th Report, Cm 3752, London, HMSO.

Ryan, P. (1994) 'Inheritance and wealth', in Glyn, A. and Miliband, D. (eds) *Paying for Inequality*, London, Rivers Oram Press.

Sacks, J. (1995) *Faith in the Future*, London, Darton, Longman & Todd.

Scarman Report (1982) Harmondsworth, Penguin.

Schmid, G. (1995) 'A new approach to labour market policy', *Economic and Industrial Democracy*, **16**(3): 420–56.

Schnaiberg, A. and Gould, K. (1994) *Environment and Society*, New York, St Martins Press.

Schumpeter, J. (1970) *Capitalism, Socialism and Democracy*, London, Allen & Unwin.

Scott, H. (1984) *Working Your Way to the Bottom: The Feminisation of Poverty*, London, Pandora Press.

Scott, J. and Perren, K. (1994) 'The family album: reflection on personal and family life', in Buck, N., Gershuny, J., Rose, D. and Scott, J. (eds) (1994) *Changing Households: the British Households Panel Study 1990–1992*, Colchester, ESRC Research Centre on Micro Social Change.

Scott, J., Braun, M. and Alwin, D. (1993) 'The family way', in Jowell, R., Brook, L., Dowds L. with Ahrendt, D. (eds) *International Social Attitudes 10th British Social Attitudes Report*, Aldershot, Dartmouth.

Shackleton, J.R. (1996) 'Unemployment and labour markets in the 1990s', *Economic Affairs*, **16**(2): 4–8.

Sherman, L.W. *et al.* (1997) *Preventing Crime: What Works, What Doesn't, What's Promising*, Washington, Department of Justice.

Shucksmith, M. (1997) 'Poverty in rural areas of Britain', *Benefits*, (19): 1–8.

Skidelsky, R. (1995) *The World After Communism*, London, Macmillan.

Sly, F. (1994) 'Mothers in the labour market', *Employment Gazette*, **102**(11): 403–13.

Sly, F. (1995) 'Ethnic groups and the labour market', *Employment Gazette*, **103**(6): 251–61.

Social Policy Research Findings 89 (1995) *The Cost of Children and the Welfare State*, York, Joseph Rowntree Foundation.

Stationery Office (1998) *Meeting the Child Care Challenge*, Cm. 3959, London, HMSO.

Strange, S. (1995) 'The limits of politics', *Government and Opposition*, **30**(3): 292–312.

Straw, J. (1998) Speech to the Lords and Commons Family and Child Protection Group at the launch of the Group's Report 'Family Matters', July 1998.

Tawney, R.H. (1984) *Equality* (4th edn), London, Allen & Unwin.

Taylor, A. (1992) *Choosing our Future: A Practical Politics of the Environment* (2nd edn), London, Routledge.

Thatcher, M. (1993) *The Downing Street Years*, London, HarperCollins.

Thomson, K. (1995) 'Working mothers: choice or circumstances', in Jowell, R., Curtice, J., Park, A. (eds) *British Social Attitudes 12th Report*, Aldershot, Dartmouth.

Timms, N. (1992) *Family and Citizenship*, Aldershot, Dartmouth.

Townsend, P. (1979) *Poverty in the United Kingdom*, Harmondsworth, Penguin.

Toynbee, P. (1997) 'A matter of life and death', *Search*, (28): 4–8.

Trickett, A., Ellingworth, D., Hope, T. and Pease, K. (1995) 'Crime victimization in the eighties', *British Journal of Criminology*, **35**(3): 343–59.

United Nations Organization (1990) *Global Outlook 2000*, New York, UNO Publications.

Utting, D. (1995) *Family and Parenthood*, York, Joseph Rowntree Foundation.

Utting, D., Bright, J. and Henricson, C. (1993) *Crime and the Family*, London, Family Policy Studies Centre.

Voisey, H. and O'Riordan, T. (1997) 'Governing Institutions for Sustainable Development: The United Kingdom's National Level Approach', *Environmental Politics*, **6**(1), Spring, pp. 24–54.

Walker, A. and Walker, C. (eds) (1997) *Britain Divided*, London, Child Poverty Action Group.

Walker, A., Alber, J. and Guillermard, A.-M. (1993) *Older People in Europe: Social and Economic Policies*, Brussels, EC.

Wilde, O. (1891/1954) 'The soul of man under socialism', in *Selected Essays and Poems*, London, Penguin.

Wilkinson, R. (1994) 'Wealth redistribution and growth', in Glyn, A. and Miliband, D. (eds) *Paying for Inequality*, London, Rivers Oram Press.

Wilson, J.Q. (1983) *Thinking About Crime*, New York, Basic Books.

Wilson, J.Q. (1993) *The Moral Sense*, New York, Free Press.

Wilson, W.J. (1991) 'Public policy research and the truly disadvantaged', in Jencks, C. and Peterson, T. (eds) (1991) *The Urban Underclass*, Washington, Brookings Institute.

Wilson, W.J. (1996) *When Work Disappears*, New York, Knopf.

World Bank (1991) *World Development Report, 1991*, New York, Oxford University Press.

World Commission on Environment and Development (1987) *Our Common Future* (Brundtland report), Oxford, Oxford University Press.

Wright, T. (1997) *Why Vote Labour?*, Harmondsworth, Penguin.

Young, K. (1991) 'Shades of green', in Jowell, R., Brook, L. and Taylor, B. *British Social Attitudes 8th Report*, Aldershot, SCPR/Dartmouth.

Young, S.C. (1995) 'Running up the down escalator', in Gray, T.S. (ed.) *U.K. Environmental Policy in the 1990s*, London, Macmillan.

Index